FINDING THE KEYS

for remembering anything

PAUL MELLOR

All rights reserved. No part of this book shall be reproduced or transmitted in any form or by any means, electronic, mechanical, magnetic, photographic including photocopying, recording or by any information storage and retrieval system, without prior written permission of the publisher. No patent liability is assumed with respect to the use of the information contained herein. Although every precaution has been taken in the preparation of this book, the publisher and author assume no responsibility for errors or omissions. Neither is any liability assumed for damages resulting from the use of the information contained herein.

Copyright © 2018 by Paul Mellor

ISBN 978-0692137819

To Max and Ben

Christmas Eve babies who are babies no more.
May you continue to grow in all aspects of your life.

Acknowledgements

I thank my parents, Don and Helen Mellor, who have instilled in me the love of learning. My dad still claims he can recall his high school locker combination. My mom can still rattle off the 50 states in alphabetical order in less than 60 seconds. Impressive indeed, but what's more impressive about these WWII veterans is their zest for life, their positive attitude, and their wonderful sense of humor. I hope my brain is just as healthy when I'm in my 90's.

I thank all my teachers from grade school to college who reminded me to study up. I thank Toastmasters International, an organization that helped me speak up.

I thank the hundreds of associations and corporations who have contacted me to speak on Memory. Oh, how I love what I do.

Table of Contents

Introduction 1

Chapter 1 6
The Basics 6
   Know Your Anchors 8
   Association Do's 10
   Exaggeration Alert 12
   Visual Cues 16

Chapter 2 19
The Anchors 19
   Loci 20
   Body Anchor Method 24
   Number / Shape Method 30
   Remembering the Bill of Rights 31
   Number / Rhyme Method 34
   How to Remember an Entire Year 37
   Alphabet Anchor Method 41

Chapter 3 44
How to Speak without Notes 44
   Linking 48
   Using Acronyms 52

Chapter 4 54
How to Remember Names 54
   You're Very Special 55
   Focus, Focus, Focus 57
   Eyes on You 58
   Listen Up Everybody 60
   Guaranteed Return Policy 61
   Thanks for Noticing 63
   Get the Picture 64
   I Can Relate to That 67
   Dynamic Duos 68

v

Table of Contents

Chapter 4 (cont.)
    Meaningful Last Names 69
    Color Me Beautiful 69
    The Right Place 70
    The Job Line 70
    Hello in There...71
    The Wild Kingdom......................................72
    The Grocery List 72
    A Simple Breakdown 72
    Feeling of Belonging 75
    MADD, NOW, and NATO............................75
    Drafting the Letters 76
    It's Story Time 76
    What's My Line? 78
    It Pays to Remember 80
    Names & Associations 81

Chapter 5 92
101 Ways to Beat Absent-mindedness 92

ADVANCED SECTIONS................................195

Chapter 6 196
Phonetic Alphabet..197
    The Rules..199
    100 Anchors 201

Chapter 7 205
How to Remember Numbers 205

Chapter 8 211
How to Remember Appointments 211

Chapter 9 215
How to Remember Important Dates 215
    Remembering Birthdates of the Rich and Famous ..223

vi

Table of Contents

Chapter 10 225
How to Remember Playing Cards 225

Chapter 11 234
Have Some Pi (60 Slices) 234

Chapter 12 236
The Directory..236

Conclusion..305

Index 306

INTRODUCTION

Introduction

Every day millions of people pace. Looking down at the floor or up at the ceiling, they walk and wonder. They ask themselves any one of many questions...

"Did I turn the iron off?"

"Did I turn the security system on?"

"Where did I put my glasses down?"

"Where's the checkbook going to turn up?"

"Where were my keys left?"

"What I told him, was it right?"

They rack their brains looking for that misplaced file, scratch their heads trying to recall the name and believe they've lost their minds when they can't remember where they've parked.

If I could only remember. That's a question millions of people ask. Yet the answer is so close it's frustrating. It's something that slipped their minds, something they can't put a finger on, and something that winds up on the tips of their tongues. Are you one of these people, or don't you remember?

As one who teaches memory skills throughout the United States and Canada, I'm amazed at the raised hands I see after I ask, "Who thinks they have a bad memory?" Many of those hands are young. They're from people who are well educated yet frustrated thinking they're losing their minds. They can't recall names, could never speak without notes, and often lose track of their parked cars. Nothing wrong with taking the bus, I say. Of course, there's pressure in remembering when to get off.

From Atlanta to Anchorage, from Hartford to Honolulu, and from Miami to Minneapolis, I've witnessed a lot of raised hands from people who struggle with their memory. If there were only a magic

Introduction

pill that would eliminate forgetfulness, oh how the demand would be. Pharmaceutical companies are trying.

They're rushing to develop a product that would lick our memory deficiencies, a pill helping us find our way through life. No doubt, the line would stretch longer than those waiting to purchase the latest iPhone.

There are products on the market claiming to improve memory. Whether it's an herb or an energy booster, every drugstore has something that states they can bolster the brain with the words *improves memory* printed somewhere on the packaging.

If the products worked, would we still need to hide our spare key? Would we still call our neighbor, *"What's-his-name"*? Would statements, such as *"I know it's here somewhere"* be a thing of the past? Unfortunately, those comments will probably never go out of use and there will always be a *What's-his-name* living on every block.

I believe we don't need pills to remember. I believe everyone with a healthy brain can improve their memory tenfold. I believe that because I've seen it. It's happened to me. It can happen to you.

I once believed people were either born with a good memory or a bad memory. Hey, some people just had it. However, for the ones who hadn't, it gave them a legitimate excuse when telling their teachers they had forgotten their homework. I never used that excuse. I had a dog, instead.

In school, the word *memory* was never one of my teacher's favorite words. "Don't memorize it," she would say. "I want you to know it." Her belief was that trying to memorize information puts the mind in a trance. Perhaps she thought the needed information entered our heads only during test time. Then it would fade into a distant memory never to come back again. Perhaps she thought it was a shortcut to learning and we would be cheating ourselves if we memorized it.

x

Introduction

If memorization and shortcuts were so bad, why did my teacher apply them? I've long left Eden Park Elementary School, but I can recall her teaching the music scale by saying <u>E</u>very <u>G</u>ood <u>B</u>oy <u>D</u>oes <u>F</u>ine. I also recall when she taught us the names of the five great lakes. Think *HOMES*, she said, and you'll remember. I did and it worked. It was *Erie* how *Superior* my mind would be. My teacher helped me remember the information by making me package the information. I could grasp it.

It wasn't until I joined the Richmond Toastmasters Club that I became interested in learning about Memory. Toastmasters, a world-wide organization founded in 1924, helps people develop and polish their communication skills. Toastmasters was a big part of my life. I enjoyed writing, rehearsing, and giving speeches. I gave speeches on a wide range of topics, but never had a genuine passion for any of the subject matter.

However, on December 31st, 1994, while others were anticipating their passion at the stroke of midnight, I was meeting mine. It was on a shelf at the Bon Air Library in Richmond, Virginia.

I found *The Memory Book*, by Harry Lorayne and Jerry Lucas. I remembered that my mother had checked the book out from her library years earlier while I was living in Cranston, Rhode Island. She's a voracious reader, and *The Memory Book* was in the middle of one of her stacks. I flipped through it but never spent time reading it. However, on that last day in '94 I brought the book home. This time I read it.

I found a topic that helped everyone, including myself. Everything we do involves memory. By learning to strengthen it we become more powerful, more persuasive, and more popular.

I believe memory is the most important topic there is, yet it's often overlooked. Who wouldn't want to improve their memory? I learned that the same techniques for remembering numbers or names can be used for beating absent-mindedness, giving speeches without notes, helping recall Bible verses, and remember playing cards. It can help in every aspect of your life.

Introduction

Yes, I have a genuine passion for this topic and learned that trying to remember doesn't have to be hard. It can be fun. The best part is that the answers to our memory problems are all in our heads.

CHAPTER 1

The Basics

The Basics

Look up the word, *patriot* in a dictionary. You can probably find it in less than 30 seconds. As long as you know how to spell the word, you could locate it promptly.

Dictionaries are organized, with each entry listed in alphabetical order. It wouldn't matter if you were holding a pocket-sized edition or flipping through the big one at the downtown library, you would find it easily.

It also wouldn't matter if you were asked to look up the word *pumpernickel* or *hemisphere* or *fondue* or *trumpet*. Since you know which part of the book the word is in, you'd turn to it quickly.

How much time would it take finding those same words in different book? Instead of a dictionary, this book would list words in no order, have no table of contents, index, or glossary, making your task more difficult. You wouldn't know where to look. You'd flip to this page and that page searching for the word in question.

The only way to find the word is to start at the beginning. You'd have to read the first page, the second page, the third page, and so on, until Presto! You found it! It's similar to when we walk into another room of our home, not remembering why we went in there. So what do we do? We go back to where we started, hoping to get back on track. Thank goodness, dictionaries are always on track.

I am grateful to Noah Webster. That big book of his is always at my side when I'm in my office. With the help of Mr. Webster, I am a freak of nature. Give me a word and I will locate it in seconds from his 1600-page tome.

If Webster's words were thrown into the book haphazardly, it would be a book seldom used. If *thunder* were next to *cantaloupe* and *jungle* next to *yodel*, who would have time to hunt? There's no order. We know the words are in there, but not even a SWAT team could get them out.

The Basics

Our minds can be like that. We struggle to think of the actor who won the Academy Award a few years earlier. "I know his name, but I just can't think of it now." Sound familiar?

Noah Webster spent 27 years compiling his dictionary, with the words strategically placed in a way that we could instantly find them. *Thunder, cantaloupe, jungle,* and *yodel,* you say? No problem. They're on pages 1494, 215, 776, and 1661.

The work might have seemed laborious putting those words in order, but look at the benefits. Any word needed could be immediately discovered. To find a word, one didn't need to memorize the pages, but memorize only the 26 letters of the alphabet. It's a system that works. And, a system is what memory training is all about.

From the outset, training our memory can seem boring, stressful, and tedious. Why spend an hour memorizing something we won't need after next week? Why spend the effort trying to remember someone's name, when I'll never see him again after this morning's meeting? And another thing, how is anyone going to change my way of thinking?

If memory were like trying to memorize a 1600-page volume with words in no order, the task would be mind-numbing. Instead, we're going to develop a system similar to Noah Webster's. It's easy to learn yet won't take 27 years to develop. To get started, we must highlight one of Mr. Webster's words. In my dictionary it's on page 51. The word is *anchor*.

Know Your Anchors

According to *Webster's*, the word *anchor* is defined as anything that gives or seems to give stability or security; to keep from drifting.

I became aware of the importance of anchors as a boy. My grandfather often took my sister and me fishing off the Massachusetts coast, near Plymouth. If he had neglected the anchor, I may be speaking Portuguese now.

The Basics

There were a lot of anchors on those fishing expeditions. The obvious one was the apparatus tied to a rope that plunged to the ocean floor. That anchor kept the boat in place. The seat was another type of anchor. It was the stability to keep me in place. The fishhook was an anchor. It kept the worm in place. The lighthouse was an anchor. It led us back to port.

The world is full of anchors. To the pilot, it's the runway. To the hunter, it's the scope. To the coffee drinker, it's the mug. It's the starting point keeping us on course.

When we're interrupted during a conversation, our minds search for an anchor when we ask, "What was the last thing I was talking about?" When we misplace out keys, our minds look to an anchor as we retrace our steps and ask, "Where was I?" When we drive on country roads, not sure when to make the turn, our anchors are the big, red barn, or better yet, the GPS.

Sadly, many people have lost their anchors. Those who suffer from Alzheimer's have not only lost their keys, they may not know what the key is for. For some, a remote control is just a stick with buttons, a bar of soap is just something that smells, and a loved one may be just a stranger in the room.

Human beings need anchors to function. Without anchors the simplest question is virtually impossible to answer. Here are a few:

>Guess which number I'm thinking of?
>Guess what movie I watched last night?
>Can we meet in Texas?

If you guessed *817* you answered the first question correctly. If not, don't feel bad. The only anchor provided was that it was a number. A question using a better anchor would have been, "Guess which number I'm thinking of between 816 and 818."

On the second question, if you had guessed *ET*, fix yourself some popcorn. You're correct, but how would you have known? It would

The Basics

have helped if someone provided an anchor by saying, "It's the letter right after *d*, and the one immediately before *u*."

Can we meet in Texas? Yes, I'd love to but where? Which county, which city, which corner? Give me an anchor.

There have been a few times, before the use of cell phones, when I had planned to meet someone at one location, but each time waited several minutes until we located each other. Whether it was my buddy at a restaurant parking lot, my parents outside a bus station, or my cousin at a ballpark, several minutes had elapsed because we didn't settle on a specific spot, and therefore couldn't find one another. Since those occasions I've learned to give exact locations for meeting someone. Anchors have kept me straight.

Knowing my anchors, I can count to one hundred in less than 60 seconds. If I talk really, really fast I can do it in half that time, but I would need to go in the order of 1, 2, 3, 4, 5, 6, 7, 8, 9, 10, 11…98, 99, 100. If I started at 35, then went to 8 and then to 11 and then to 73, I would be unsure of myself if 23 or 62 got mentioned. I would have to rely a lot on my memory. I would need a very, very good memory to recall all those numbers without repeating or omitting the others.

I don't like to rely on my memory. I prefer to develop strong anchors to take the pressure off remembering. That's why, in Mr. Webster's dictionary, I turn to page 86. It's there I find *association*.

Association Do's

It's Christmas morning when your teenager opens the gift box with the car keys. Stand back and grab your angel; not him, the one on top of the tree. Johnny is going bonkers. It's an amazing grip the power of association has on people. Did anyone tell your son he only got keys? Who said he's getting a car? His associative juices got the better of him.

Your boss just phoned. She wants to see you in the morning. Why is your head spinning?

The Basics

It's your surgeon's first day on the job. Your surgeon's first day? Why are your first thoughts to phone your priest?

Everything we do links. Everything has association. An iPod is an association with listening to music. A pencil is an association with writing, a chair with sitting, an oven with cooking, a tub with bathing, a doorbell with alerting, and the Division of Motor Vehicles with ... waiting.

It's a never-ending list how quickly we react to association. For instance, a woman with a baby is sitting next to you on a cross country flight. With that in mind, you associate irritability, fussing, and crying. Then, you wonder what the baby will do.

To build a better memory we must harness the power of association. Try memorizing the following lists:

List #1
Egg, eggshell, Shell gasoline, Gasoline Alley, alley cat, catfish, fishbowl, bowling ball, ball of fire, fire truck.

List #2
Fire truck, bowling ball, egg, alley cat, Gasoline Alley, eggshell, ball of fire, fishbowl, Shell gasoline, catfish.

The first list flowed. It rolled off our tongues. When we got to *egg* we automatically shifted into *eggshell*. Once we got to *eggshell* we pulled into *Shell gasoline*. From *Shell gasoline*, we didn't think about *eggshell* anymore. Instead, our minds went to *Gasoline Alley*. It was easy because we associated one word into another.

Each word became an anchor, reminding us to pivot to the next. When we got to *fishbowl* our minds leaped to *bowling ball*. If we got interrupted during the reciting of this list, we'd stop and search for our anchor, by asking, "Where was I?" Psst, bowling ball. "Oh, that reminds me, the next words are *ball of fire*."

The list would have taken much longer to memorize without anchors and associations. Each of those words, beginning with *egg*, was an

The Basics

anchor at one time. After *egg* was an anchor, *eggshell* took its place. The power of association reminded us the next word was *Shell gasoline*. Then <u>Gasoline</u> *Alley* was an anchor, which by association reminded us that <u>alley</u> *cat* were the next words.

Anchors are the starting point. We would wander without them.

Using the power of anchors and association, recall the series of words, beginning with the anchor *egg*, _____, _____, _____, *alley cat*, _____, _____, *bowling ball*, _____, *fire truck*.

In List #2, the words were not in an order that we could grasp. It was difficult to recall that *bowling ball* came after *fire truck*, or *Shell gasoline* came after *fishbowl*. We would need a supercharged memory to recite those words in order.

Unfortunately, life is more like List # 2, than #1. We have lists to remember, tasks to perform, and topics to address that don't flow as easily as A, B, C. Therefore, anchor and association need a little more assistance.

With the inclusion of *exaggeration* we can make any list flow effortlessly.

Exaggeration Alert

The cow jumped over the moon. London Bridge is falling down. My Bonnie lies over the ocean. (Hey Bonnie, I told you not to walk over London Bridge).

Let's not forget about Humpty Dumpty on a brick wall, the little old woman who lived in a shoe, and that bough that's about to break.

No wonder kids are running away from home. Do we really think that our children will drift into a pleasant sleep after listening to those bedtime stories?

The Basics

Those classic nursery rhymes have one thing in common: they're exaggerated stories that stay with us generation after generation. If Humpty Dumpy hadn't fallen, if the bough hadn't broken, and if the old woman had lived in a convalescent home, who would remember?

Exaggeration doesn't live just in story books. It is found on the front pages of our newspapers and on the evening news. It's the fire on Main Street, the murder on Elm, and the day the circus came to town. It's the story that's different, out of the norm. It's the one that catches our attention.

There are many people, myself included, still keeping the newspaper of September 12, 2001. Spectacular events, happy or sad, remain fixed in our memories. Dates, not only September 11, 2001, but also November 22, 1963, and December 7, 1941, will always, and should always, be remembered.

In my seminars I ask attendees what they were doing on that November day in 1963. Many people remember. I hear, "I was taking a spelling test." "I was watching my mother iron a shirt." "I was reading my law book in class." "I was at a diner in downtown Indianapolis." "I was talking to my friend Ellen." They recite their actions with conviction and without hesitation.

One Texas gentleman I asked knew exactly where he was on November 22, 1963. He and his 5th grade class were standing on a curb in downtown Dallas, Texas. He remembers waving to the President of the United States. Shortly after returning to school, he learned what the rest of America already knew.

Those who remember the Kennedy assassination apply anchors and association. I was somewhat surprised when one senior citizen couldn't recall what he was doing on November 22, 1963. "No idea," he said. "Are you sure?" I asked, finishing the sentence with "JFK." "Oh, now I remember," he replied. "I was walking down the hallway. I was holding a cup of coffee ..."

The Basics

When I mentioned *JFK* it anchored his memory to that tragic event. He was able to associate that horror to what he was doing when he heard the news. He couldn't recall what he was doing the day before or after that November day, but when the President was shot, he remembered. That was the anchor.

It's not just tragedy taking hold of our memory, but other extraordinary events as well. We vividly remember the day we got married, the game-winning hit, finishing a marathon, and the birth of our children (shot par that day).

Why can we recall, with such clarity, events that happened so long ago, but not events that happened yesterday or the day before? The mundane just doesn't cut it.

Knowing the bizarre, unusual, exaggerated, or extraordinary event embeds in our minds, we have to connect that power to remember. We must use our imagination.

In your "mind's eye" visualize your *mattress*, your *sink*, a *basketball*, an *elephant*, and a *trampoline*.

Did your mind move from one image to the next? If so, it probably zipped at top speed. You visualized these images quickly, but "saw" them one at a time. There is no correlation between any of these six objects. Therefore, there is no association, and we desperately needed that *A* word to remember.

Here's another test: Visualize a *fish* and a *hook*. Imagine a *clown* and a *balloon*. Now picture an *umbrella* and *rain*. This section is easier to recall, because there's an association. We can picture the fish attached to the hook, we can mentally see the clown holding colorful balloons, and we can imagine rain pounding the umbrella.

If the words were rearranged, we would have to create an association using exaggeration. For instance, try to memorize the order now: *umbrella, balloon, fish, clown, rain,* and *hook*.

The Basics

The anchor is the *umbrella*; that's the starting point. The next word is *balloon*, which we have to connect to the anchor. Since there is no immediate association between the two, we'll use exaggeration to bring the words together.

The image is exaggerated when we put the *umbrella* into the *balloon's* world or vice versa. For instance, imagine *balloons*, with some escaping through an opening, under an *umbrella*. That's weird.

Other images include: *balloons* stuck to an *umbrella*, an *umbrella* popping *balloons*, an *umbrella* inside a huge *balloon*, or a hot air *balloon* shaped like an *umbrella*.

From *umbrella* we associate *balloon*. *Balloon* is now the anchor. That's what we know. Next, an association must be made to remember *fish*. Using exaggeration we can mentally see a *balloon* catching a fish. Or, we can mentally see *fish* stuck in *balloons*.

The anchor moves to *fish*. The next word is *clown*. Imagine a *clown* eaten by a *fish* or a *clown* with a *fish* head.

Now the *clown* takes over the anchor. Note that we're not bringing the other words into play. We'll think of them only if called upon. Instead, we're linking only two words together; never trying to think of more than two at a time.

Clown to *rain*. Imagine *clowns* dancing in the *rain*. Visualize *rain* puddles of *clowns* or it's *raining clowns*.

The Basics

The anchor moves to *rain*. *Rain* to *hook*. Imagine it's raining *hooks*. This will keep the kids from going to school.

Remember that these are my connections; you'll make your own. Yes, there will probably never be a time when you have to remember an umbrella held by balloons. However, life comes at you fast, and you have to be fast to be able to remember lists and tasks and speeches and names and a lot of everything else.

Mentally seeing exaggerated images is effective brain training. The rest of this book goes into specifics, but it's imperative to acquire this memory principal of success: exaggeration is paramount. I am not exaggerating.

Visual Cues

It's easier to remember the words *hot dog*, *kite*, *marble*, and *balloon* than the words *vital*, *totally*, *gripe*, and *exact*. Visuals are memorable. They have texture, shape, and color. It's about tangible nouns and action verbs.

Rarely do you see empty red double-decker buses on the streets of New York or short lines for Chicago's boat tours. People pay money to experience the sights. Sights are memorable. Words are not. For instance, take the word, *giraffe*. Don't visualize the tall, dark orange, brown and white animal, with the 18-inch tongue leaning over to pluck green leaves off a tree. Instead, visualize the letter *i* between the letters *g* and *r*. Can you do that?

The brain is more powerful than the computer sitting on your desk or the one held in your hand. Ask the computer to conjure up a picture of a giraffe and the wait begins. First, you to turn the machine on; second, you have to let it warm up; third, you have to log in; fourth, you have to type *giraffe*; and fifth, you have to wait. How long did it take your brain to see the African animal? It's no contest. The brain wins.

The Basics

Seeing the image in our "mind's eye" helps us retain the information. We can picture our grandparents' home and a ballet dancer on stage. We can taste the lemon, smell the bread, and we cringe when the fingernails approach the chalkboard. Our memories are in pictures, and we develop them each day.

The following exercise helps you narrow an image from vague and fuzzy to one that is crystal clear.

Vague Image	**Clearer Image**
nutrition	apple
wood	rocking chair
transportation	train
pottery	clay pot
fluffy	pillow
height	ladder

Continue with remaining list ...

bounce	_____
bright	_____
heavy	_____
slow	_____
wake-up call	_____
strong	_____

Once you come up with an image, it's easier to connect it to something you already know.

So far, in remembering each list, we never attempted to remember more than two things at the same time. Remember? We went from *egg* to *eggshell* to *Shell gasoline*. When we got to *gasoline*, we automatically recalled *Gasoline Alley*, without holding onto the previous words.

The Basics

We remembered *umbrella* held by *balloons*. Then we remembered *balloons* connected to the *fish*. From *fish* we mentally saw the *clown* *followed* by the *hooks*.

Just like saying our *ABC's* or counting to 100, we never need to connect more than two items at the same time. A trained mind is like a dictionary with anchors along the way, attaching new information to what we already know.

CHAPTER 2

The Anchors

Loci Method

Location, location, location. That's something any realtor says is most important. Memory experts say the same. One anchor system, known as Loci, has been utilized for ages and is still in use today when we utter the phrase, "in the first place."

Long before the tape recorder, fax machine, telephone, and computer, information had to be remembered. The ancient Romans could memorize lengthy speeches by mentally associating parts of their speech with objects in their home.

For example, the first part of their speech would be associated to their door; the second part to a table; the third part to a vase or column or statue. By going in order, beginning in the first place, orators didn't need notes because they were able to make exaggerated associations with each object.

The method is effective not only for speeches, but also for remembering tasks and lists.

To construct a Loci Method of your own, write down ten objects in one room of your home. These items will act as anchors helping you recall information. Choose these items while you're away from the room you're going to use. This way, you're able to focus while visualizing them in their location.

Choose items that are stationary instead of items that will be moved or discarded, such as the rolled-up napkin on the counter or the newspaper on the table. Be very specific with each object. For instance, focus on the handle of the refrigerator, not the entire appliance; the grill instead of the entire oven; or the rotating plate instead of the microwave itself.

Other possible objects include *trash can, flower pot, dishwasher, wall painting, faucet, blender,* and *toaster*.

The Anchors

To start, begin in the kitchen.

Object # 1 _____   Object # 6 _____

Object # 2 _____   Object # 7 _____

Object # 3 _____   Object # 8 _____

Object # 4 _____   Object # 9 _____

Object # 5 _____   Object # 10 _____

After finishing writing these anchors, turn your eyes away from the words and visualize each object. The result is being able to mentally see each item, in order, quickly. Practice until you can visualize your anchors in less than ten seconds. It's imperative that you know your anchors.

Once your anchors are in place, you can retain any list of items by associating what you want remembered to that anchor.

Let's attempt to memorize these ten objects; *paintbrush, flowers, hat, newspaper, marshmallows, parachute, penguin, horseshoe, frog,* and *trombone.*

Visualize the first object in your kitchen and associate it with the first object from our list (*paintbrush*). Exaggerate the image by enlarging the *paintbrush* and dumping gallons of paint on your first anchor. See it in your "mind's eye." Afterward, visualize your next anchor and associate that object with the next object on the list (*flowers*).

If your anchor is *faucet*, imagine the flowers spewing out of the faucet. The exaggeration, coupled with the action of the flowers exiting the spout, is an image that's remembered. It's not graphic enough if our visuals were watering the flowers from the sink.

16

The Anchors

There should be no confusion if an item on your list is also one of your anchors. For instance, if you wanted to remember *flowers*, and *flowers* was one of your anchors, then just imagine your lovely flowers attacked by another set of flowers.

Moving to the next Loci we come to the *dishwasher*. We look inside and what do we see? Of course, it's a huge hat.

After *dishwasher* our next anchor may be the *candle* on the counter. If so, then visualize *candle* with the next object to be remembered (*newspaper*).

Associate the remaining seven objects to each one of your anchors. Make sure that you visualize those objects colliding with each anchor. Use a lot of action and make it ridiculous. It's the ridiculous that helps us remember.

When you need to remember your list, just look to your anchor and your image will show up in living color.

Once you have your ten anchors, write down ten more in another room. Focus on fixed objects, such as *lamp, fireplace, bureau,* or *ceiling fan*. It won't take long before you have 50 or more anchors. Don't despair if you have a small home with few objects. If you have only a refrigerator you already have ten objects. You have *butter, mustard jar, ice cream carton, head of lettuce, frozen dinner, Dr. Pepper, Chinese take-out, pizza slice, spoiled milk*, and the empty *ice tray* that you keep forgetting to fill.

Some of my anchors are on my college campus, my childhood home, and homes of people I know. Any object can be an anchor, as long as it can be organized in your mind. Even if you rearrange your furniture or restock your refrigerator, you'll still be able to recall your anchors. Periodically, mentally revisit those anchors beginning ... in the first place.

When you want to remember a different list, you won't be confused by the original list. Your memory will naturally kick in when you use the techniques of exaggeration.

The Anchors

The Loci Method is great because it anchors your memory, not allowing it to drift, since you already know where to look.

In remembering a list, most people try to stack the information. They try to remember too many things at once. A trained memory is like a dictionary or efficient filing system. Once you have preset anchors, you can attach anything you need remembered to that anchor.

Body Anchor Method

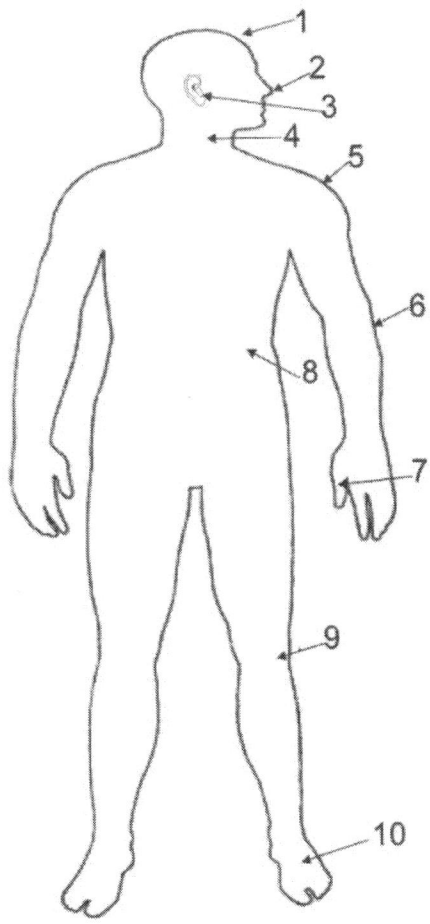

Body Anchor Method

This system works well because you're always with half of what you need to remember. It follows you wherever you go. It makes no difference if you're at the gym, in the pool, at work, on the couch, or on a plane. The Body Anchor Method is a memory aid you can't get rid of. Unless you have an out of body experience.

# 1 represents your head	# 6 represents your elbow
# 2 represents your nose	# 7 represents your thumb
# 3 represents your ear	# 8 represents your waist
# 4 represents your neck	# 9 represents your knee
# 5 represents your shoulder	#10 represents your foot

Associate what you need to remember with each body part. Let's try it. Here's your list…

# 1 Plant flowers	# 6 Take shirts to cleaners
# 2 Mail birthday card	# 7 Oil change for car
# 3 Order tickets	# 8 Return library book
# 4 Buy toothpaste	# 9 Call plumber
# 5 Buy soup	#10 Make bank deposit

To remember the list, associate each numbered body part to a task in a very ridiculous manner. Focus and visualize.

~ Flowers drooping over your head.

~ Birthday cards flying out of your nose.

~ Tickets hanging from your ears.

~ Toothpaste sticking in your neck.

~ Cans of soup spinning around your shoulder.

Body Anchor Method

~ Shirts wrapped around your elbow.

~ Oil dripping from your thumb. Although that could happen, a better image may be using your thumb, instead of the dip stick, to check the oil.

~ Books hanging from your waist.

~ Plunger is swinging from your knee.

~ Money stuck on your foot.

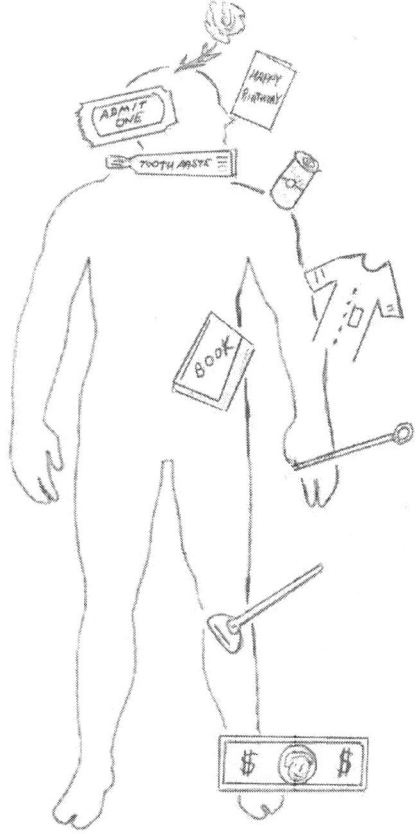

Test your memory on page 29

Body Anchor Method

A common thread to these associations was action. Did you notice? The objects weren't just lounging around, they were doing something. They were hanging, dripping, or swinging. They were flying or sticking or wrapping. With action we remember.

We experience action at concerts. The performer doesn't stand still; they move, dance, and jump. The stage moves, too, with its flashing lights and neon signs. All that movement makes the experience memorable. Our minds notice when objects move.

In the early days, Las Vegas casinos lured customers with their flashing lights and neon signs. Today, they've gone it a step farther. They've added towering fountains that almost seem to dance right in front of your eyes. They have volcanic explosions where you can feel the heat. They showcase pirate ships that tilt and rock while buccaneers swing on ropes high above.

Action gets people's attention.

We see action at sporting events, especially with the movement of a ball. After a game, ask the third baseman how many times the ball went to him. He'll know exactly. "It was seven. The first one was a slow roller, the second was hit to my left, the third was..." He remembers because he did something. He moved. Ask the right fielder how many times the ball was hit to the third baseman and he won't remember. Why? He was not involved. Unlike the third baseman, it meant nothing to him.

The same is true when we drive. If we're not behind the wheel making the turns and stepping on the gas, the likelihood of us remembering the way to Grandma's house is slim. We weren't active. We looked out the window, watched the cows, thought about the big project on Monday, and paid no attention to that red car that cut us off on Highway 62. The driver not only remembers the incident but can take you back to the spot three months later.
  Adding a dose of action to every link creates memorable images.

The Body Anchor Method is useful when you're in a conversation and you don't want to interrupt, yet you want to remember what to

Body Anchor Method

say. As a reminder, take the key word of your statement or question and link it to a body part.

For instance, when your friend tells you about her daughter's cooking class, this may remind you of the new cookbook you saw at the store. Rather than interrupting her, simply associate a cookbook covering your head. Once your friend finishes her story, you'll go to your anchors to retrieve the information.

When your son bounces in from school, excited by telling you he's the team's new pitcher, you may not want to cut short his gusto. Instead, associate a trash bag wrapped around your waist or elbow and you'll be reminded to tell him to "pitch the trash."

Sometimes there are things you do want to remember that you do not want to discuss. For instance, when your friend mentions she's taking her new phone to get repaired, you're reminded about the repair you need to get on your son's bike. Rather than reaching for a pencil to jot the thought down, or rudely stopping her in mid-sentence with, "Hey, remind me ...," use your body anchor. Associate your thumb caught in the bike's spoke. If you anticipate grimacing, you can always associate the bike riding over your friend's phone. Each method you're reminded.

A salesman told me how he used the Body Anchor Method to sell a car. Early in the conversation, he recalled the prospect saying he had a tee time later that day. The salesman associated golf clubs to one of his anchors which reminded him to direct the customer to the larger car with the bigger trunk. "*Mr. Jones, look how easily your clubs can fit in here.*"

It's happened to every person who has ever had a conversation. Sooner or later we're going to think, *I forgot what I was going to say*. The Body Anchor Method prevents that, but you have to act quickly. As soon as you think of what to say, without wanting to interrupt the speaker, mentally throw your key word on a body part. Who *nose*, from *ear* on out, this method may be all your *knee-d*. Anything less would be a total *waist*. Go *a-head* and try it.
From page 30, match the picture to the body part.

Body Anchor Method

Birthday Card	Head
Money	Nose
Flowers	Ear
Book	Neck
Dip Stick	Shoulder
Tickets	Elbow
Toothpaste	Thumb
Plunger	Waist
Soup Can	Knee
Shirt	Foot

Number / Shape Method

Numbers are boring. They sit there and do nothing. They're not colorful, playful, or memorable. The Number / Shape Method changes that. The shape of the number takes on an object, thus making it memorable.

1 is shaped like a rocket.

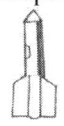

2 is shaped like a swan.

3 is shaped like a pitchfork.

4 is similar to a sailboat.

5 is similar to a saxophone.

6 resembles a golf club.

7 is shaped as a diving board.

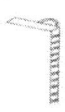

8 represents a snowman.

9 looks like a flagpole.

10 is a bat and ball.

Number / Shape Method

If you notice an object other than what's listed, make that your choice. For instance, the number 1 resembles a pencil, 2 resembles a coat hanger, and 3 looks like an unfinished heart on its side. With a little imagination, the number 4 looks like a roof, 5 looks like a fish hook, and number 6 resembles a cherry. The number 7 looks like a cane, 8 looks like a racetrack, 9 looks like a bent needle, and 10 looks like an ice fisherman's pole placed down by the opening in a lake. If you reach back and use your imagination, you'll see it too.

Decide which object works best for you. This is your list. Each number will represent a specific object. This visual will be your anchor to hang new information to what you need to remember.

Remembering The Bill of Rights

To remember the Bill of Rights, the first 10 Amendments of the U.S. Constitution, associate the main idea to each one of your anchors. Here's an example.

1 = rocket The 1st Amendment represents freedom of speech. To remember, link what we know (*rocket*) to what we're trying to know (*freedom of speech*). Imagine a public speaker, standing atop a rocket, lifted off to space. Rocket means 1. Speaker means freedom of speech. By linking them, it strengthens our memory.

2 = swan The 2nd Amendment is about the right to keep and bear arms. Imagine a *swan* with huge arms. The arms are waving a huge gun. The image is absurd and ridiculous, but memorable.

3 = pitchfork The 3rd Amendment states that no soldier shall, in time of peace, be quartered in any house without the consent of the owner. To remember, associate *pitchfork* to the key word in that amendment, *quarter*. Now, imagine quarters spinning on a pitchfork.

Number / Shape Method

4 = sailboat The 4th Amendment is about unreasonable searches and seizures. Visualize a sailboat with thousands of flashlights guiding its path. It's ridiculous, but it works. Having the sailboat searched isn't bizarre enough.

5 = saxophone The 5th Amendment provides that no person can be forced to be a witness against him or herself. Taking the fifth means we don't talk. Visualize a tongue being used to clog a saxophone. Hey, that hurts!

6 = golf club The 6th Amendment represents the right to a speedy and public trial by an impartial jury. Associate jury to golf club and it sticks in our mind, especially if a jury box is speeding on the fairway.

7 = diving board The 7th Amendment is about the preservation of trial by jury. Imagine a diving board preserved in a glass jar. Another image could be a diving board used as a preservative on your bread. By remembering the key word, *preserved,* we'll easily remember the 7th Amendment.

8 = snowman The 8th Amendment is about unnecessary cruel and unusual punishment. People shall not be allowed to be tortured or be imposed with excessive bail or fines. Imagine setting fire to a snowman. That's cruel. Another visual is pitching bales of hay at a snowman. *Bales* reminds us of excessive *bails* or fines. Although the spelling is different, bales and bails are pronounced the same, and that makes it memorable.

9 = flagpole The 9th Amendment states that "the enumeration in the Constitution, of certain rights, shall not be construed to deny or disparage others retained by the people." In other words, it states that any rights that weren't specifically listed would not be forfeited. This includes, marrying, raising a family, and moving from place to place. Once we understand what this amendment states, all we have to do is associate the key word, which is *List*, on a flagpole to remind us of this important amendment.

Number / Shape Method

10 = bat and **ball** The 10th Amendment recognizes that states are allowed to do many things at the local level. For instance, traffic and child custody laws are in the domain of the states. The key word is *state*. Picturing a state is difficult, but picturing a *steak* isn't. The word *steak* is similar to *state*. Visualizing hitting a ball with a *steak*, instead of a bat, reminds us that the state plays an important role in the 10th Amendment.

We've just learned the Bill of Rights and all we did was link two items ten times.

Number / Rhyme Method

The Number / Rhyme Method is another way in remembering. Choosing a word that rhymes with a number makes it memorable.

1 = bun, gun, run, sun
2 = shoe, glue, zoo
3 = tree, sea, key
4 = door, floor, boar
5 = hive, dive, chive
6 = bricks, sticks, kicks
7 = Kevin, heaven
8 = gate, bait
9 = sign, pine, wine, dine
10 = hen, pen, men

Choose only one word for each number. For instance, if you chose *Sun* for 1, picture a place when you were under the sun. Was it at the beach? Which beach? Were you in the water or sun bathing? Each number picture should take you to a specific place where you saw this object. For example...

2 = shoe Visualize a particular shoe, in a particular place.

3 = tree Mentally see a tree.

4 = door Which door are you referring to? Go to it.

5 = hive Imagine a huge beehive.

6 = bricks Which bricks? Were they a part of your house, chimney, walkway, or stacked behind your garage?

7 = Kevin If you don't know someone named Kevin, here's your chance. Another image is Heaven. Visualizing rain or clouds may be better than picturing Heaven's Gate, since gate represents 8.

Number / Rhyme Method

8 = gate Visualize a particular railroad gate.

9 = sign Is it a yield, stop, or right of way sign? Choose.

10 = pen Get one in your head. That's your visual for number 10.

Going to the store to shop? Associate each item needed to each anchor. Here's your list: (1) ice cream, (2) bread, (3) toothpaste, (4) English muffins, (5) milk, (6) baking powder, (7) yogurt, (8) corn, (9) onions, and (10) spaghetti.

(Memory Quiz on following page)

Visualize seeing the sun inside an ice cream cone.

Associate bread stuffed in your shoes.

In your "mind's eye," picture lettuce covering the tree. And while you're at it, associate English muffins spinning on your doorknob.

Five represents hive. Imagine dumping milk over all those bees.

Imagine baking powder covering the bricks, and remember to see yogurt spilled over your friend, Kevin.

Ears of corn, instead of a gate, are coming down at the railroad crossing. Try to see that. After you do, look at the stop sign made of onions. That's sweet.

For number 10, associate spaghetti wrapped around a pen.

This system won't keep you walking back and forth the entire grocery store. For example, once you reach for the bread and then notice the English Muffins, you'll remember to grab them, even though it's farther down your list.

The next day, if we have to remember another list, the previous list will fade from our memory. The action-oriented image helps us to remember. To prove it, as you're reading these pages, imagine

Number / Rhyme Method

squirting ketchup all over this paragraph. Now, look away for a moment, and then come back to the next paragraph.

As you're reading these words, imagine highlighting, with a yellow marker, the entire paragraph. Go ahead and do it. I know this goes against everything you've stood for. You've never been one to write in books but do it with this one.

Okay, snap out of it. When you were reading about highlighting the page, were you still looking at the ketchup stain? Fortunately, our brains keep us straight. It's difficult to imagine two separate bizarre images at the same time.

Keep the Number Rhyme Anchor Method simple by associating each number to a particular place.

Memory Quiz

Use the alphabet peg to remember this list...
Allow 2-minutes

Using the words below, fill in the blanks to its position as seen on previous page.

Yogurt, Ice Cream, Baking Powder, Lettuce,

English Muffin, Onions, Bread, Corn, Spaghetti, Milk

1 (bun)_____   6 (bricks) _____

2 (shoe) _____   7 (heaven) _____

3 (tree) _____   8 (gate) _____

4 (door) _____   9 (sign) _____

5 (hive) _____   10 (pen) _____

How to Memorize an Entire Year

(in less than 2 Minutes)

Whoever said, "Death and Taxes are the only certainties in life," didn't own a dog. Visit a dog owner's home and the countdown begins when Fido will be asked to roll over, shake your hand, or simply sit. Dog owners relish in showing you their four-legged friend's latest trick.

Don't despair if you have no pet. With your new memory, you can be just as engaging. Your bag of tricks will have people flocking by your side, asking "Do it again, will you?" You'll be happy to oblige, especially since you won't be asked to chase down a Frisbee.

You know you're special because you're the only person in the room who understands anchors, association, and exaggeration. To prove your point, you're about to show everyone how you can memorize an entire calendar. When they give you a date on the calendar, you'll be able to tell them what day of the week it falls. It will also help you get invited to more parties.

To memorize a 365-day calendar, there are a few basics we need to know:

1) There are twelve months, beginning with January and ending with December.
2) There are seven days in each week, beginning with Monday and ending with Sunday.
3) Simple Arithmetic.

How to Memorize an Entire Year

Begin by creating visuals for each month.

January	Ball Drop at Times Square
February	Snowman
March	Marching Band
April	April Showers
May	Flowers
June	Graduation Cap
July	Fireworks
August	Beach
September	School Bus
October	Halloween
November	Thanksgiving Turkey
December	Christmas Tree

Next, we take the numbers 1 through 7, representing the seven days of the week, and transpose them to visuals.

1 = Bun
2 = Shoe
3 = Tree
4 = Door
5 = Hive
6 = Bricks
7 = Rain (from Heaven)

How to Memorize an Entire Year

In 2019, the following days are the first Monday's of each month:

            January 7   July 1
            February 4   August 5
            March 4   September 2
            April 1   October 7
            May 6   November 4
            June 3   December 2

To remember January 7 is the first Monday of the month, visualize the Times Square *Ball* falling from the *Heavens*. When we see that visualization, we not only have memorized the first Monday of the month, but the other 30 days as well.

For example, what day does is January 23? If we know January 7 is a Monday, we know seven days later that the 14th is a Monday, and seven days later the 21st is a Monday. Two days later is Wednesday the 23rd.

What day falls on January 12th? By knowing that January 7 is a Monday, we only have to do simple math to know the answer. Five days from the 7th is Saturday the 12th.

For February 4 visualize a *Snowman* walking through a *Door* or a *Snowman-shaped Door*.

For March 4 visualize a *Marching* band stuck in a huge of *Door*.

To remember April 1 is a Monday, simply associate a *Shower* spewing hamburger *Buns*. Once we commit that to memory, we've also remembered the other April days.

For May 6, visualize *Flowers* stuck in *Bricks*.

For June 3, *visualize Graduation Caps* covering *Trees*.

For July 1, *Fireworks* display of burger *Buns* shooting into the air.

How to Memorize an Entire Year

For August 5, a *Wave* of *Beehives* rolling onto the shore.

For September 2, picture a *School Bus* stuffed *Shoes* or the *Bus* is shaped like a giant *Shoe*.

For October 7, imagine holding a *Trick or Treat Bag* candy reaching to the *Heavens*.

For November 4, imagine carving a *Turkey* with a giant *Door* or a *Turkey* is walking through a *Door*.

For December 2, visualize a *Christmas* tree decorated with *Shoes*.

By remembering these 12 images, we've memorized the entire 2019 calendar of 365 days. Also, we can easily do the same for 2020 even though it's a leap year.

Remembering the calendar is similar to finding the word in a dictionary. It's all about mental compartments. Your friends will think you've spent months memorizing all 365 days. However, what they don't know is that you've established a dozen anchors, a starting point for each month. With that starting point, you know every day of the year.

This system comes in handy in other ways, too. When you're asked if you want to go to the drive-in movie on the 7th of next month, you can reply "Sorry Charlie, Thursday's are when I wash my hair."

Alphabet Anchor Method

This system enables you to recall up to 26 items. Since the objective is to create a picture, the *sound* of the letter will represent a visual image. For example, *elephant* and *envelope* begin with the letter *E*, but are pronounced L-*ephant* and N-*velope*. Once you pronounce the letter, you're on the way to pronouncing the word.

LETTER	VISUAL
A	Ape
B	Bee
C	Sea
D	Deed
E	Eel
F	Effort (from weightlifter)
G	Jeep
H	H-Bomb
I	Eye
J	Jay Bird
K	Cake
L	Elephant
M	Emcee
N	Envelope
O	Odor (from skunk)
P	Pea
Q	Cue Stick
R	Arch
S	S-Curve
T	Golf Tee
U	Unicycle
V	Venus
W	W. C. Fields (cigar smoke)
X	X-Ray
Y	YMCA
Z	Zebra

Alphabet Anchor Method

Attach what you want to remember to each item.

Want to remember to return library book, send letters, and sharpen pencils? Then, associate *book* to *ape*. See the ape throwing millions of books around the cage.

Letters to *Bee*. See bees carrying letters from flower to flower.
Pencils to *Sea*. See millions of pencils floating in the sea, or a giant wave of pencils is about to crash upon you. Get the point?

This system is perfect for locating your car at the mall. Can't remember you parked in *K*? You will when you associate your car as a cake (K-ake). By associating your car with cake, you'll be reminded of where you parked when you ask yourself, *where's my car? Oh yeah, cake. I parked in K.*

Memory Quiz

Use the alphabet peg to remember this list…
Allow 5-minutes

A	Book (Apes are throwing books)	N	Calendar
B	Mail (Bees carrying mail)	O	Sunrise
C	Pencils (Sea full of pencils)	P	Blanket
D	Wrestling Mat	Q	Lamp
E	Trumpet	R	Soccer Net
F	Toll Booth	S	Calculator
G	Poster	T	Penguin
H	Cell Phone	U	Moon
I	Waterfall	V	Kettle
J	Paint	W	Ketchup
K	Music Box	X	Bike Pump
L	Soldier	Y	Fountain
M	Wedding Cake	Z	Drum

Alphabet Anchor Method

Using the words below, fill in the blanks to its position as seen on previous page.

Waterfall, Kettle, Pencils, Moon, Trumpet, Wedding Cake, Sunrise, Cell Phone, Soldier, Toll Booth, Wrestling Mat, Music Box, Calculator, Mail, Penguin, Fountain, Poster, Bike Pump, Drum, Soccer Net, Blanket, Books, Paint, Ketchup, Lamp, Calendar

A	_____	N	_____
B	_____	O	_____
C	_____	P	_____
D	_____	Q	_____
E	_____	R	_____
F	_____	S	_____
G	_____	T	_____
H	_____	U	_____
I	_____	V	_____
J	_____	W	_____
K	_____	X	_____
L	_____	Y	_____
M	_____	Z	_____

CHAPTER 3

How to Speak Without Notes

It has been said that the brain is a wondrous thing. It starts working the moment we are born but tends to stop the moment we stand to speak in public.

That statement was probably delivered with notes.

There's nothing wrong with speaking with notes. It shows that we care about our message and about the people who are present to listen. Nothing is worse than listening to a speaker who doesn't care about his message. Seeing a speaker with notes tells us, hey, at least the guy's trying.

Effort aside, it tells us something else. Does the speaker realize we're in the room? He hasn't brought his head up since he stepped behind the lectern 30 minutes ago. Watching the top of a speaker's head has a direct correlation to the inside of our own head. We start daydreaming. *Jamie's soccer practice is tomorrow… must wash uniform tonight; chicken in freezer … must take out tomorrow; proposal due on Friday … must look for new job on Thursday.*

A speaker who is glued to his notes may lose his audience, but he does help them organize their lives. Daydreaming will do that for you. We don't want our audience to daydream.

Whether we want to inspire, motivate, inform, or humor the audience, our goals are to connect with them. Notes get in the way.

Can you imagine how ineffective comedians Jimmy Fallon, Conan O'Brien, or Ellen DeGeneres would be if they used notes? Granted, they may lean toward cue cards, but the words aren't held in their hands. Watch George Carlin's four-minute monologue, *I'm a Modern Man* on *YouTube* and see if he would have been just as effective as if he had clutched 3x5 note cards.

Yes, Martin Luther King and John F. Kennedy succeeded by using notes, as did that fella in Gettysburg, but most likely, their stage was a bit bigger than the one we'll stand on.

Our stage may be a hotel ballroom, a high school auditorium, or the

How to Speak Without Notes

office break room. We want a clear pathway to our audience, void of lecterns and note cards that get in the way of our message.

There's pressure in delivering a speech without notes, but there are rewards when speaking without them. You're one speaker who maintained eye contact, spoke confidently, and gestured without fumbling for printed words.

Giving a speech is no different than sitting down at the coffee shop with our best buddy. We talk, don't we? We communicate our thoughts freely, openly, and easily. We're not pulling sheets of paper out from our breast pocket with the words, *Thank you for having me here today*. When we discuss one topic, it reminds us to talk about another.

Conversations advance because of reminders; attaching new information to what we already know. The following exchange between Bob and Judy is an example.

Bob: "Hi Judy, how's George?"
Judy: "He's great. He got a new job downtown."
Bob: "Which reminds me, I went downtown to the concert last night."
Judy: "Which reminds me, my son wants concert tickets for Christmas."
Bob: "Which reminds me, for Christmas, we're cutting down a fresh tree this year."
Judy: "Which reminds me, a tree blocked the road to Mount Vernon."
Bob: "Which reminds me, Mount Vernon, how's Martha?"

Notes are the *Which reminds me*'s in public speaking. When we finish with one topic, we glance down to see what we talk about next.

For instance, if we tell three people, on three occasions, about our week-long vacation to New York City, our story will not be told the same to each person. Yet, the message will be the same.

How to Speak Without Notes

We'll talk about our experience of riding on a subway, standing on the observation deck of the Empire State Building, attending a Knicks game, and skating at Rockefeller Center. We don't need notes for that. We've experienced it and we remember it. However, what we may need notes for is recalling the order we visited them, as well as the sights and sounds we heard along the way. Note cards keep us on track.

Usually, when note cards are used, only key words are printed reminding the speaker as to what to talk about next. The word *Subway* will automatically trigger his mind to talk about his journey beneath New York's street. He'll talk about the mad rush to find a seat, how others were grabbing onto poles, and how some were grabbing onto others.

The next word on the note card will read, *Empire State Building*. This reminds the speaker to talk about the long line waiting to get to the top, the wind whipping once he reached the top, and the view of all those yellow cars below. One thought will remind him of another. But what happens after he finishes talking about the Empire State Building? He must pivot to another NYC adventure and remember.

Good thing he has notes, because his next card reads, *Knicks*. In his mind, he's saying, Oh, which reminds me. *We went to Madison Square Garden and watched the Knicks beat the Cavs. It was fun. During the game ...*

From *Knicks* the next card may read, *Skating*, a reminder to talk about the adventure on ice.

If he could only remember without using notes, his stage presence would be stronger. He'd be free to gesture and his eyes would be on the audience. He can still accomplish all this and use notes. The best part is, the notes will never be seen by the audience.

It's almost impossible to think of two things at the same time. We can think of things very, very quickly, but it's difficult for our mind to see two images at once. Try it for yourself. Can you think of a *giraffe* and a *phone* at the same time? How about thinking about a *moose* and a *letter opener*? Try thinking of a *ping pong table* and the *Chesapeake Bay Bridge-Tunnel*.

Linking

If you're like most people, your mind moved from one image to the next at rapid speed, but the images were not combined.

Let's take the four subjects in the earlier speech - *Subway, Empire State Building, Knicks,* and *Skating* - and commit them to memory. To do this, we must remember that premise about how we make conversation. We attach new information to what we already know.

The first part is *Subway*. Once we discuss this we have to pivot to *Empire State Building*. By attaching new information (*Empire State Building*) to what we already know (*Subway*) we are able to remember. However, a subway and a building don't go together. I've never witnessed a building board a subway. I've never seen a subway ride an elevator to the top floor.

Each time I've passed through New York City subway turnstiles nothing unusual has happened. It's been relatively mundane. Yes, I've been crammed with the masses and the subway car does rock, but the lights have never gone out and the windows have never broken. Plus, the people have kept to themselves.

However, if I saw the President of the United States, the Pope, or a 16-foot alligator on the train, I would remember. It's out of the ordinary, it's different, it doesn't happen every day.

The power of remembering two things at the same time is to create unusual images that are combined into one.

To remember *Subway* and *Empire State Building* one image needs to be made. Standing behind the solid yellow line and seeing the Empire State Building come down the track is an experience long remembered. It wasn't expected. It's also memorable. It's that exaggeration that helps us lock in the information.

How to Speak Without Notes

If you want to speak without notes, create one of these crazy pictures. Don't worry, you're not going to laugh out loud. Instead, you're going to move smoothly from your *Subway* story to your *Empire State Building* experience.

Once we talk about the Empire State Building, we move to the New York Knicks. Applying the same principal, we associate new information (*Knicks*) to what we already know (*Empire State Building*). Notice that we're not including *Subway*. We stepped out of that subway car when we started speaking about the Empire State Building. The subway is long gone.

Crazy, bizarre, ridiculous. That's the connection we want to make between *Empire State Building* and *Knicks* basketball. We want to put the building where the ball goes or put the ball where the building goes. For instance, imagine dropping thousands of basketballs off the Empire State Building. Can you mentally see them speeding through the air like tiny, orange parachutes falling to the ground? Why do we throw thousands of basketballs, instead of just one? The volume enables us to embed that image into our mind. If it were only one, we may not see it. With thousands, they're everywhere.

Another image we could create is seeing the Empire State Building playing basketball. The ref may call "foul," but spectators call it memorable.

From Knicks basketball we speak on ice skating. We remember the order because we're connecting new information (*Skating*) to what we already know (*Knicks*). And what do we do with the Empire State Building? It's back on the corner of 5th and West 34th where it belongs.

Bouncing a basketball outside a skating rink is not memorable. We want to mentally see an image that's totally ridiculous. It's the ridiculous that we remember. Remember?

Imagine ice skates on a basketball. A crowd would gather for that. The basketballs are skating on the rink.

How to Speak Without Notes

It takes only a split second for our mind to see that image. The more bizarre and action-oriented the visual, the more it becomes cemented in our memory.

Can you remember the list? The first word was Subway, and that reminds us of _____ and that reminds us of _____. That reminds us _____.

Did you mentally see the Empire State Building on the subway track? Then, did you "see" the Empire State Building playing basketball? From basketballs, did you visualize the balls skating on ice? One image kicks into another.

We can confidently give this speech because we've added color and pizzazz to our brain. Instead of physically seeing the words on note cards, we're mentally seeing the images we created. We can do this with any speech we give.

For most speeches, we don't want to memorize it word for word. However, there may be times when we must, such as reciting the *Gettysburg Address*.

In rehearsal, read the speech from a piece of paper. Then, place the paper down and attempt to recite it from memory. If you stumble, go back to the paper and see where you can link the last word you're able to memorize, to the next word. Start at the beginning and keep practicing.

If you're giving a speech without notes, you must have an exit strategy. That's not to say yell *"FIRE!"* or consider a fainting spell, but it means that you have to know what to do if you do forget. You don't want to be standing on stage in front of 200 people and say, *"Four score and seven ... bear with me for a moment."*

If you got to *"Four score and seven years ago,"* and forgot, you can counter with, *Yes, Abraham Lincoln was on his way to giving an inspirational...*

If you're unable to recall the word or sentence you need, pause and ask a question on what you have just said. Speaking on education? Ask, "How much time do you read to your children?" Speaking about fitness? Ask, "What are some of your fitness goals?" Speaking about the budget? Ask, "Wouldn't you agree we have to cut expenditures?" This extra pause may be the time you need to get back on track.

In rehearsal, fight your way to the end of your speech if you do forget. You won't have the luxury of walking back to your kitchen table to glance at your notes during your big speech. Afterward, begin the speech again. If you find yourself stuck, pause, slow down, repeat what you have said, and somehow get through your talk. This is rehearsal, so now's the time to throw yourself into the fire, if only the simulator.

Do you know how many stage actors forget their lines? More than we know, I'm sure. They may not remember, but somehow, they get through it. That's why they're called actors. The audience doesn't have a clue.

Singers and musicians can't get away with it so easily. Deep into the 2008 *American Idol* competition, artist Brooke White forgot her lyrics. She stopped and started over. Judge Paula Abdul wasn't so sympathetic, stating that as a performer you just can't do that, and if you have to ad lib.

Speakers have it easier. We can slow the pace, speed the pace, ask for a glass of water, and ask for the heat to be turned down. We can stand still, sit on a stool, walk about, or kneel. We can ad lib. Piano players, and those who play the harp, can never get away with all that. If a musician can't remember the tune, everyone in the audience will think, that didn't sound right. If a speaker doesn't remember the speech, the audience may not be aware.

Whether it's Vegas, or Branson, or down at the neighborhood bar, singers have to get it right. There's only one way to sing "The

How to Speak Without Notes

Impossible Dream." Motivational speakers have hundreds of ways of delivering it.

Be authentic. The audience doesn't want you to be someone else. They're not looking for a speaker who looks and sounds like Elvis. They came to hear you. You have an advantage. You know the words you're going to say, while the audience doesn't. So, if you do forget, just go down a different road, preferably one that doesn't come to a dead one. Try to avoid looking frazzled and out of sync and say something. We ad lib with our friends, don't we?

Using Acronyms

An effective method many speakers use for remembering a speech is applying acronyms. This way, if you do forget, the audience can help you out. If presented properly, they'll never know you had a mental lapse.

No matter what your topic is, pull out a key word and draft your speech using the letters from that word. If your speech is about growing roses, then make *ROSES* the basis of your talk. *R* can represent *Rain*. We need rain to make them grow. *O* stands for *Oxygen*. They need to breathe and they need light. *S* could stand for *Soil*, *E* for *Environment*, and *S* for *Sweet* smelling. Since you're already familiar with your topic, you can easily pivot from one segment to another.

In your opening remarks, state the key word to the audience. Not only does this help you to remember the speech, but it keeps the audience on track, as well. They now become participants. They know after you speak about the first *R*, you're going to mention an *O* next. The beauty of this system is that if you forget, you can ask, "What do you think the *O* stands for in growing roses?" You may hear *Oasis* or *Observation* or *Organic*. This question and answer period allows you to start thinking really hard what your *O* stands for. And, perhaps they may give you a better answer than the one you had planned to use.

How to Speak Without Notes

Giving a talk about Education? If so, use *TEACH*. *T* stands for *Time* management, *E* stands for *Effort*, *A* for *Achieve*, *C* for *Clarity*, and *H* for *Habit* or *Handwriting* or *Humor* or *Honors*.

Are you motivating your sales staff? If so, use *SALES*. *S* stands for *Service*. *A* stands for *Accountability*, *L* equals *Leadership*, *E* for *Engage*, and *S* for *Smile*. Each word automatically reminds you what your message is about. For instance, being *Engaged* means conversing with the prospect, asking open ended questions, showing that you care, and you're available to assist. You'll know to share examples and systems relating to that key word. Plus, your acronym method creates a device for your salespeople to remember for the entire day. Using acronyms is an easy-to-follow system helping not only the speaker to remember, but also the listener.

When drafting your speech, make sure a dictionary or thesaurus is nearby. The latter is a great, outstanding, wonderful, terrific, splendid, majestic, and impressive tool. Use it.

Senator and statesman Daniel Webster (1782-1852) said, "If all my talents and powers were to be taken from me by some inscrutable providence, and I had my choice of keeping but one, I would unhesitatingly ask to be allowed to keep the Power of Speaking, for through it, I would quickly recover all the rest."

Speaking is power. You gain more of that power when you relinquish your notes.

CHAPTER 4

How to Remember Names

How to Remember Names

It's your parents first nightmare, a time they could have avoided months earlier, instead of putting it off until the last minute. They could have easily consulted family, friends, and even professional help from numerous books they browsed through the past nine months. Instead they waited, thinking this day would never come.

Now, as they hold you, adore you, and kiss you, their fears are becoming more evident. After gently placing you in your warm crib, they look frantically at each other asking the question they should have answered a long time ago, an answer that will be carried with you forever.

"What are we going to name it?"

They have to name you something. Names are important. There's a lot of pressure with naming a child. For the first few weeks, it may seem strange identifying this newborn by its name. Before long, you'll realize there couldn't have been a better choice.

No matter which name is chosen, it will be the right one. Your child will put that name on all their books and papers, write it when buying a home, and give it when looking for a job. The name will represent who he is, and he'll carry it wherever he goes. It will be the first thing she says when she meets someone. It will be the first thing she looks for after she's quoted in the newspaper, and nine times out of ten, it will be the first thing he writes to check if his pen has any more ink.

In today's fiercely competitive world, the edge goes to the person with the best memory. It's that simple. Since we're all in the people business, it pays to remember names.

You're Very Special

Outside the Dolby Theatre in the hours leading up to the Academy Awards ceremony, hundreds of people wait patiently hoping to catch a glimpse of their favorite stars. The moment these celebrities step out of their limos, fans are calling their names. Why are they

How to Remember Names

able to remember their names so easily? They don't know these people. They never invited them to their homes. They don't share an office cubicle. They remember their names because they are interested in them. To remember someone's name we must be interested in the person who owns it. You may think it's easy to recall a celebrity's name because we see him in our living rooms, whereas the folks we meet will never grace magazine covers or be seen on television and movie screens. Still, it should be easier to remember these people because we've spoken to them and they've spoken to us.

We shook their hands, exchanged business cards, and sat next to them. We remember them because their son plays ball with our kids, they live in our neighborhoods, attend our churches, and know some of the same people we know. That's why we remember them. We have common bonds.

The more interested we are in the people we meet, the more likely we'll remember their names. Each person we meet today is different from the person we may meet tomorrow. Each has a special quality and uniqueness. The people we meet are experts. They know about subjects we don't. They might be practiced in pottery, music, photography, dog training, American history, or woodworking. They're talented, unique, and have a lot to offer. Yes, every person we meet knows something we don't.

Treat each person as the most important person in the world because they are. They're taking time out of their life to be with you when they could be talking or doing business with someone else. See each person as an individual and act interested.

Whether you're a school teacher talking to a student, a shop owner meeting a customer, or a salesperson talking to a client, focus your attention on that person and show an interest. You may want to visualize this person as your mother's cousin or best friend, or the person you're meeting is about to give you a check for $100,000. It's hard to forget her now.

Whether you're speaking to the checkout person at the grocery store or the person you're introduced to at the meeting, show a genuine interest in what they're saying. Remember, you're in the people business each day of your life. You can't get along without them. They're the ones who sell you the paint at the hardware store, the ones you call to order a pizza, and the ones we trust when we send our children to school. Actually, they're just like us. They work hard, are loved by others, and want to live happily ever after.

Showing an interest in everyone we meet is the first step in remembering their name. How do you remember a name? You start by showing an interest. That interest will compound as others will be interested in you.

Focus, Focus, Focus

Think back when you first learned to drive. You were focused on the job at hand, making certain mirrors were in the correct position; your seat belt was securely fastened, and turn signals came on at every turn. You never considered talking on the phone or turning on the radio. By concentrating on the road, you eliminated distractions. However, after a few weeks you might have added a few. You were able to put cream in your coffee, munch on french fries, and call your friend about the bad drivers hogging your lane.

Our concentration level might have slipped since our first day on the road. The same holds true when meeting people. After meeting one, then another, and then another, our concentration level subsides. We begin thinking about other things. At the party we may be thinking about the tray full of shrimp, instead of the person standing in front of us. The chandelier in the center of the room may appear more sparkling than the people below it.

If you want to make a good first impression, it's important to concentrate. If not, the person you're with may not give you a second chance.

Usually, when we're meeting someone for the first time, we're not in familiar territory of our home or backyard. Instead, we're sitting in a hotel meeting room, shopping in aisle three, or strolling on a

How to Remember Names

city sidewalk. There are distractions all around us. Couple that with trying to remember a name and the pressure to concentrate is on. Focus on the individual when you're ready to introduce yourself. Avoid thinking about the next person you're going to meet. Concentrate. You only get one chance to make this first impression. Take advantage of it.

The first word spoken when meeting someone is our name. That's why it's called an *introduction*. Unfortunately, it's usually the first word forgotten. The name escaped us. It went over our heads and out the window. Thirty minutes into our conversation we're still wondering, *Whom am I speaking with*? The embarrassment is too overwhelming to reintroduce ourselves. We weren't concentrating.

Concentrating on remembering a name can take place hours before you meet someone. Driving to a business meeting where you know you're going to meet new people, concentrate not only on the road, but also on the people you're going to encounter. Anticipate meeting these people and remind yourself to focus on the names when they are given.

At work, when you're on your way to the Accounting Office, concentrate on the people you know you're going to see. Remember? There are four people in the department. There's Barbara, Judy, Henry, and Lynn. By going over the names in your mind, you won't be caught off guard when you bump into them.

So far, we know we're going to be interested in the person and we're going to concentrate when the name is given. We're two steps ahead in the game before we even meet the person.

Eyes on You

When it comes to spectators, you can't beat tennis fans. They look to the left. They look to the right. They look to the left. They look to the right. If you ever want to borrow money from a tennis fan, begin your question with, "Do you mind…" instead of "May I…" because they're constantly shaking their head from side to side. Not all tennis fans appear to be in disagreeing form; they just keep their

53

How to Remember Names

eye on the ball. If you look right when you should be looking left you're going to miss all the action. The same applies with remembering names.

Keeping your eye on the ball, or person, keeps you in the game. It's virtually impossible to remember someone's name if you're not looking at the person who's providing it. If, after being introduced, you hear a comment on how nice your shoes are, don't count on that person to remember you. They were looking at your feet, instead of your face.

Watch people meet and notice where they're looking when the name is given. They're looking up, they're looking down, they're looking at the light fixture, the salt shaker, the tie on the person standing to the side. Often the eyes don't lock with the other person they're speaking to, and therefore, neither does the name. The next time you make a purchase, take note whether the clerk is more interested in your face or President Grant's.

Looking people in the eye shows that you're confident and that you care about the person. It's essential for remembering a name.

If you enter a party and the host/hostess wants to introduce you to everyone, you're in deep trouble. You've now lost control of the situation. Often, the host already has low expectations of your ability for recall. That's why during the introductions, he'll rapid fire the names to you as quickly as a mud puddle finds your five-year-old's new shoes. He feels it's his obligation. When it's all over, the only name you remember is your own.

You may encounter another host who shouts, "Hey everybody, this is Josh. Say hi to Josh." This system does work. Hours later, your memory is as sharp as ever when you whisper to your host, "Tell everybody I'm leaving."

If you plan to go to the party, take it upon yourself to make the introductions. Concentrate on one person at a time. Look each person in the eye, make a comment or two, and then move to the next person. One person, one name, nothing complicated. Focusing

How to Remember Names

on an individual by looking at his face will greatly enhance your ability for recalling the name.

For the rest of our lives we'll always have a vivid picture of our own mother. Why? She kept telling us, "Look at me when I'm talking to you." There's a lesson in that. If you want to be remembered and want to remember others, look the person in the eye and give the person a big smile. Who can forget a friendly face?

Listen Up Everybody

In the rotunda of the Virginia State Capitol in Richmond stands the most famous statue of George Washington. Sculpted by Frenchman, Jean Houdon in 1785, the figure is life-like. No wonder. It is the only statue Washington posed for. When visitors approach the statue they are in awe. Their full attention is directed at Washington. They look at him, walk around him, and study the magnificent detail of our first Commander in Chief. When people walk away from the rotunda there's no doubt whom they just met.

However, imagine what would happen if Washington, all of a sudden, came to life. As we're gazing up at him, Washington begins to move his arms and legs, bends forward and speaks. If so, what would we do? We may ponder what the President thinks of us and if he likes what we're wearing. We may be thinking of something clever or witty to say to see if we can make old George laugh. When Washington stood still we thought about him. However, when he comes to life, we start thinking about ourselves, and therefore, we fail to listen.

The problem when meeting people is that they're not statues. As we study them, they study us! We want to make a positive impression by saying something intelligent and of value. In doing so, we're not listening when the name is announced, because we're engrossed in ourselves. How can we remember a name if we don't hear it?

Many people who may not hear the name don't bother about asking for clarification. If it were *Judy*, *Jenny*, or *Janet*, who cares? I'll never see her again, and if I do I'll just say *Hi* and leave it at that.

However, months later when you do see her, you may wish you had listened closer to her name when it was first given.

Listen for the name. Lean slightly forward, pay attention, and you'll make that person feel rich. For instance, if you're unsure if the name was *Marie* or *Maria*, ask. There's nothing wrong with saying "Did you say your name is Maria?" "Please say your last name again?" People won't be offended, they'll be flattered. They'll remember you because you're the only person who took the time to want to remember his name.

If the name you hear is unusual, don't hesitate to ask about the origin of it. "Is that a Russian name? I've never heard that name before. Tell me about it. Is it a family name?" People enjoy talking about their name. Remember, they've owned it for years and they're proud of it. They take it with them wherever they go. Chances are, they'll give you hints as to how to remember it. "It's Mollisee; rhymes with policy." "It's Losee; like a low C." "It's Bumberger; like a bad hamburger."

How is your name memorable? If you haven't already, think of ways to make your name meaningful to others. The time you take to do this will be greatly appreciated by those you meet.

The names *John*, *Mary*, and *Michael* aren't the most popular names. More people are named *Mac*, *Buddy*, *Friend*, *Hey*, or *Chief*, especially by those who have poor listening skills. If you haven't heard the name the odds are not in your favor you'll remember it. There's a reason why we have two ears and one mouth. By taking the time to listen for the name you're taking the time to learn it.

Guaranteed Return Policy

Potatoes can be very hot to the touch, especially those that have been cooking for 60 minutes. I learned this when I reached into the oven to pull one out. When I grabbed hold of it, I got rid of it immediately. It's a lesson I've long remembered. Names are like hot potatoes. When you're handed a name, get rid of it immediately. Throw it back where it came from. You'll remember the name easier when you repeat it to the person who gave it to you.

Make your first reply the name you just heard. It will reinforce the name. "Hi, my name is Jerry, what's your name?" "Jerry, hi. My name is Sam." It's one thing to hear the name; it's another to say it. Allow the name to sink into your head and then let it roll off your tongue. Getting into the habit of repeating the name enhances our ability to remember. Before long it will be natural for you to repeat the name. Everyone you meet, throw their name right back. "Cindy, how are you?" "Ed, glad to see you." "Cy, thanks for stopping by."

By saying the name at the beginning of the conversation it takes pressure off our minds, than if we had to remember the name at the end of the conversation. It's much easier to remember it's Jack we're speaking to when we say "Jack, nice to see you," versus "Nice to see you ... um, Jay? Jim? John?" By the time we say to *Nice to see you*, we've already forgotten the name, because we're thinking about what we're going to say.

Continue to use the name during the conversation but be careful not to overdo it. Try saying the name at least three times during the conversation. "Jeff, you're in an interesting business. What would you say, Jeff, is your biggest challenge?" "I look forward to seeing you again Jeff. Have a great night."

Repeat the name to yourself several times, but don't lose track with what is being said. Knowing the name of your jumpmaster is one thing; not knowing how to deploy the parachute is another. If you're standing with new acquaintances, quickly go over their names in your mind. Look at the person to your right and say to yourself "Al, Al, Al." Now, the person across from you, "Steve, Steve, his name is Steve." It only takes an instant to repeat the names in your mind. This exercise will help you secure those names into your mind.

Jot the name down if an opportunity presents itself. Many times at meetings a guest will introduce himself. Take advantage of the moment by writing the name on a piece of paper. Trace the name and circle it. Draw an arrow in the direction where the person is sitting and quietly repeat the name. Again, it takes only an instant to do this. You're not writing a mathematical equation or listing the lakes in Minnesota. You're writing a name. That's it. It's easy and simple, yet powerful when you present it to the person at the end of the meeting.

Repetition, whether saying it, thinking it, or writing it, bolsters our memory. When someone tells you her name, pretend she's saying, "repeat after me."

Thanks for Noticing

Whoever said, "No two snowflakes are exactly alike," didn't spend last winter in Buffalo. I could have sworn I spotted two that were identical. If I were asked which one was responsible for closing schools, I'd have a hard time identifying them in the police line-up. "I think the second from the right is the one, but then the third from the left looks familiar too."

People, on the other hand, are nothing like snow, even though some may act like flakes.

We are different and rare in every way. An exhibit at Disney World flashes a sign that is forever changing. It shows the number of the billions and billions of people in the world. Fortunately, names aren't included. So many people, each with two eyes, a nose and a mouth; yet they all look different. Our job is to study the faces we meet and find something that's distinguishable.

Look closely at the eyes. Are they small, large, close together, or far apart? What color are they? Are they blue, brown, or green? What about the eyebrows? Are they thin, bushy, or one straight line? Choose one hundred people off the street and you'll find one hundred different pairs of eyes and eyebrows.

Study the face some more. Look at the forehead. Is it wrinkled or smooth? Is it large or small? See any freckles? Drop down to the nose and what do you see? Is it pug, narrow, or wide? Is it crooked or straight? Look at the chin. Is it cleft or prominent in any way? Does the jaw protrude? Any dimples? Are the lips thin, full, or

How to Remember Names

about average? How do the teeth look? Are they straight? Is there a gap in the middle? What about high cheek bones? What color is the hair? Is it curly, straight or balding? Are the ears large or small? After studying all these features it's no wonder why people look different.

Watch the news and study faces of the reporters. What do you notice first about their face? Study the people in the commercials and the shows. How are they different? Look at photos in the newspaper and study the faces. Study people at the mall. Make mental notes of lips and lobes, chins and cheeks, and brows and bangs.

If you're unable to find one outstanding feature, don't fret. By taking the time to study the face, you're farther along than most people who don't even look at the face and thus can't remember the name. Get into the habit of studying every face you see. Therefore, it will become second nature when you see one feature stand out.

Get the Picture

Our parents didn't know any better. It's not their fault. They gave us names such as, *James*, *Mary Ann*, *Susan*, *Barbara*, *Peter*, *Tiffany*, *Martha*, *William*, *Ken*, *David*, and *Carol*. It might have meant something to them, but for the rest of us it means nothing. What's a *Susan*? What's a *Daniel*? How can I remember the name *Deborah*? I don't even know what it is.

Our parents didn't know that. If they wanted our names to be truly memorable they would have given us names such as, *Bookshelf*, *Radioknob*, *Keyboard*, or *Frozenyogurt*. These names mean something. "Your name is *Curtainrod*? Hey, I know what that is. I have one of those. By the way, whatever happened to *Dipstick*?"

Most names don't have any significant meaning and they're difficult to remember. In order to retain information for a long time, we have to associate that new information to something we already know.

We're more apt to remember a guy named *Barsoap* than we are a guy named *Phil*. Why? We know what a bar of soap is. We've seen it, bought it, and used it. We can relate to this guy's name,

How to Remember Names

because we know what a bar of soap is. When we see him we think of soap. When we see Phil there's a struggle to remember his name because it doesn't remind us of anything. Unless your name is *Phil*, you know someone with the name *Phil*, or you wished your name was *Phil*, it may be hard to remember his name. Therefore, the key to remembering names is to make them meaningful. Visuals help to accomplish that.

Names that we had trouble remembering because they had no meaning will come alive. They're no longer going to lie dormant. They're going to get up and walk, and if we can make them run, so be it. These names are going to be enlarged. They're going to fly. They're going to be involved. Every name we hear will be significant, spectacular, and memorable. John Doe won't be any ordinary person. He'll be unforgettable, because we'll make him memorable.

Boring, lazy, humdrum names will be exchanged for vibrant, energetic, and exciting names. Let's take the name *Steve*. What word sounds like *Steve* that's meaningful? It must be a name that's tangible and useful. How about *Stove* or *Sleeve*? We know his name isn't *Stove*, but we know what a stove is.

We're associating what we know and are familiar with (*Stove*) to something unfamiliar (*Steve*). By linking the two it's difficult to break them apart. The consonant letters in *STeVe* are *STV*. By placing vowels in and around those letters we come up with *Stove*. *Sleeve* is also similar, because we're keeping the *S* and *V*.

Another example is the name *Jim*. What's a *Jim*? I don't know, but I know what a *Gym* is. By associating *Gym* to *Jim* we can't go wrong. We come out with the same sound. We also come out looking smart because we remembered his name. Of course, we needn't tell him how we remembered.

How about the name *Brenda*? Taking the consonants and throwing out the vowels we get *BRND*. What word do you see? *Brand* is one word but it's hard to picture. We want a word that we can visualize and understand. The word *Bread* comes close. The letters *BRD*

How to Remember Names

jump out. *Blender* is another word. We now get the letters *BND* which is similar to *BreNDa*. If we picture a *Blender* on *Brenda*, we'll remember her name. We won't be mistaken of calling her *Blender*, even though we may crave a strawberry milkshake when we see her.

The name *Evelyn* is similar to *Violin*. *Cheryl* with *Shovel*. The sounds are comparable. *Beverly* to *Beverage*. *Ray* to *sunRAYS* and *Bruce* to *Bruise*. The examples listed are just that. You may come up with better images. The bottom line is, you have to remember the name. As long as you remember the name, it doesn't matter what you think of. The only goal is to remember the name and recall it easily.

Once we have an image of the name we can connect it to the outstanding feature on the person. If Cheryl's outstanding feature is her long hair, we visualize *Shovels* instead of hair coming down her face and shoulders. It's an image not soon to be forgotten.

The more bizarre and ridiculous the picture, the more likely you'll remember the name.

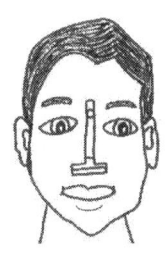

If you meet *Nick* and notice his nose, mentally see a razor (representing *Nick*) replacing his nose. Each *Nick* you meet will be associated with *Razor*.

Each association will mean one specific name. For instance, don't be worried that you'll call *Blanche* by the name *Avalanche* when you see her. You won't. The association will remind you of the name. Once you get to know Blanche, the image of the avalanche will melt and you'll see her as *Blanche*. Again, we're attaching new information to something we already know.

Visualize *Dollar Bills* when you meet someone named *Bill*. Seeing hundreds of dollar *Bills* flying around *Bill's* nose creates a more vivid picture than seeing just one. Weeks later when we run into Bill, he's already reminding us of his name. You can take that to the bank.

The more we drown him in bills, the easier it will be to recall his name. He may change his tie, his shirt, and jacket, but that face is going to be with him no matter where he goes or what he does.

Practice with the associations provided at the end of this section or create your own. With a little effort, you'll have standard pictures for every person you meet. Meeting people will begin to take on a new adventure. Everyone has a name and because of that, a picture. Our job is to get that picture in focus each time.

I Can Relate to That

Of the four *Beatles*, Paul McCartney is the one I recall the most, not that I don't like John Lennon, but I always felt connected to Paul. It's a bond similar to what my sister feels toward Jackie Kennedy, my mother to Helen of Troy, and my friend to Lawrence of Arabia.

Many of us may have difficulty remembering names, but that isn't the case when meeting people who share our names. "Your name is Percy? Hey, that's my name too."

Does the person you're meeting share a name with anyone you know or know of? If so, use your imagination and link the two together. Imagine the two as best friends or roommates.

Meeting a *Donald*? If so, imagine he lives a floor below Donald Trump or was Trump's college roommate.

Meeting a *Fred*? Pretend his grandfather was the brains behind the Fred Flintstone character. The image immediately creates an "Oh, Wow." It's those "Oh Wow's" that help us remember.

Meeting a *Jennifer*? Imagine she's best friends with Jennifer Lopez. Perhaps she'll get you a backstage pass.

It takes a split second to see those images, but it's that split second that helps us remember.

How to Remember Names

Dynamic Duos

What's Frank's wife name? Who is Jay married to? Our new neighbors are Sheila and what's-his-name.

It's one thing trying to remember a name; it's another when you have to remember two of them. However, many times we'll know the name of one, but not the other. No surprise. We work with Cindy, bowl with Larry, and Jason mows our lawn. Howard is our accountant, Sal is our mail carrier, and Wendy teaches our daughter how to play the piano. It would be nice to remember the names of the people they live with.
If you remember one, it's easy to remember the other by using visuals and association techniques.

Ryan and Shelly are engaged; Tina's young son is David; Mitchell and his little sister, Tracy live next door; and Tyler and Sophie are a great couple. How do we remember all that?

At first glance, the name *Ryan* creates no visual. However, when you say the name s-l-o-w-l-y, a picture evolves. The name *Ryan* becomes *RYE-in*. Imagine a *Shell* sandwich on *Rye* and you'll remember *Ryan* is married to *Shelly*. If there's *Mayo* on a *Shell*, you'll know it's *Michelle* (Ma-Shell), instead.

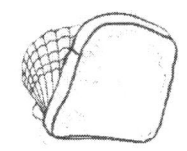

The name *Tina* isn't memorable until you realize there's a *Tea* or *Tee* in her name. The name *David* doesn't mean much either, but it does when you remove the vowels; *DVD*.

Spin a *DVD* atop a *Tee* and that's an image that sticks. It also sticks in Tina's mind that you remember her son's name.

Mentally *Trace* over a catcher's *Mitt* and you'll know that the two kids next door are *Tracy* and *Mitchell*.

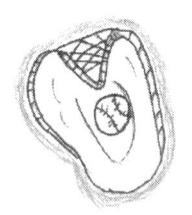

Visualize sewing a tie, and you'll always remember *TIE-ler* (Tyler) and *SEW-phie* (Sophie) go together.

Concerned about remembering the next *Sophie* you meet who's married to Tom Pierson, not Tyler? That hazard is avoided when you incorporate their last name in the association. Imagine <u>*Tomatoes*</u> <u>*Sewn*</u> onto your <u>*Pierced*</u> ears.

It makes no difference what the last name is; there's always something memorable to come out of it.

Meaningful Last Names

Every name has meaning. If not, it will rhyme or sound like something that is meaningful. No matter how long or hard to pronounce, breaking it down into syllables helps us see pictures.

Color Me Beautiful

There are colorful last names, such as *Green*, *Redford*, *Goldberg*, *Silverstein*, *Pinkston*, *White*, *Blackman*, *Copperfield*, *Browning*, *Blue*, and *Gray*. Think of the people you know with a color in their name. You'll come up with quite a few. Visualize dumping paint on their head. Their name will tell you which color to use. It will be an image that will have a lasting impression, but not on them. The more paint the better.

Once you apply the coat you won't have any trouble knowing if it were on Mr. *Greenberg*, *Greenwell*, *Greenwood*, *Greenfield*, or *Greenbaum*, or plain old Mr. *Green*. Mentally seeing the green paint will remind you it's Mr. Greenfield. Depending on which *Green*, you can go a step farther and visualize him painting the field green, the well green, the wood green, or the bomb green, without having it blow up in your face.

How to Remember Names

We all come in many shapes and sizes. Some of us come in different colors. So be ready with your paintbrush when one comes to you.

The Right Place

It would be simpler to remember someone's name if it also told us where she lived. Many names do tell us that. We can imagine Joe, the football great, lived in Montana, or Kirstie, the actress, slept in the Alley. Since they don't, we have to imagine they do. The people we meet come from many places. They come from *Rivers*, *Holmes*, and *Waters*. They live in *Meadows* and *Fields* and *Woods*.

Browse through the newspaper or phone directory and you'll find names with places, such as *Hall*, *Ward*, *London*, *Jordan*, *Starr*, *Moon*, *Houseman*, *Parish*, *Lane*, *Lancaster*, *Barnes*, and *Barnhill*.

Some of the names might be deceiving. You may not see a place, but if you look closely you can see the *Bar* in *Barton*, the *Car* in *Carlton*, and the *town* in *Townsend*. Look a little closer and there's a *Trailer* right in front of you when you're introduced to Miss *Traylor* and the *Grave* in Mr. *Gravely*.

Go to the kitchen and you'll meet a lot of people. There's Mr. *Stover*, Mrs. *Stewart*, and Dr. *Rangely*. Look over there and you'll see Mr. *Sinkler*, Mr. *Spooner*, and Mrs. *Washburn*. It's not *being* in the right place at the right time that matters, but *seeing* the right place at the right time.

The Job Line

Many last names are working hard putting in long hours each day. Be on the lookout for these names, such as *Taylor*, *Miller*, *Weaver*, *Shoemaker*, *Barber*, *Mason*, *Hunter*, *Parker*, *Butcher*, *Farmer*, *Marshall*, *Letterman*, *Bishop*, *King*, *Chancellor*, *Foreman*, and the *Blacksmith*, who we prefer to call *Smith*. These names are begging you to remember them, because they're all doing something.
Visualize throwing knives at Mrs. *Carver*, bricks at Mr. *Brickman*, and nails at Mr. *Carpenter*. You'll never mistake Ms. *Cooke* with Ms. *Baker*, by associating a chef's hat on the former and flour on

How to Remember Names

the latter. Occupational names are working when you may think they're not. There's a *Cop* in *Koppel*, a *Bailiff* in *Bailey*, and a shortstop in *Glover*.

Look in the backyard and you'll see the workings of Mrs. *Gardner* and Mrs. *Douglass*. Could they be planting Mr. *Rose* or Mr. *Bush*? There are numerous employed names in the workforce. Although it may take an effort finding them, they're working hard each day to be remembered.

Hello In There

It would be easy to remember a person's name if they were called *Handcuffs*, *Guitarstrings*, or *Peneraser*. Those names are simple to recall because they're all things. We've seen handcuffs, played with guitar strings, and used pen erasers. We can visualize those objects. At first glance, most last names aren't things, but with a sharp eye and imagination, you'll find them.

Brockington is a name that may appear strange. What's a *Brockington*? I've never seen one of those. Therefore, it's hard to remember, because it's a new word. But wait, let's break it down and find words within that name we are familiar with. We see a *Rock*, a *King*, and a *Ton*. There's also the word *Rocking*. The word *Brock* is similar to the word *Broccoli*. With a little imagination, we can picture a king lifting broccoli that weighs a ton.

We've now taken a name, which at first didn't mean anything, and made it memorable.

Most everyone is carrying something. There's a *Harp* in *Harper*, *Staples* in *Stapleton*, and a *Key* in *Keaton*. There's a *Full Lip* in *Phillips*, a *Meltdown* in *Melton*, and a *Mart* in *Martin*.

There's the *Goodman* family who feels well, the *Kaufman* family who can never shake their cold, and the *Pleasants* who are always doing fine. There are the *Nuckols* and *Nichols*, the *Branches* and *Buckmans*, the *Coles* and *Chapmans*. Things are everywhere. No matter whom you meet, whether it's late at *Knight*, middle of the

How to Remember Names

Davis, or at high *Noonan*, you'll find something memorable about a name.

The Wild Kingdom

The *SPCA* is understaffed. They have no control of the thousands of animals running through city streets, walking on country roads, or shopping in neighborhood stores. Perhaps you're one of these roaming creatures. If so, you're not alone. There are many names that are animalistic and they could be living in your community.

Keep your eyes open for *Byrd*, *Cowens*, *Hawkins*, *Lyons*, *Salmon*, *Henderson*, *Robins*, *Fox*, *Lambert*, *Wrenn*, *Deerfield*, *Fowler*, *Swanson*, or *Morgan*, who's usually atop the horse. Don't overlook Mr. *Finley*, Mrs. *Barker*, Professor *Doggett*, and Rev. *Catlett*, either.

Be careful not to be tickled by Mrs. *Featherstone*, scratched by Mr. *Clauson*, or be chicken of Mrs. *Cox*. Take good care of yourself by not smoking *Camels* with Mr. *Humphrey*, pigging out with Mr. *Hamilton*, and monkeying around with Miss *Gibbons*. If you do, the *Hunts* will track you down, while the *Carter's* will cart you away. So watch out! It's a jungle out there.

The Grocery List

Associate products to people who have brand names. Visualize wrapping Mr. *Reynolds* up, heating Mrs. *Campbell*, or camping with the *Colemans*. Don't hesitate to drive Mr. *Ford*, grab a bite with Miss *McDonald*, or wipe down with Mr. *Scott*. Sit down for tea with Mrs. *Lipton*, dunk donuts with Mr. *Duncan*, and munch out with Mrs. *Graham*. Careful now, names can fill you up.

A Simple Breakdown

Any last name can be broken down to something memorable. Think of *Blacksmith's hammer* when you meet a *Smith*, *Smyth*, or *Schmidt*. Don't worry about being confused which name it is. You'll know it because you've already listened carefully for it. You have looked the person directly in the face, and repeated the name.

How to Remember Names

Names that end with *Witz*, think *Wits* and visualize a huge brain. Names that end with *Son* tell you whose son it is. Is it Joseph's son, Peter's son, or Albert's son? Think *Beer Stein* when introduced to names that end with *Stein*. Visualize *Men* with names that end with *Man*. Some of them might be mighty like Mr. *Strongman* or weak like Mr. *Holloman*. Put skis on people whose last name end with *Ski* and put *Buns* on people whose last name ends with *Berg*. If you know someone with the same name, associate that person to your new friend.

Everywhere you look and everyone you meet has a name that means something or is doing something. Who are you going to meet today?

How to Remember Names

In the following exercise, pick out common word(s) from each name. Say the name slowly and record as many words as you hear.

Rozelli _____

Massenburg _____

Gianotti _____

Gustafson _____

Hauser _____

Abernathy _____

Marandino _____

Rembecki _____

Saunderlin _____

Schaefer _____

Skoracky _____

Taliaferro _____

Tonetti _____

Voelcker _____

Cheverton _____

Page 91 offers ideas to finding meaningful words.

Feeling of Belonging

We all belong to something. We may work in the computer room with five other people, wear the same uniform as twelve others on the basketball team, or be one of ten on the Board of Directors. No matter who you meet, they can be associated with a group.

The method for remembering groups is fun. It always works, whether it's the three people who work at the cleaners, the young family of four who live down the street, or the members of the Lakeside Baton Club.

MADD, NOW, and NATO

Mothers Against Drunk Driving, *National Organization for Women*, and the *North Atlantic Treaty Organization*. Acronyms help us remember.

Ask most people if they know the names of the nine Supreme Court Justices and the answer will be "No." They may know one or two, but all of them are too many to recall. Without acronyms it would be difficult to remember.

To remember the Justices who were in office at the beginning of 2018, we could repeat the names over and over; Roberts, Alito, Ginsburg, Sotomayor, Kennedy, Breyer, Thomas, Kagan, and Gorsuch. But who wants to do that? It takes too much effort. It's better to form an acronym; taking the first letter of each last name to form a word or phrase.

BGG SKATR K. Imagine Big skater Kay skates down the Supreme Court steps.

STAGG BRKK. Imagine a Stag broke the justices.

GRABS T G KK. Imagine that he grabs two great keys to unlock the Supreme Court building.

How to Remember Names

There are many other combinations you could use that will jumpstart your memory for remembering the Justices or any other group. Rearrange the letters to come up with a memorable acronym.

Drafting the Letters

Another method used for remembering a group is called Acrostic. The first letter of the names you want remembered form a meaningful sentence. Here's one example to recall the Justices:

The **S**upreme (**K**)ourt's **R**ulings **B**y **G**uys/**G**als **A**re (**K**)aring.

It's Story Time

If statements aren't exciting, we can make up a story.

The *Cagey* (Kagan), *Gorgeous* (Gorsuch) *Robber* (Roberts), a doubting *Thomas* (Thomas) with *a Lead Toe* (Alito), climbs the Supreme Court building full of *Briar* (Breyer). Then, drinks a bottle of *Gin* (Ginsburg), as well as the *Mayor's Soda* (Sotomayor) right out of the *Can* (Kennedy).

Think of memorable links with the following groups:

Rose Bowl Grand Marshals (2014-2018)
Scully, Zamperini, Burns, (Louganis, Evans, Felix), Sinise

_____
_____
_____
_____

Moon Walkers
Aldrin, Armstrong, Shepard, Conrad, Bean, Mitchell, Scott, Irwin, Young, Duke, Cernan, Schmitt

_____

_____

_____

_____

_____

National Teachers of the Year (2014-2018)
McComb, Peeples, Hayes, Chaffee, Manning

_____

_____

_____

_____

_____

_____

No matter which group many there are methods for remembering.

What's My Line?

In the 1950's and 60's, *"What's My Line?"* was one of television's most popular game shows. A panel of four people asked *Yes* or *No* questions to guess a contestant's occupation.

Today, many of us are still playing the game. We may know the person's name, but aren't sure where they work or vice versa. This can be especially embarrassing after we ask "How are the trucks running?", and then learn that the station he works at is the radio, not the fire.

Knowing what people do for a living reinforces our ability to remember them. It also demonstrates that we're taking an interest.

Here is a partial list of President Trump's 2018 Cabinet and suggestions for remembering their name and position.

James Mattis / Department of Defense. *Mats* are draped over *Da fence*.

Mike Pompeo / Secretary of State. Writing *SOS* on your *Palm*.

Ryan Zinke / Department of Interior. *Tearing* up a bottle of *Zinc*.

Nikki Haley / Ambassador to the U.N. *Hail* storm is hitting the *U.N.* building.

Alex Acosta / Department of Labor. Enter *Labor* market and it will *Cost* you.

Sonny Perdue / Department of Agriculture. *Agriculture* sure is '*Purdy.*'

Elaine Chao / Department of Transportation. Having a bowl of *Chow* on the *Train*.

Betsy DeVos / Department of Education. *Da vase* is on the *Edge*. (edge-ucation)

How to Remember Names

In the examples below, associate the name to the job by linking them in a bizarre and unusual way. If the name has no meaning, change it slightly to form a memorable picture.

Mr. Montgomery, an accountant.

Mr. Perkins, a computer analyst.

Mrs. Drummond, a physical therapist.

Mr. Ferguson, a postman.

Ms. Wilton, a pharmacist.

Mr. Appleton, a golf pro.

Mrs. Rodriquez, an architect.

Miss Sullivan, a lawyer.

It PAY$ To Remember

The ability to remember a name and recall it easily gives you an instant advantage. No matter what your profession, you'll be stronger and more influential because of your memory proficiency.

For a banker it demonstrates courtesy. For a lawyer it demonstrates confidence. For a librarian it demonstrates compassion. Because we remember the name, the teller exhibits competence, the attorney displays persuasiveness, and the librarian gets the overdue fine.

A restaurant stays busier, an organization becomes more productive, and a sales force hits quotas when its owners, leaders, and salespeople take the effort to remember names.

Nothing makes you more powerful, more persuasive, and more popular than remembering a name and recalling it easily. Whether you're a politician campaigning for a vote, a manager looking for a result, or a store owner looking for repeat business, a strong memory is essential.

We all come into this world owning nothing, except a name. Through the years we protect it, correct others who mispronounce it, and feel a slight resentment if someone forgets it. By remembering a person's name, it makes that person feel good and makes them want to know us.

There's no better sound than the sound of our own name.

Names and Associations

Aaron	**Iron**	Anita	**A Knee**
Abigail	**Abdomen**	Ann	**Raggedy Ann**
Adam	**Adam's Apple**	Annette	**A Net**
Adele	**Farmer in Dell**	Anthony	**Ant**
Adrienne	**Aid (Red Cross)**	Antoinette	**A Twin Net**
Agnes	**Agony**	April	**Showers**
Al	**Ale**	Archie	**Arch**
Alan	**Allen Wrench**	Arnold	**Arm**
Alex	**Axle**	Art	**Artist**
Alexandria	**Licks Hand**	Arthur	**Author**
Alfred	**Alfredo**	Ashley	**Ashtray**
Alice	**In Wonderland**	Audrey	**Audio**
Alisha	**Leash**	Augustus	**Gust of Wind**
Alma	**Alma Mater**	Avis	**Rent A Car**
Alonzo	**A Loner**	Barbara	**Barbed Wire**
Alfreda	**Alfredo**	Barry	**Berry**
Alton	**Altar**	Bart	**Bartender**
Alvita	**Cheese**	Beatrice	**Bee**
Amanda	**A Man**	Becky	**Beak**
Amy	**Bullseye (Aim)**	Bella	**Bell**
Andre	**Hand Dry**	Ben	**Bench**
Andrew	**Hand Drew**	Benjamin	**Franklin**
Andy	**Raggedy Ann**	Bernard	**Burr! Nod**
Angel	**Halo**	Bernice	**Burning**

How to Remember Names

Bertha	**Birthday**	Calvin	**Calf**
Bess	**Boss**	Cameron	**Camera**
Beth	**Bath**	Carl	**Curl**
Betsy	**Betsy Ross**	Carmen	**Car Men**
Betty	**Betting**	Carol	**Car**
Beulah	**Beauty**	Caroline	**Caroling**
Beverly	**Beverage**	Carrie	**Carry**
Bill	**Dollar Bill**	Carson	**Cars**
Billy	**Billy Goat**	Carter	**Cart**
Blair	**Bear**	Cathy	**Cat**
Blanche	**Avalanche**	Cecil	**Seal**
Bob	**Kabob**	Chad	**Chaps**
Bonita	**Bow and Arrow**	Charles	**Prince**
Bonnie	**Bonnet**	Charlie	**Horse**
Boyd	**Boy**	Charlotte	**Charcoal**
Brad	**Braid**	Cheryl	**Shovel**
Brandi	**Brandy**	Chip	**Chips**
Brandon	**Branded**	Chris	**Crisscross**
Brenda	**Blender**	Christy	**Crusty**
Brent	**Bent**	Chuck	**Throw**
Brett	**Barrette**	Cindy	**Cinder**
Brian	**Bran**	Claire	**Eclair**
Bridget	**Bridge**	Clarence	**Clarinet**
Brittany	**Britain**	Clark	**Clock**
Bruce	**Bruise**	Claudine	**Claw**
Buck	**Buck (deer)**	Clay	**Clay**
Bud	**Flower Bud**	Clem	**Climb**
Byron	**Red Baron**	Cleo	**Cello**

How to Remember Names

Clete	Football Cleats	Debbie	Dobber (Bingo)
Cliff	Cliff	Dee	Letter D
Clint	Clint Eastwood	Deidre	Deed
Cody	Code	Della	Deli
Colin	Colon (:)	Delores	Dealer (Cards)
Colleen	Collar	Demetri	Diameter
Connie	Cone	Denise	Den
Constance	Constable	Dennis	Dent
Cornelius	Corn	Derek	Oil Derrick
Cory	Apple Core	Dexter	Deck
Courtney	Court	Diana	Dye Hand
Craig	Creek	Dick	Duck
Crystal	Crystal Bowl	Dion	D Flashing On
Curt	Curtain	Dolan	Dole Pineapple
Cynthia	Cinders	Dolly	Dolly
Cyrus	Citrus	Dominic	Domino
Daisy	Daisy	Donald	Trump
Dale	Doll	Donna	Dinosaur
Dan	Dandelion	Doreen	Door in Rain
Dana	Great Dane	Doris	Door
Daniel	Boone	Dorothy	Wizard of Oz
Darla	Dollar	Dot	Polka Dot
Darlene	Darling	Douglas	Dug Glass
Darren	Deer	Drew	Draw
Darryl	Barrel	Duane	Drain
David	DVD	Dudley	Milk Duds
Dawn	Rising Sun	Duke	Dukes (fighting)
Dean	College Dean	Dustin	Dust

How to Remember Names

Dwight	**Light**	Eugene	**Jeans**
Earl	**Hurl**	Eva	**Eve**
Ed	**Mister Ed**	Evelyn	**Violin**
Edgar	**Cigar**	Everett	**Mt. Everest**
Edie	**Eat**	Faith	**Prayer**
Edith	**Eat Dish**	Faye	**Hay**
Edna	**Head**	Felecia	**Felt Leash**
Eileen	**Eye Lean**	Felix	**the Cat**
Elaine	**Lane**	Ferguson	**Fur**
Eleanor	**Elephant**	Florence	**Floor Rinse**
Elise	**A Lease**	Floyd	**Floor**
Elizabeth	**Lizard**	Forrest	**Forest**
Ellen	**Lion**	Foster	**Fist**
Elliott	**Alley**	Frank	**Hot Dog**
Elmo	**Eskimo**	Frasier	**Fraser Fir**
Elsie	**Elf**	Fred	**Flintstone**
Emile	**A Meal**	Freda	**Fried**
Emily	**Meal**	Gail	**Wind**
Emma	**M & M's**	Garland	**Garlic**
Emmett	**Mitt**	Garrison	**Carry Son**
Eric	**Rock**	Gary	**Garlic**
Erica	**Rock**	Gavin	**Gavel**
Erin	**Errand**	Gene	**Jeans**
Ernie	**Urn**	Genevieve	**Generous**
Ervin	**Curved Van**	Geoff	**Chef**
Estelle	**A Stall**	George	**Bush**
Ester	**Ether**	Gerry	**Cherry**
Ethel	**Lethal**	Gertrude	**Girdle**

Giles	**Gel**	Hillary	**Hill**
Gill	**Fish Gill**	Holly	**Holly**
Ginger	**Ginger Snaps**	Homer	**Home Run**
Gladys	**Glad**	Hope	**Hop**
Glen	**Glue**	Horace	**Whole Rice**
Gloria	**Glory**	Howard	**How are you**
Gordon	**Accordion**	Hubert	**Sherbet**
Grace	**Grease**	Hugh	**Hoe**
Grady	**Grate**	Ian	**Eel**
Graham	**Cracker**	Ida	**Eye Drops**
Greg	**Egg**	Ingrid	**Grid**
Guy	**Big Guy**	Iola	**Eye**
Gwen	**Gown**	Irene	**Running Eyes**
Hal	**Hail**	Iris	**Iris Flower**
Hank	**Honk**	Irvin	**Curved Van**
Harley	**Harley Davidson**	Isaac	**Eye Sacks**
Harold	**How Old**	Isabelle	**Icy Bell**
Harrison	**Hairy Son**	Israel	**Rail**
Harry	**Hairy**	Ivan	**Eye on Van**
Harvey	**Carve**	Jack	**Jackrabbit**
Hattie	**Hat**	Jackie	**Jacket**
Hazel	**Hazel**	Jacob	**Hiccup**
Heath	**Heart**	Jake	**Shake**
Helen	**Heel**	James	**Jam**
Henry	**Hen**	Jamie	**Blue Jay**
Herman	**Hermit Crab**	Jane	**Chain**
Hershel	**Hershey Bar**	Janet	**Janitor**
Hilda	**Hill**	Janice	**Janitor on Ice**

How to Remember Names

Janine	**Chin**	Karen	**Car**
Jason	**Chase Son**	Karl	**Collar**
Jay	**Blue Jay**	Kate	**Kite**
Jean	**Jeans**	Kathleen	**Cat Leans**
Jeff	**Chef**	Kathy	**Cat**
Jennifer	**Gin**	Katie	**K Tie**
Jerome	**Go Home**	Kay	**Special K**
Jerry	**Cherry**	Keith	**Key**
Jessica	**Jester**	Kelly	**Kilt**
Jill	**Chill**	Kelvin	**Kettle**
Jim	**Gym**	Ken	**Can**
Joan	**Phone**	Kendall	**Candle**
Jody	**Cup of Joe**	Kermit	**the Frog**
Joe	**Cup of Joe**	Kerry	**Carry**
Joey	**Kangaroo**	Kevin	**Cove**
John	**Bathroom**	Kim	**Comb**
Joseph	**Show Stuff**	Kirby	**Curb**
Joshua	**Shower**	Kirk	**Keg**
Joy	**Joy Stick**	Kristen	**Christmas**
Joyce	**Joist**	Kristy	**Crusty**
Juanita	**Wand**	Kurt	**Curtain**
Jud	**Shed**	Kyle	**Coil**
Judith	**Chewed Dish**	Lance	**Lancer**
Judy	**Chewy**	Larry	**Lard**
Julia	**Jewelry**	LaToya	**Toy**
Julius	**Julius Caesar**	Laurie	**Law**
June	**June Bug**	Laverne	**Lavatory**
Justin	**Just in Time**	Lawrence	**Rinse**

81

How to Remember Names

Leah	Hawaiian Lei	Lydia	Lid
Lee	Lee Jeans	Lyle	Aisle
Lenora	Lean	Lynn	Linen
Leon	Lion	Lynnette	Hair Net
Leonard	Leopard	Mabel	Table
Leroy	Lawyer	Madelyn	Mad Lion
Leslie	Less Sign (<)	Mae	Maid
Lester	List Her	Maggie	Magazine
Letitia	Lettuce	Malcolm	Milk
Lewis	Boo Us	Marcia	Marshmallow
Lila	Lie Down	Margaret	Margarine
Lillian	Lily	Maria	Marinate
Lincoln	Chain Link	Marie	Marry Me
Linda	Lint	Marilyn	Monroe
Lindsay	Lint in Suds	Marion	Mirror
Lisa	Pizza	Mark	Marksman
Lloyd	Loud Music	Martha	Mart
Lois	Lois Lane	Martin	Mart
Lonnie	Loan	Marvin	Marvelous
Lorenzo	Lawman	Mary	Little Lamb
Lorraine	Rain	Mason	Mason Jar
Lou	Loop	Matthew	Mat
Louise	Sneeze	Maureen	Listerine
Lowell	Low Well	Max	Ax
LuAnn	Love Hand	Maya	Migraine
Lucille	Loose Wheel	Megan	Megaphone
Lucy	I Love Lucy	Melissa	Molasses
Luke	Luke Warm	Merna	Morning

How to Remember Names

Michael	**Muscle**	Olivia	**Olive**
Michelle	**Shell**	Oral	**Mouth**
Mickey	**Mouse**	Orlando	**Florida**
Mike	**Microphone**	Orville	**Oar**
Mildred	**Mildew**	Oscar	**Scar**
Miles	**Smiles**	Otis	**Oats**
Minnie	**Mouse**	Owen	**Oh Win**
Missy	**Messy**	Paige	**Page**
Mitch	**Mitt**	Pamela	**Pan**
Mona	**Moan**	Patricia	**Pat Dish**
Monica	**Harmonica**	Patty	**Patty Cake**
Monte	**Mount Horse**	Paul	**Pole**
Morley	**More More**	Pearl	**Pearl**
Morton	**Morton Salt**	Peggy	**Peg**
Muriel	**Mural**	Penelope	**Pen**
Murray	**In a Hurry**	Penny	**Penny**
Myron	**My Run**	Perry	**Pear**
Nancy	**Nun See**	Peter	**Peat Moss**
Naomi	**Name**	Phillip	**Full Lip**
Natalie	**Gnat**	Phoebe	**Frisbee**
Natasha	**No Touch**	Phyllis	**Fill Less**
Nathan	**Gnat**	Porter	**Pour**
Nick	**Razor Nick**	Preston	**Press On**
Nicholas	**Nickel**	Priscilla	**Cinderella**
Nicole	**Coal**	Queen	**Queen Bee**
Nora	**Norway**	Quincy	**Squint**
Norma	**Normal**	Quinton	**Twin**
Odell	**Odor**	Rachel	**Reach**

How to Remember Names

Randolph	Running	Sabastian	Sub Bath
Randy	Ran	Sabrina	Subway
Ray	Sunray	Sadie	Sad
Reba	Rub	Samantha	Cement
Rebecca	Rub Back	Samuel	Uncle Sam
Reggie	Ridge	Sandra	Sand Dry
Regina	Raging Bull	Sandy	Sandy
Reid	Read	Scott	Cot
Renee	Run Away	Sean	Yawn
Richard	Rich Man	Seth	Seed
Rick	Rickshaw	Shannon	Share
Rita	Reading	Sharon	Sharing
Robert	Robber	Sidney	Sud Knee
Robin	Robin	Sonya	Sun
Rodney	Rod Knee	Sophia	Sofa
Roger	Over and Out	Sophie	Soap
Roland	Roll	Stacy	Stay
Ronald	Reagan	Stephen	Stove
Rose	Rose	Stuart	Stew
Roslyn	Raisin	Sue	Sushi
Ross	Rust	Sylvester	Silver
Roy	Roy Rogers	Sylvia	Silver Bowl
Ruby	Ruby	Tamara	Tambourine
Rufus	Roof	Tammy	Tummy
Russ	Rust	Tanya	Tan
Rusty	Rusty	Ted	Toad
Ruth	Tooth	Teddy	Teddy Bear
Ryan	Rye Bread	Terrence	Terrier

How to Remember Names

Terry	**Terry Cloth**	Wallace	**Wall Lace**
Thelma	**Thermos**	Walter	**Wall**
Theodore	**See a Door**	Wanda	**Wand**
Theresa	**Tear**	Ward	**E R Ward**
Thomas	**Tom Tom**	Warner	**Warn Her**
Tim	**Timber**	Warren	**War Inn**
Tina	**Tiny**	Waylon	**Whale**
Todd	**Tardy**	Wayne	**Wine**
Tom	**Tomahawk**	Wendall	**Window**
Tony	**Toe Knee**	Wesley	**Vest**
Tracy	**Trace**	Whitney	**Witty**
Travis	**Traveler**	Wiley	**A Whale**
Troy	**Toy**	Will	**A Will**
Turner	**Turning**	William	**Will Yum**
Ulysses	**U.S. Grant**	Wilson	**Wilting**
Valerie	**Veil**	Winfred	**Win**
Vanessa	**Van**	Woodrow	**Wooden**
Vaughn	**Horn**	Wyatt	**Why Eat**
Vera	**Voice**	Xander	**Sander**
Vernon	**Fern**	Xavier	**X**
Veronica	**Harmonica**	Yasmin	**Yes Man**
Vic	**Vacuum**	Yvette	**Email Vet**
Victoria	**Victoria's Secret**	Yvonne	**E Van**
Vincent	**Cent**	Zachariah	**Sack of Rye**
Virgil	**Fur Gel**	Zachary	**Sack**
Virginia	**Virginia Ham**	Zane	**Zany**
Vivian	**Visa**	Zelma	**Sell More**
Wade	**Wading**	Zoe	**Sewing**

How to Remember Names

Ideas from Page 74

Rozelli	Row silly, rose sill e
Massenburg	Messy burger
Gianotti	Gee, a knot tea/tee
Gustafson	Gust of wind, Gust of sun
Hauser	House her, How Sir
Abernathy	Ab burr gnat thee
Marandino	Marry Dino, Marinate D, No
Rembecki	Rim beak key, Rum with Becky
Saunderlin	Sauna land, Thunder lint
Schaefer	Shave fur
Skoracky	Score rack key, score a wreck
Taliaferro	Tell a ferret, tell a fairy
Tonetti	Tone net tea/tea, Toe net tea/tee
Voelcker	Vulcher, Vulgar
Cheverton	Shove a ton, Chevy ton

CHAPTER 5

101 Ways
for
Beating Absent-mindedness

101 Ways for Beating Absent-mindedness

Our brains are always working. Even when we sleep our brains never completely shuts down. It's active. Of course, sometimes it works at the wrong job.

We might be looking directly at our Algebra teacher, nodding to everything she says, but our brains are somewhere else. It's thinking about the upcoming party. At work, when we should be paying attention to what we're supposed to do, our brain is thinking about what we want to do, which has nothing to do with what we're doing.

Information is constantly coming at us - from our kids, our bosses, our customers, and advertisers who want us to be customers. We turn on the radio and someone is telling us about a game and who should win, or a special order that we should place, or a date and time of an upcoming show.

Driving on the highway, we look at signs and stores and scenery. Our brain is moving at a pace that no car could keep up with. It's no wonder why we forget. Our brains are somewhere else, and it doesn't care whether we've locked the door, brought the file, or remembered our wallets. Our brains are long down the highway doing other things while we're only there for the ride.

The following pages offer valuable systems, strategies, and solutions to save time, save money, and save face. You'll get through your day without the frustrations, the fluster, and the fumbling of finding things, losing things, and trying to remember what to do next.

101 questions and answers on battling an enemy you meet each day:
A-B-S-E-N-T-M-I-N-D-E-D-N-E-S-S

— a long word you can begin to cut into pieces, today —

1 There's a set of identical twins in my class. How can I tell them apart?

As a father of identical twin boys, Max and Ben, I learned early to tell them apart. After feeding them a bowl of spaghetti, I clean the face of only one. Sometimes I forget whose face it is.

Twins have been known to play tricks on parents, teachers, and dates who come to the house. "Gee, Stanley, you've never treated me this well before. And another thing, how'd you get so smart in Math?"

When you're dealing with twins, look for the differences instead of the similarities. Do you notice any freckles, blemishes, or outstanding facial feature, as slight as it may be, that differentiates the two?

Does Frank have a chipped tooth? Does Hank have a look of youth? Does Sandy have a twitch? Does Mandy have a stitch? Is Ray's voice high? Does Clay often sigh? Look closely and you can find something different about them.

Associate the name to the facial feature. Visualizing *phil-ing* in Phil's freckle or posting a *bill* on Bill, helps to tell them apart.

Also, from a parent, dress them differently. They're more than a set of twins, they're two individuals.

#2 **Sometimes I forget which door I entered the mall. How can I remember?**

Architects knew what they were doing when they designed these places. So many doors, but they all look the same. Maybe I should continue shopping until I remember which door I came through.

Take note of the first stationary thing you see upon entering. Go ahead and touch it. I know you have no intention of buying a leather handbag, but pick it up, look inside, and smell it. The washing machines? Go over and lift the top and spin the dial. The televisions? Touch it. The lingerie? Well, that's up to you. The point is you're getting your senses involved. You're active. You're using your sense of touch, smell, and sight.

Note the merchandise you veered from after each turn. Was it the kiosk with all the calendars? Was it the perfume counter? Was it the jewelry store with the balloons in front? Take note and you'll remember when you have to retrace your steps.

Once you're ready to leave the mall, you'll remember what you were sniffing and grabbing when you came in. But please, keep away from the mannequins.

3 **I forget to turn the headlights off after driving through tunnels. Do you have any suggestion for remembering?**

The highway department has asked me to make sure you're referring to *daytime* travel.

Many tunnels have signs reading *Check Headlights* upon exiting. Those that don't have ruined many a vacation when Dad can't start the car after the family eats at the roadside picnic table. Don't blame Dad. No one reminded him to turn the lights off after that mountainous tunnel 320 miles ago.

When you turn the lights on approaching a tunnel, make a game of it. Ask your daughter in the back seat, "When you see daylight shout, *"Lights."* If you're alone shout, *"Lights On"* when you're turning them on. It's just another trigger for your mind to remember.

Blast the a/c or the heater to its max. This is similar to the string tied to your finger reminding you to do something. However, if you wind up at your destination half frozen or sweating profusely, find another route on the way back without tunnels.

 # 4 I can't recall if I owe Larry $10 or $20. How should I go about paying him back?

Give Larry a $50 bill and ask for change. Then, don't say anything.

The best medicine to improve one's memory is to lend money. The worse medicine is to be on the receiving end of a cash advance.

This question should be for Larry, "How do I remind people to pay me back?"

If we want to get our money back, it's important that we, in a nice way, put reminders out to the owner of the extended hand. Tell the recipient it's a custom of yours to have things down on paper. In fact, let the other person write the IOU, and after you both sign it, make copies.

Have the person write out your address on an envelope. A couple of days prior to the due date, put the envelope in the mail. When he sees his handwriting on the envelope, he'll know what it's for.

Communicating when and how the money is to be paid back is vital. Will he send it to you? Will you pick it up at his work or at his house? Will he make installments? When is the full amount due?

Before you dole out money, make certain all parties know when, how, and if the money will be paid back.

101 Ways for Beating Absent-mindedness

 # 5 It took me three innings to find my way back to my seat. How can I remember which section and seat I'm in after I go for a hot dog?

Sit in most stadiums and you'll notice all sections look the same. The only difference is the view of the field. So, before you jump up and mutter, "Excuse me, excuse me," watch a couple more batters. When the batter steps out, or when the pitcher looks in, locate the tunnel taking you to the concessions. Count the number of rows you'll pass to reach that site. You'll need that information later.

As you're turning to go down the ramp, glance upward to the section you came from. See it? It's that big, yellow sign up there reading *302*. You'll have to remember that because your boyfriend is holding the ticket stub. Which reminds me, why isn't he getting the popcorn and beer?

Pay attention when you make the turn because the food is in both directions. Armed with your peanuts, pennant, and Pepsi in the big plastic cup ($2 extra if you opt to get it with the home team logo) you'll be back to your seat before you miss a pitch. The reason? You had correct change, no one wanted mustard, and you took the time to make a mental dry run.

Upon entering the ballpark, you save additional time when making mental notes to locations of concessions and restrooms.

6 There's a special television show I want to watch next Sunday. How can I be sure to remember it?

The invention of cable television and the remote control have done more damage to our memory than we admit. By the time we flip through the food, fishing, and fashion network, we've forgotten the program from where we started. Some people claim they have 100 channels. I believe they have half that but can't recall they've gone by each channel twice.

We've noticed in the television section that the special on Whales is coming on Sunday night at 7.

Do you know that red pen you have in the junk drawer by the sink? Go get it. Circle the listing for the program along with the other must-see shows for the coming week.

Put the newspaper listing atop the TV. I know it will go better on the coffee table or underneath the television but put it on top. And for your remote, which is underneath the cushion to the chair, put that on top of the TV listing. This way the three most important things are connected.

If you don't plan on being near the television until the Sunday special, put the listing on something you will be near. The refrigerator will work better than the stove. We want this to be a night of big fish, not big fire.

Find a teenager to set up a digital recording device for you. That will work, too.

7 The pot roast is always getting burnt. How do I remember to take it out?

The best solution is a timer. They're inexpensive and come in many sizes. However, on this rare occasion when the 24-hour store is closed and your oven's clock is untrustworthy, you must depend on other means.

Once the pot roast is in the oven, look at your watch and determine what time it needs to come out. Your actions at the next hour will decide whether your family sits down to a wonderful meal or if your dog sleeps through the night soundly with a full stomach.

If you're off to watch television, bring something with you from the oven, other than the pot roast, to remind you. For instance, keeping an oven mitt on your lap could be the memory jogger that something is cooking nearby.

If the roast is scheduled to be ready right before the news hour, visualize the lead story being a giant pot roast falling from the sky. Once the news comes on, you'll be on your way to the kitchen.

Put the mitt on if you're reading a book or magazine. Hopefully, you'll know which hand to use to turn the page.

Keep in mind, your family is behind you. Ask them to refresh your memory when the magic time arrives. And for your dog? Promise him a bone, instead.

#8 **How can I remember to re-charge my phone?**

If after every three days your friends aren't calling, it probably has nothing to do with you. When in doubt, look to the phone. Feed it some juice.

Make it a habit when you insert the charger into the phone, or remove it from the phone, the process is done on your bed. When you settle down for the night, the stretched charger cord is in your way. As the phone is charging, place the unit on the floor or nearby drawer. In the morning, bring the cord, with the phone attached, to the bed. This way, the cord is in plain sight every day, reminding you to 'charge up.'

The key is putting the charger somewhere in your home where it's preventing you from accomplishing your usual routine. For instance, placing the charger across your toothpaste, cereal bowl, or coffee maker will force you to touch it. And, it's that 'touching it' that you need. Your friends will be happy too. You're finally answering your phone.

9 The doctor says I should eat fiber each day, but some days I forget. How can I remember?

When it's a matter of maintaining good health, these are the times we can't afford to forget. Get in the habit of setting aside a particular time when you will eat fiber, preferably for breakfast.

As reminders, leave the cereal box on the counter before you go to bed or tear off the boxtop to keep on the counter. It also wouldn't hurt to tape a sign onto the refrigerator reading, *Have you had your fiber today?*

Mentally connect the *br* in BReakfast with the *br* in Bran you need. Your morning is now complete.

10 After asking and receiving directions, I still get lost. How can I remember what I'm told?

Before you rush out of your car and ask, take a deep breath. I know you're running late, you're getting lost, and you're lashing out. So, take a minute to settle your nerves. You're a little upset. Reach in the glove compartment and get a pad and pencil. What? You say you forgot to put them in there. Oh well, you'll just have to rely on your memory.

If you're with a friend ask him to go with you. Four ears are better than two. If possible, have the person who's giving directions stand by your car, the starting point to your journey. Like the time you stood to get married, repeat back what you heard. *"Okay, I turn left at Rosemont Avenue. Is that correct?"* Use the word "correct" instead of "right" which might confuse you. *"Then, I take my first left immediately past Windham Baptist Church, correct?"*

Try to get landmarks instead of the number of lights. You may lose track when you pass the 4th, or was it the 5th, traffic light. Plus, you'll wonder if he meant those blinking lights just past his business. Seeing the bowling alley and the golden arches are easier to remember than traffic lights. It wouldn't hurt to ask, *"If I've gone too far what will I see?"* This will save you from driving for miles.

Because *left* and *right* are difficult to picture, visualize a *Loaf* of bread to represent Left and a *Rose* to represent Right. When you hear "turn right onto Boxwood Boulevard," you can quickly imagine boxes of roses and you'll remember which way to turn six miles later.

#*11* **I keep forgetting to take my umbrella. How should I remember?**

It's Monday morning and you're getting ready for work. The weather report calls for showers later in the day. However, it isn't until you pull into your parking space that you realize you forgot something. Not only are you dripping mad for forgetting, but soon you'll be dripping wet.

Before turning in for the night, check tomorrow's forecast. Is rain expected? If so, while it's on your mind, pull out the umbrella and hook it onto the knob of the door from which you'll be leaving. Once you try you'll stay dry.

Spend a few dollars to get extra umbrellas. Leave one at work and put another in your car. Minimize the time two of your umbrellas are in the same location. After returning from work, hook the "work umbrella" to the doorknob to take back with you the next day. Your trusted umbrella won't let you down when the rain comes.

12 I left my shaving cream at the hotel. I hate when that happens. How can I prevent this?

You awoke before the sun to drive to the airport. The crying baby four rows back kept you from napping and the connecting flight out of Atlanta never showed up. Hours later you make it to Portland. Hopefully, it's the one in Oregon because that's where the meeting is. You're so tired you throw your luggage onto one bed and sleep in the other. The last thing on your mind is organizing your stuff.

Start organizing your stuff. Put your socks, underwear, and T-shirts in the drawers. Hang your clothes in the closet and put your shoes on the rack above. Rearrange all that hotel propaganda, such as the menu from Starlights Restaurant, the brochures to the wax museum, and the hard cover book of all the Econo Lodges throughout North America off to the side.

Loose change goes in the ashtray or in one of the plastic cups. Place toiletries in the corner of the sink. You'll have to slide the glass jar with the paper on top, the tiny shampoo container, and the coffee maker out of the way. Make certain the hotel key and your wallet are near your change and your wristwatch is not on the bed. Now don't you feel better? You're settled in.

Upon checkout, one grab with each hand airlifts your toiletries from the corner. Gather clothes from drawers and empty out the closet. If the cord to the iron connects to the wall, leave it. It ain't yours. Put your luggage by the door, then go to the far end of the room. Walk slowly back and start scanning the room. Pick up towels in the bathroom and drop them into a corner. Find any socks in there? Look in the tub and underneath the sink. With key in hand your memorable stay is over. You didn't forget anything.

13 My goal is to swim ten laps in the pool, but some days I lose count. How can I remember?

This is the case where a pad and pencil won't work. Maybe you can scratch the wall with a waterproof marker. But then, maybe the *YMCA* would cancel your membership.

When you decide to do an even number of laps, one question is already answered for you; the end of the pool where you'll finish. The pressing issue is the number of times you have to go there. Instead of doing ten laps, just think of touching one end five times. Mentally, this may also get you through the tough workout.

Once you make the turn coming back shout, "*One*," in the water. Don't worry, no one will hear you. The next turn coming back shout, "*Twoooo*." You'll save yourself from shouting, "*Fivvve*," because you'll be done, and because you will have remembered.

Not only are you promoting good health by swimming, but you could also promote each finger and thumb to each lap. Competitive swimmers would frown upon such advice, but each time you do a lap, touch the wall with a different finger and thumb. When the last is used, you're finished.

Dedicate a lap to a loved one. As you're moving effortlessly through the water, focus on a different member of your family during each lap. Say to yourself, "*Bobby, this one's for you, my special grandson.*"

 # *14* I ate the most wonderful crackers at my friend's house. However, I had forgotten the brand when I went to the store to buy them. How could I have remembered?

The hors d'oeuvres were nicely placed on the silver platter. You mentioned to Barbara how good everything was, especially the crackers and dip. "Remind me to pick up some at the store," you say to her.

Hey, who do you think she is? Superwoman? She spent all day preparing this meal, polished up the silverware, and made sure all coats made it to the spare bed. Now you want her to remind you to get crackers at the store? She has enough going on.

If your phone is equipped with a camera, take a picture of the crackers and set the new photo as your screen saver. A screen saver of a box of crackers should motivate you to quickly buy the crackers and re-set your screen saver.

If no camera, back at the party house make your way to the kitchen and take hold of the box. Associate the Golden Crisps turning your teeth golden, or that you're eating Gold. Associate the *Ritz* tasting so *Right,* or that it's so Ritzy. Associate the brand into your taste buds so when you're at the store searching for that good tasting cracker, you'll remember.

If the box is empty, ask the hostess if you can tear off the box top; a reminder to get some at the store.

Trace the brand name with your finger and study the picture on the box taking note of shapes and colors. At the grocery store the box of crackers will seem to be leaning toward you when you look in that direction. You've already held the box and traced the name. All that's left is getting the dip.

15 I forgot to set my alarm clock last night. How can I remember tonight?

Why blame your memory? It's easier to lay blame on the non-working alarm. Either way, one of you needs to be adjusted, and since it's you who's reading this, here are some suggestions.

If you wear a nightcap, pajamas, or your favorite T-shirt, drape it over the alarm clock as you're getting dressed for the day. That night when you reach for your PJ's, you're going to be alarmed because that's what your hand will be on when you grab your garment. Of course, make sure the curtains are drawn as you're doing this.

Another method is to place the clock on the bed each day. This will remind you, as you settle in for the night, to set the alarm and to put it back on the nightstand.

16 How can I be sure to carry enough business cards?

It's embarrassing not to be carrying a business card when we know there are 873 of them in our desk drawer. It can also work to our advantage. Get the other person's card and promise to send yours in the mail. This gives you a good reason to add a short note and the recipient is less likely to lose the card. Also, the cards he got at the networking function are stuffed into his jacket and won't be seen until the wedding he attends two months later.

Tuck several cards in your wallet. Keep several at home, at the office, and in your car. Put some in the pockets of your suits you plan to wear.

Keep other cards in a visible place in your wallet or purse. When you're down to your last few cards, fold one and wedge it between your car keys or slip it into your shoe. When the card pops out at the end of your day it will be your cue to stock up. And please, do it now while it's on your mind.

 # 17 **I have a tendency to repeat myself. How do I remember what I've already told someone? I have a tendency to repeat myself.**

Don't you just hate that? You're cornered at the party and Lou is telling that same story ... again. Doesn't he remember he's told you this six times? Evidently not, because here comes the part when the canoe tipped over and Helen's tuna fish sandwich came apart.

It's a good thing we don't do that, or do we? Do we tell the same story to the same person twice?

Sometimes what we have to say is so good we want to tell the story again. The problem is, the other person may not want to hear it again. To help remember what you've said, engage yourself in a true conversation. Look at the person and don't hog the speaking part. If you do, your listener will only be listening to when you come up for air in order to get his 'two cents' in.

When you tell the story about visiting Wall Drug, ask questions along the way. *"Frank and I went to Wall Drug. Have you been out there, Beth? It's one big drugstore near Mount Rushmore with everything imaginable. We bought Suzy a pair of moccasins. And I tell you, Beth, she loves them..."*

Sometimes when you pose those questions, get ready, the other person may run with it for 30 minutes. Then use your lasso, the one you got at Wall Drug, to bring her back.

Eye contact, questions, and the listener's name will help prevent you from telling the same story. If you're still unsure, a simple statement, such as *"Stop me if I've already told you this"* will be much appreciated.

18 My checkbook didn't balance. How can I remember to record the ATM withdrawals?

It's amazing to see the many withdrawal receipts outside an ATM machine. And secretly, don't you want to read some of those balances to see how well people in your community are doing? I wonder how many of those transactions, represented by those floating receipts, were recorded.

One way to make sure the money is recorded is to bring the check register with you each time you make a withdrawal. However, sometimes this isn't practical. Instead, the receipt is your link so be sure to take it after each transaction.

As you're stuffing the receipt into your pocket or purse, you think you'll remember to record it later. However, the *later* is a month afterward when the call comes from the dry cleaners to remind you.

The receipt needs to be in the same spot after each visit to the ATM, preferably a wallet or purse. Avoid mixing it in with the clutter you already have in there. Take a rainy Saturday to clean it out.

The coupon for Happy Jack Pancakes has expired so remove it from your wallet. The pass for one free game of miniature golf should be removed, too. Remember? You got it while you were in Morehead, Minnesota. You live in South Jersey now.

Place the receipt with your dollars or wrap it around the ATM card. Each day when you record your entries, you'll always know where to find your ATM receipts. You'll be overly charged with excitement when you keep those receipts together. It's a different "overly charged" feeling you'll get from your bank.

19 I'm afraid to leave my seat in a darkened theatre. How will I remember to find my way back?

The show is just about to start, but sadly, so is the urge to use the restroom. Your aim is making it to both seats in time.

Theatres aren't what they used to be. Today's typical movie house is a condominium. There are eight movies playing at 7:45. You might make it back in time for the movie but when you settle down in your seat, you'll be confused when you look up and see *Snow White*. *"Isn't this supposed to be a romantic comedy?" And come to think of it, who's this guy beside me?"*

Before you hand the tickets to the usher, use your time wisely. Ask yourself if you need to use the restroom. Also, ask your date if she wants *Goobers* or *Raisinets*.

As you make your way down the long corridor, note the entrance to your movie. It's #5, right beside the fire extinguisher and across from the big poster of Dwayne Johnson.

Before you walk down the aisle deciding where to sit, stand to the side and make that decision. *"Okay, it's going to be in the middle section, 3/4's of the way up on the left hand side."* Good choice. Now, count the rows you're walking past to get there.

The movie might be awful, but the next day Holly will tell her friends how thoughtful her date was. *"... and when I said I had to use the restroom, Joey whispered, 'remember, we're eight rows from the top.'"*

#20 **I'm sure my neighbor doesn't remember my name. How do I tell him without making it embarrassing?**

The greetings come each time you're raking leaves or walking to the mailbox. It's always "*Hey there.*" The few times you do talk you've noticed that Ned, from next door, doesn't know your name. You'd like to tell him, but how? You could lend him your power tools with your name engraved on them. At least he'd know your name. Of course, there's that chance he'd forget to return your drill.

If he's not going to say your name, then you must. You can give him your name without his realizing what you're doing. It's a foolproof method when you say, "*It was such a beautiful morning I said to myself, Harold Beasley, get up and take a long walk. So, I did and I feel terrific.*"

People want to call you by name, but their memory isn't as good as yours, so help them out.

Avoid the phrase, "*You don't remember me do you?*" If you haven't seen someone for a long time, don't assume they'll remember you. Wipe the uneasiness away by saying, "*Janet, hi, Phil Kendall from the Little League banquet.*" She'll respond, "*Of course, Phil, how are you?*"

At every White House State Dinner there's a gentleman standing in the receiving line next to the President. His only job is getting the name of the person next in line, so he can whisper it into the President's ear.

We aren't so lucky. There are moments when we have to whisper our own name to others. When it's done right we won't have to whisper it to the same person again.

#21 How do I remember which page I left off in my book?

You've just read the last page and a half when it occurs to you that you read those words last night. No wonder this book is taking so long to read.

If possible, finish a chapter before you put the book down, and say out loud the title of the next one. This action will help you remember when it comes time to pick up where you left off.

A bookmark would be most helpful. If you have small children suggest that they make Mommy a special bookmark. This also instills the world of reading to them and your family's love of books. Of course, your two-year-old will suggest the bookmark consist of peanut butter.

If you don't finish the chapter, read the last paragraph out loud, and emphasize the final sentence. Then, lay the bookmark horizontally across the page lining it up with the stopping point. Days later you won't have to glance up and down pages 131 and 132, because the bookmark will indicate where to begin.

 # 22 **After leaving the mall, I spend more time searching for my car than inside searching for bargains. How can I remember where I parked?**

Every day parking lot malls are filled. However, many of the vehicles are never driven again because the owners have given up looking. It's one reason why city buses continue to pick up passengers outside the doors of Macy's.

To save on bus fare, take a moment after getting out of your car and look at the building you're soon to walk to. What do you see? Is it the letter 'R' in Barnes & Noble? Is it the green awning to the Mexican restaurant? Walk directly to that landmark. As you're doing this, count the number of parking spaces, with and without cars, along the way. Once you walk that straight line to the building, you're free to go left or right to your entrance.

After exiting from your shopping spree, you'll be reminded of the landmark and where you parked. You'll also recall that it was 12 car spaces away, because you became aware of your surroundings before you shopped.

23 How can I remember definitions?

Vocabulary building is wonderful, only if you know what the words mean. To get a handle on it, tweak the word so they create pictures. Here are some examples.

Concede. By breaking this non-visual word into syllables, we get a very visual *con seed*, as in a conman planting seeds. To remember the definition of concede; to yield, or surrender, we can picture a conman holding up seeds as if he's surrendering.

Condone and *Condemn.* The words sound alike, but there's a mammoth difference in their meaning. It would be a bit embarrassing if you, as principal of an elementary school, told the PTA members that you "*condone any student who cuts class.*" The word you wanted to say was *condemn,* to disapprove of strongly; whereas *condone* means to forgive or overlook.

Creating visuals helps us remember. *Condone* sounds like *con-dough-n.* Making dough is good. *Condemn* sounds like *con-dem,* similar to *demolition.* Destroying things is bad.

Not sure what *congruent* means? You wished you had when your preteen has math homework. You might have known 20 years earlier, but now you're not too sure. You would have remembered if your teacher told you, "as they *grew, ants* (*con-grew-ant*) are in agreement having identical shapes and size."

The definition of *connoisseur* is one who is well-versed, having expert knowledge. To put it another way, a *con-knows-sir,* is a *sir who knows.*

And now, you're one who knows how to remember definitions.

#24 **At times I forget and call my boyfriend by my old boyfriend's name. I really like this guy and don't want to jeopardize things. How can I remember?**

This situation is quite common. Beginning a new relationship after a long one it's easy to blurt out, *"Keith, pass the salt,"* when you meant to say *"Antonio, pass the pepper."*

The rules of thumb are to date or marry people with the same name. You can't go wrong. Calling your new guy by your old guy's name won't matter. No need to tell him you slipped when you said *"Stephen,"* when you meant to say *"Steven."*

Get in the habit of calling your boyfriend *"sweetie"* or *"honey."* He'll never know you dated those same guys when you lived in West Texas three years earlier.

Don't apologize to Bruce when you begin to say your ex-husband's name. Keep your cool after you mistakenly say, *"Hey, Jack."* Continue the sentence with *"... son Hole, Wyoming is beautiful this time of year. Let's go."*

All of us, men and women, are bound to slip every now and then, so before it happens think of a recovery plan. *"Sharon... (oops)... a life with you makes me so happy."* Annette will be happy, too.

25 I think I forgot to turn the iron off. Help me to remember?

The story goes ... the husband became annoyed at his wife's insistence that she left the iron on that he decided to do something about it on their next trip. So, ten miles down the road when she said, *"Harold, turn around. I know the iron is on,"* Harold remained calm. He steered the car to the side of the road, got out, opened the trunk and quietly handed his wife the iron.

If you have a large area to iron and the board remains up, it's easy to forget whether the iron was turned off. Therefore, you must make it memorable.

After ironing, loop the cord around the board and make a karate chop between the board and the outlet. Silly yes, but the action convincingly forces your mind to remember the iron is off. Don't be embarrassed, no one is watching you iron, anyway.

If the iron belongs on the shelf, then say what you're doing. *"I'm putting the iron away."* Also, tie a handkerchief to the handle after each use. The action of tying the knot will help you remember that it's off.

If you're still unsure whether the iron is off, get an outlet cover. Each time you iron, put the cover at the end of the ironing board or in your hand, and then plug it back in after ironing.

Have you ever thought of dry cleaning?

#*26* **My son claims he never received his allowance. I can't remember if I paid him. How can I be sure?**

When you see Jimmy offering bribes to the McDonald's customers to be first in line, you'll know you've paid him too often.

If there's confusion as to whether the money was paid, remember this, you're the parent. You get the final say.

To avoid a misunderstanding, put a chart on the refrigerator showing the work needing to be done and money needing to be paid. Sign your name in ink after each payment is made. I'm not implying your kid is a rat, but a penciled checkmark could be erased by anyone, if not by him, then by that friend who stops over much too often.

Teach your youngster early business skills. Like any employee, have him bring you his time sheet where you can sign it and then reward him. Keep a copy for yourself.

Set a time each week when the allowance is paid. Keep in mind that you ARE the payroll department, so avoid paying the money days before or when the mood strikes your kids. They might fuss and rage, but they're not going to leave you to work for the competition.

#27 How do I prevent losing my keys?

If you want to avoid being laid off, become a locksmith. You'll stay busy. Faulty memories keep you working.

Keys are just waiting to be lost. They're small, always on the go, and have lots of friends looking just like them. Sometimes we think they've packed up never to return. Who knows? Maybe they've migrated south becoming one of the Florida Keys.

Keys help get us to work, help get us our mail, and play a vital role in keeping us warm when the winds start to blow outside. With all their importance, it behooves us to protect them. They need a home just like we do.

Find a place near the entrance to your door to keep your keys. Hang a key hook or put the keys in a specific corner of a drawer. Reinforce this by repeating the process 10 times. In your hand, then on the hook, in your hand, then on the hook, in your hand, then ... It will become second nature when you come through the door to automatically put the keys where they belong.

Find a place or object that identifies with the keys. For instance, you could put the _K_eys in the _K_ettle, or hook the _K_eys to the _K_alendar, or place the _K_eys inside the _K_upboard. Whichever spot you chose, make it permanent.

Be verbal if you put your keys down in an unfamiliar place. *"I'm putting the keys by the plant."* This prevents you from becoming absent-minded. Also, visualize keys instead of leaves dangling from the plant. Later, you'll be reminded as to what they were doing, and you'll find them quickly.

#*28* **I'm taking a trip overseas and want to learn new words and phrases. How can I learn in a short time?**

You're 55 years old. You have a master's degree and you're a corporate vice president. Yet there are millions of 6-year olds who can speak better Japanese than you. Don't be too hard on yourself. It's not your fault. Those kids live in Tokyo. You live in Toledo.

To learn a new language, link the English word to the foreign meaning in a bizarre and imaginative way. The connection makes it memorable.

In Spanish the word *umbrella* is *el paraguas* (ehl-pah-rah-gwahs). Locking that to memory, we can visualize an umbrella held up by parakeets. Hundreds of parakeets are flying inside the umbrella. The visual connection reminds you that the word is *el paraguas*.

In German the word *store* is *vorrat* (fo-rrat). Visualize a store for rats and you'll know the German translation for *store*. It may also keep you away from window shopping in Berlin.

In Italian the word *morning* is *mattino* (maht-tee-noa). Imagine stepping out of your bed in the morning and landing on a mat covered with tees.

Linking the two words visually speeds the process to learning a new language. Reading out loud and listening to audio tapes helps you master your new voice. Whether you ask for directions in Denmark or a menu in Manila, you'll be ready for your trip.

#29 How can I remember my dance steps?

A survey concludes that couples are marrying late. The reason may be that they're still learning how to dance so they'll be ready during the reception. The couple with four left feet must do a couple of things right.

"Step together, step. Step together, step. Backwards, pivot, step to the side, and step together, step." Please, make up your mind.

After the dance lesson, sit with your instructor and have the steps written out. This allows your brain to soak in the information while your feet are still.

Take the dance notes home and push aside the furniture. Be careful not to throw your back out, unless it's your wife's idea to take the dance lesson. Place objects on the floor where your dance steps are to go and number them. Objects, such as newspaper, stapler, paperweight, napkin, the car from Monopoly, or a sock will do.

You're ready to dance. Step on the book, then the stapler. Pivot on the napkin and slide the car off to the right. Each step is different and memorable. You're not just taking steps, but you're moving from one destination to another. When you get to the napkin you'll recall what to do. That's when you pivot, and that's what dancing is all about. It's going from one place to another through a series of steps, some short, some backward, some to the side.

After you master these early steps find more objects around the house and place them on the floor. With each step, you'll be landing on something new and the association will help you remember.

Practice the steps while waiting in line at the post office. No one will ever know. Soon, you'll be ready for Saturday night.

30 **How can I remember my golf strokes?**

A round of golf takes less time if the guy ahead of you, the one in the plaid pants and sneakers, wouldn't stand by the flag counting the number of hits it took to get him there.

Perhaps, you're one of those guys or gals, who after making the putt, slowly walks back to the cart unsure if a 4 or 5 goes on the scorecard. One number you are sure of is the number of golf balls it took to reach the green. *"Put down an 8 for me on the lake hole."*

Bring a dollar worth of dimes with you the next time you head for the links. Put them in one pocket. After each swing, transfer one dime to the other pocket. Also, transfer a coin on the easy par 3's when you're positive you'll remember the strokes. Your four-foot putt could turn into a 40-yard chip if there's a steep hill nearby. Then, on your final putt add another coin. 5 coins equal 5 shots.

If you run out of dimes put *10* on your card and pick up your ball. Your partner, and those patient souls behind you, will thank you.

Why use dimes? They're small and easy to handle. They make less noise than a pocketful of quarters or silver dollars. Plus, those are the coins you always lose on the 19th hole.

101 Ways for Beating Absent-mindedness

 # 31 **How can I remember my wife's dress and shoe size? I often want to surprise her but can never recall her sizes.**

If you're a man you'd like this question addressed. If you're a woman you'd like the address of the questioner.

On the back of one of your business cards write the measurements of your mate. Be sure to mark out the front of the card. This is one card you don't want to hand out. It's a good idea to write your own sizes, too. Sometimes we forget if we wear a size 10 or 10 ½ shoe. Carrying a reminder card is a time saver.

When your spouse is not in the house, go to the closet and check the sizes on dresses, blouses, and shoes. Write the number on a large sheet of paper. Draw a huge *3* and lean it against her dresses. Put the *3* on a coat hanger. Then, mark a huge *6* and put it on top of her shoes. It takes little time, but the action of writing those numbers helps you remember. Minutes later when you throw the numbers away you'll be surprised that the numbers stay in your mind.

Use the Number/Rhyme Method to help you remember. If the shoe size is **8**, associate her wearing the shoes when she's running late and **8** rhymes with *late*. A dress size **4** drapes over the door with **4** rhyming with *door.*

Tuck important information to your mate's favorite color, style, and size into your purse or wallet. Shopping will become less stressful when you walk in those stores armed with all the answers. Won't she be surprised!

*32 How can I remember to get my car's oil changed?

When most people hear a knock they get up. However, when it's from their car's engine they get down. To keep from feeling that way make sure your car gets its regular check-up. If you forget, your Toyota will let you know.

Many service stations apply a clear plastic sticker in the upper corner of the windshield indicating your car's next visit. It's a reminder you can't miss. However, if you don't want that Grease Monkey decal up there you'll have to find another way to remember.

If you're unsure when to bring your vehicle in, call the service station asking when you last visited. They'll give you the answer.

Setting the trip odometer to zero the day of your auto's oil change gives you an accurate reading. Once those numbers reach 4000 to 5000, you'll remember to take your car in.

Make a notation in your appointment book for three months out. Seeing the word, *car* in mid February will ring a bell. You could write the number of miles, instead. All you need are the last few digits. A written *8661* written on October 15 will have a special meaning for you.

Another system reminding you to take the car in is to associate the month to the car. Think about *MARCHing* in to take the car in, or checking the car's E*xhaust* in *August*, or changing the oil of your *Jalopy* in *July*. You'll be reminded when the new month comes in.

Keeping your car running smoothly depends on a sharp mechanic and a sharp memory.

#*33* **How can I remember to bring my gym pass each morning?**

It's not that you lack the motivation to work out; it's just that you can't remember where you put your gym pass.

Place the gym pass in the path of your morning routine. To recap, a routine is what you do without thinking. You go to the bathroom, you pour yourself a cup of coffee, you grab your gym bag, and you go to the car. Two miles later, your routine continues when you shout "I forgot my gym pass."

Place the pass on your coffee maker. If your routine is a cup of joe, you'll have to touch the pass to get to your coffee. Once it's in your hand, keep hold of it. Put it into your pocket or tuck it into your shoe. You've already remembered it once, so avoid looking for it a second time.

Immediately after presenting your pass, put it into an envelope and place it into your gym bag. The envelope is much easier to find than searching for the small pass amongst the socks and shorts. The pass would appreciate it, too.

Upon exiting the gym, keep the pass in your hand, so you can leave it in your car. You've never forgotten your car, have you?

Purchase a hole punch machine to attach the pass to your set of keys. If you're on a budget, a hammer and nail will work, as well.

If you continue to forget your pass, invest in home exercise equipment. Who needs a gym pass?

101 Ways for Beating Absent-mindedness

 # 34   I have trouble remembering if I've already added an ingredient to a recipe. How can I remember?

Your sponge cake didn't turn out the way it usually does. For some reason, it's a bit salty, and why do I still have all these eggs?

It's easy to get lost in your excitement of preparing a meal or dessert. Surrounding you is the bag of flour, brown sugar, salt, paprika, walnuts, eggs, baking soda, and everything else you need to make this concoction. You're doing everything correctly. The instructions include putting all the necessary ingredients on the counter. However, what's not included is how to remember if you've used them.

Be organized with the ingredients. After each use, transfer the remaining contents to the opposite side of the bowl. When you see the bag of sugar on your left, you'll know that ingredient has already been added. Hold off on discarding the eggshells. Instead, move them to the other side, as well. It's nice to maintain a clean work area, but once the eggshells are discarded, you're back to relying on your memory.

Say what you're doing as if you are rehearsing for your own cooking show. Say, "I'm adding the flour. Look at it go into the bowl. Now, I'm adding the vanilla. The vanilla has been added."

Line up the ingredients against the back wall of the counter. Once they've been added, keep them off the wall. In doing so, you won't feel your back is up against there too because you've remembered.

.

35 How can I remember the Books of the Bible?

The minister is telling you to flip to *Philippians*, but you're still trying to find *Zephaniah*. Sometimes it's a job to find *Job*, numbing to find *Numbers*, and not so E Z to find *Ezra*.

While sitting in your pew waiting for the service to begin, take a look at the program and make note of the books of the Bible the preacher will cover. It's a time saver when you can follow along, instead of following behind.

Buy a Bible with tabs showing where each book begins. You won't have to fish for *Ephesians* because you'll know where it is. Many Christian bookstores sell bookmarks with the books of the Bible listed. A quick glance will guide you where you need to turn.

Use the link system, and a little imagination, to remember the books.

Imagining a bottle of GIN EXITING the LAVATORY that's NUMB from the DEW, tells you the first five books are *Genesis*, *Exodus*, *Leviticus*, *Numbers*, and *Deuteronomy*.

If you think I'm JOSHING, then tell the JUDGE. He'll find the TRUTH under the laws of UNCLE SAM, yes UNCLE SAM and all the KINGS men. BOTH of them. It's been CHRONICLED on TWO occasions.

Remember that story and you'll know the next books are *Joshua*, *Judges*, *Ruth*, *1 Samuel*, *2 Samuel*, *1 Kings*, *2 Kings*, *1 Chronicles*, and *2 Chronicles*.

The link pattern can take you all the way to *Revelation*, even if you start, "In the beginning..." Think you have a bad memory? Miracles do happen.

36 I often forget to add a fabric softener sheet. How can I remember?

After you remove the clothes from the dryer and clean the lint filter, (oh yeah, that too) put a fabric softener sheet into the dryer. It may feel lonely for a few days, but it will start mingling when the underwear and shirts come to town later in the week.

You could also put the whole box of sheets in the dryer. When you open the door to the dryer, that orange box cannot be missed. Take a sheet out and put the box on top of the machine. You'll never forget again.

Think of the sheet as a welcoming mat for the wet clothes. There's a mat by every door. Your dryer is no different. Spread the sheet on the bottom of the dryer, and then add clothes. Your sweaters will love you for it.

37 It took me 30 minutes to find my way out of my friend's neighborhood. How can I remember the maze?

You find your way back to Bob's house an hour after the party. *"Sorry to bother you again Bob, but how do I get out of your neighborhood?"*

How can you get lost? The house is only one hundred yards from the main road. Yet, like a football player scrambling up field, you keep searching for an opening, one that breaks free to get you home.

Look for landmarks each time you turn onto a street. Is it a right by the house with the flagpole? Are you turning by the house with the big elm tree? Are you making a left by the house with the pink flamingo? Pay close attention each time you're making turns, even though you're focused on arriving at the house on time.

Quickly turn your head over your shoulder to see streets you've passed. They'll be reminders when you leave later that night. Focus on landmarks if neighborhood street signs are hidden from view by weeping willows or broken street lights.

Make sure you know the exact address. Just knowing that the house is *329 Bartlett* isn't enough. It just so happens Mr. Bartlett is the neighborhood developer, and he has a big ego. Is the address Lane, Avenue, Drive, Circle, Terrace, or Court? You'll need to know.

Bring written directions and always ask the key question after you thank your host. *"Bob, how do I get out of here?"*

Psst. G ...P ... S.

#38 How can I remember the Quadratic Formula?

When you put 2 and 2 together, it's easy to see why so many people have trouble with Math. Math is hard to figure. Sometimes it just doesn't add up and the confusion multiplies.

$$\text{Quadratic Formula}$$

$$x = \frac{-b \pm \sqrt{b^2 - 4ac}}{2a}$$

The last letter in *Formula* is an *a*. In the alphabet, the letter following *a* is *b*. And that's MY Bee (as in mi-nus), plus or minus. It's so hot that 2 b's go inside looking 4 an a/c. Negative; no luck. The stay until 2am.

The techniques for memorizing formulas are the same for remembering any abstract piece. Finding familiar patterns and connections help make it memorable.

#39 Have you seen my glasses?

As we're putting our glasses down, we're already on our way to do something else. We might put them down as we walk into the kitchen, about to step outside, or settle back for a short nap. Our mind is seldom in focus when we lay down our glasses. And, without glasses it's difficult to stay in focus. Know what I mean?

Get in the habit of keeping your glasses in a permanent place when they're not across your nose. Sure, it's simpler to lay them down anywhere, but it's not that simple to remember where that place is 15 minutes later.

When you finish reading, put your glasses against the lamp. You can't read The Gazette without a glow and without glasses. You know where the lamp is, so put your glasses against it. Avoid putting your specs on objects that will be moved, like papers. Family members may push them aside when searching for the comics or television section. Like a feather in the wind, your glasses will surely land somewhere else.

Follow the lead of your Kindergarten teacher or Librarian and attach a chain to them. Even if you lose your head your glasses will be in good company.

Remove your glasses with both hands. This forces you to pay closer attention to what you're doing. If the right hand doesn't know what the left hand is doing, it only needs to ask.

Another effective hint: as you're putting your glasses down, imagine they're bursting into flames on the object you put them on. Hours later, you'll recall where they are.

#40 How can I remember laps I've run around a track?

If you lose count as to the number of laps you're doing, don't despair. One of your feet will let you know when you're on your last leg.

Your mind has to be alert when you run laps versus running from point A to point B. With track work you run from point A to point A, and continue doing so unless you remember where B is. The scenery all looks the same.

Pick up pebbles before beginning. Each one represents the number of laps you plan to run. Throw down a pebble after each lap. If you're in competition, replace the pebbles with tacks and throw them in your competitor's lane. Your odds of winning now increase.

If you'd rather your hands be free, then say out loud the lap you've just completed. Repeating *"One, One, One,"* then, *"Two, Two, Two,"* and so on, will help you remember.

The alphabet game will help you remember, as well. After each lap think of places that begin with A. As you're running say, *"Asheville, Atlanta, Atlantic City, Athens."* After your second lap think of places beginning with B. Say to yourself *"Boston, Baton Rouge, Bakersfield, Bristol."*

You'll be better in geography using this system, and once you get to Zanesville, you'll be a better runner, too.

#*41* **Police need a description of the man who robbed the store. I'm having trouble remembering. How could I have paid more attention?**

Go back to the spot where you saw him. Were you seated behind the counter? Were you in front of the canned goods in the third aisle? Wherever it was, go there and put him in the picture. When he was standing close to you, was he taller than the top shelf? How much room was left from the top of his head to the doorway when he bolted?

Money and merchandise might have been stolen, but the fixtures remain fixed. If you remember whether he reached above the counter for the cigarettes, or that only the top of his hat was visible when he walked by the Mountain Dew display, then you can determine his height.

Can't recall if he was right or left-handed? You do remember the weapon, don't you? Which side of his body did your eyes go to? When you recall that you solved another piece. What's the first thing you noticed about him? Dirty fingernails? The mole on his chin? The tattoo on his hand? The gold filling in his mouth? His high cheek bones? If you remember the long blond hair, that may lead you to the dangling earring. That may remind you of something else. It's easier to recall in bits than trying to remember everything at once.

As soon as possible, write down as much as you can about the individual. As difficult as it may be, try to keep your emotions in check and start writing. Your act may prevent him from doing his next act.

42 I spend time looking up words that I should know how to spell. How can I become a better speller?

You can't tell the education level of a good speller, but you can get a hunch from a bad one. *Reatting a lettur ful uf mispeled wurds izn't verry becomeing.*

It's not uncommon to go to the dictionary looking up words we should know how to spell. Words such as *necessary, maneuver,* and *efficiency* can be tricky.

Every word is made up of patterns that can help you remember. Be sure to look for them the next time you're stumped.

Here are 10 examples....

vacuum...U, U must vacUUm.
necessary...Is the CESSpool neCESSary?
kitchen...C a HEN in the kitCHEN?
martyr...Y be a martYr?
maneuver...The MANE U brush must be MANEUvered.
pavilion...There's a LION in the paviLION.
patient...PA, TIE the PATIEnt down.
bachelor... Do you ACHE to be a bACHElor
manicure...I C U R getting a manICURe.
efficiency...I C I ENtered an effICIENcy.

There are hints to every word. The key is finding them.

#43 How can I remember to take the chicken out of the freezer to thaw?

You're sitting in front of the television when you start thinking about tomorrow's dinner. It's going to be chicken. Did the commercial about *chicken* remind you? Or was it the wings of *Delta Airlines*, instead? Either way, the chicken needs to come out of the freezer tomorrow morning.

If there's a sticker on the package, take it off and stick it onto your bathroom mirror. Hopefully, when you awake the next morning you'll still gargle, not cluck, and will remember to open the freezer.

As soon as you're reminded to take the chicken out, write *Chicken* on a piece of paper and put it in your cereal bowl or a place where you're bound to look tomorrow morning. Don't put the note on the freezer door, unless you eat frozen waffles each morning. The note must be in a place where your eyes are going to look before you leave for work.

Attach a string from the freezer door to the floor. You'll be reminded the next morning when you reach for your milk or eggs.

Wow, all this work just for chicken. Sorry, didn't mean to ruffle your feathers.

#*44* **My partner and I often lose count of the score when playing tennis. How can we remember?**

Start playing with people who are less talented than you. Stronger players always know the score.

The rules of tennis say the server announces the score by saying his score, then the opponent's. If you're holding the ball and say "*Love serving 30*" it means you're not winning. Be consistent, even if your backhand isn't, when keeping score.

If your opponent doesn't want the responsibility of scorekeeper, then it's your job. Give the score before each serve, making sure your opponent can clearly hear you. After you hit your last ball over the fence and into the woods, repeat the score. "*Okay, it's 30 all, your serve when we continue,*" as both of you enter the poison ivy.

Sometimes your opponent will be adamant that he's leading by a point. If so, let it go. Give him the benefit of the doubt and continue playing. It's not worth losing a friendship over and it will make you more determined to win the next point that you unjustly lost.

Recruit someone in the neighborhood to keep score. This way, all three of you have a job to do. If you still can't get it over the net, at least your memory will serve you right.

#45 How can I remember what I just read?

You think you've subscribed to three newspapers. Instead, you're only reading the same story again and again in the same newspaper about Russian Potato farmers.

It's frustrating when we can't comprehend what we've just read. It's time consuming, too.

If possible, find a quiet place to read. Noise from the television, radio, and kids jumping on you are mental blocks when you're trying to read and comprehend.

Read slowly and put yourself in the picture. Imagine being there and try to feel the story.

Pick out key words and link one story to another and you'll remember much easier.

The CRUISE SHIP was on its way to HAWAII when a KANGAROO jumped onto the BUFFET TABLE. The animal, covered up to its neck with ROAST BEEF, swung on a CHANDELIER to shake off the food. Suddenly, a FIRETRUCK entered the room and a PENGUIN got out and pulled the kangaroo off. Then, a MARCHING BAND began to play, until the DRUMMER walked into a LEMON PIE.

The 11 capitalized words piece the story together. Try it and see.

Cruise Ship ... Hawaii ... Kangaroo ... Buffet Table ... Roast Beef ... Chandelier ... Fire Truck ... Penguin ... Marching Band ... Drummer ... Lemon Pie.

46 How can I remember where I parked my car after my plane trip?

I've seen it happen. July, 2017, five minutes after midnight at Baltimore/Washington Airport. I'm sitting on the shuttle bus as we enter the huge, full parking lot when a woman approaches the driver, saying *"We can't remember where we parked."* The look on her husband's face, sitting by the three children, wasn't good. Does the story have a happy ending? I don't know. I got off at the next stop.

The excitement of our trip, planned for months, is upon us. We jump out of our car and onto the shuttle looking forward to the flight. Five days later we wished we had looked backward to our car.

Count the car spaces to the shuttle stop and look up at the lot #. Can you remember it? Is it #5? Hey, that's the number of children I have. Is it #13? It's bad luck to lose my car. Is it #24? That's the first two numbers of my phone number. Is it T? If so, think *Tea*. Is it L? If so, think *L-ephant*. Try to find a memorable connection.

The people at Walt Disney World in Florida understand this. That's why parking lots are named Sleepy, Happy, and Bashful. They make them memorable so Dad doesn't feel Dopey for not finding the car.

On your parking ticket, write the location to where you parked. Days later when you grab your ticket, you're also grabbing your car.

#47 My daughter is in the school play. How can she remember her lines?

How do I get to Carnegie Hall? The same is true when it comes to school plays. You practice. However, if you learn a few memory tricks you can still plan to go out with your friends.

Bring the script wherever you go and read your lines when you have minutes to spare.

While at home go through your blocking or movements, reading aloud a sentence at a time and overemphasizing each word. Continue when you have the sentence down cold. Link the last word to the first word of the next sentence. Find patterns that will aid your memory. As an example, look at the first two sentences of Lincoln's Gettysburg Address.

Four score and seven years ago, our fathers brought forth on this continent a new nation, conceived in liberty and dedicated to the proposition that all men are created equal. Now, we are engaged in a great civil war ....

Note the pattern in the first sentence with the word *four*. There's 4 score and brought 4th. That's memorable. How can you remember *conceived* and *dedicate*? Conceive is a beginning, while DEAD-icate is an ending. That's a memorable pattern. How can you remember *created equal* to *Now, we are engaged..?* Think of equal rights. That's what NOW (National Organization for Women) stands for. *Equal rights* to *NOW* is a memorable connection, especially when you're married or *engaged*. Then, you hope you don't get into a *great civil war* with your partner.

You can find patterns throughout every speech or script. So look for them, practice, and ... break a leg.

101 Ways for Beating Absent-mindedness

 # 48 How can I remember which way the one-way streets go? I'd save time if I knew beforehand and wouldn't have to circle back.

It would be nice if we knew ahead of time which way traffic flows on Dearborn. If we knew, we'd take the next exit coming up onto Clairmont, instead. We are sure of one thing: The downtown one-way streets either go left or right. So let's set ourselves straight. Hopefully, away from oncoming traffic.

Create a visual image for the four directions; *north, south, east* and *west*. Create a visual image for the street name. Associate the two in a crazy fashion.

The word *north* is hard to picture, but the word *knot*, sounding similar to *north*, isn't. Visualize a huge rope tied in knots. *North* is now *knot*. *South* is similar to *Mouth*. *East* is similar to *Yeast*. Visualize yeast, or dough rising. *West* sounds like *vest*, and that can be visualized. The nouns *knot, mouth, yeast,* and *vest* are easier to picture than *north, south, east* and *west*.

Canal Street runs South. Main Street runs West. Laurel Street runs East. Madison Street runs North. Unless you use your imagination, it will be difficult to remember.

Now, read and visualize ... The *Canal* is flowing into your *Mouth*. In fact, hundreds of mouths are lapping up the canal. On the horse's *Mane* is a huge *Vest*. The *Laurel* wreath is covered with *Yeast*. See the dough hanging from the greenery. I'm *Mad*, because I'm tied up in *knots*.

Without reviewing, which direction do Canal, Main, Laurel, and Madison go? Congratulations, you did it!

#*49* **I'm receiving an award and want to thank people in my department. I'm afraid I may forget some names. How can I remember?**

It's a memorable evening and you'll want to thank the folks who made it all happen but be careful. Where do you draw the line?

If you thank the people in your department, shouldn't you thank Judy and Ted who came in from another department helping you those last two weeks? How about your husband and the moral support he gave you? Your parents coming in from Akron will be there. Don't they deserve to be thanked?

Avoid reading a laundry list of names. It's better to write them each 'thank you' notes. In your acceptance speech, say what the award means to you and how you couldn't have done it without a strong support of team players, certainly too many to name here.

If you do want to thank a few people, create an acronym using their names. To remember to thank Gary, Tom, Cheryl, Hugh, and Sue, you can think of **GoaT CHeeSe**, or **SHaGgy CaT**. Be consistent with their names. If you're unsure of Hugh's last name don't mention the last names of the others.

Avoid using notes when offering thanks. You sound more sincere when looking at the people, instead of a paper, when saying their name. You've watched the Academy Awards, haven't you?

Before speaking find the key people in the audience. When acknowledging them you'll know where to look, instead of standing behind the lectern scanning the room like a bounty hunter.

101 Ways for Beating Absent-mindedness

 # 50 I came home from work and realized I had left the stove on. How can I remember to turn it off?

As you know, turning the oven or stove off isn't your only task. You have to hurry to stir the beans, remember to take the bread out, and keep your eyes on your one-year-old making sure he doesn't fall over in his highchair. Turning off the stove? That's the least of your concerns. Come back after dinner and we'll discuss it then.

Get in the habit of using both hands when you cook. One hand holds the pan, the other hand stirs the rice. One hand removes the pan, the other hand turns off the stove.

Incorporate the *DIAL* system when cooking. *D*elivering *I*ncredible *A*ppetizing *L*eftovers reminds you to check the dials. Or, *O*ffering *F*amily *F*ood, reminds you the oven needs to be turned *OFF*.

A pat on the back is always appreciated after a job well done. Do the same with your stove top. You couldn't have cooked the meal without them. So give a quick pat on the four coils to say 'thanks.' Of course, it's best to wait after dessert is served.

#51 How can I remember recipes without going to the file?

While visiting your daughter up north you learn the recipe to her favorite cookies is at your home down south. If your memory can't dish up the recipe you won't be dishing out the dessert.

From *The Woman's Day Book of Baking*, here's a recipe for Maple Butter Thin Cookies.

1 cup all-purpose flour
½ cup cornstarch
½ cup confectioners' sugar
1 cup butter
¼ cup maple syrup

Mix flour, cornstarch, and confectioners' sugar. Add butter and syrup and mix with hands until smooth. Chill 1 hour. Shape into 1 inch balls and place at least 3 inches apart on an ungreased baking sheet. Bake in preheated 300°F oven for 20 minutes. Now, let's make it memorable. Creating a story, with the lead actors being ingredients and measurements, helps us remember the recipe.

FLOWERS (flour), wearing a huge CAP (cup), attack an ear of CORN (cornstarch) HALF its size, when boxing great SUGAR Ray Robinson steps in ripping both of them in HALF. ADD to that, a BATTER (butter), wearing a CAP (cup), pays a QUARTER for SYRUP and MIXES it SMOOTHLY on an UNGREASED SHEET. A CHILL falls over the crowd for the next HOUR. Then, everyone INCHES up rolling into a BALL, 3 INCHES from each other, including the .300 hitter. 20 MINUTES later, the heat is off.

That's good brain food for remembering recipes.

#52 How can I remember to take the clothes out of the dryer?

You've noticed you're running out of socks and underwear, yet the hamper is empty. Hmmm, perhaps they're in the dryer.

Your clothes have had quite a night. They've been soaked, spun, and hung out to dry, at least in the dryer. Isn't it about time you get them out of there?

If you're not within earshot of the loud buzzer signaling your clothes are done, good luck. You'll have to rely on your memory to get them out.

After you toss in a fabric softener sheet (see #36 if you forget), and clean the lint filter, bring the box into the family room or kitchen. It's out of its element. Seeing the box will remind you the clothes are in the dryer. Also, leaving a laundry basket within view will tell you something is up.

Leave the door open to the laundry room. The sight of the dryer, as well as the sound emitting from it, is a constant reminder for you that your work is not done.

Leave a few coat hangers near the dryer, reminding you to hang some of those shirts that are not allowed in. Without the hangers, you may think, this time I'll let it go. However, when your shrunken shirts come out, *letting it go* is what you'll do.

53 A family moved in across the street. How can I remember their names?

The moving van just pulled away leaving a new family behind. Of course, the family isn't new. They became new when they left their old neighborhood. Now, this new family is beginning a new life in a new town. They hope it's their last move. It's starting to get old. But then, what else is new?

Three weeks later (admit it) you introduce yourself. You meet husband Ken, wife Phyllis, daughters Courtney, Sheila, and son Matt. You figure, if the mother doesn't call all their names for dinner you'll never remember.

Write the names on a 3x5 card as soon as you have a chance, filing it in the kitchen drawer with the names of the other families on the block. Next time you see them playing in their yard, get the card and reacquaint yourself with the names.

Make an effort to call out their names when you see them. After a few weeks of *"Hi Ken,"* you'll start to remember. Tweak the names to make it meaningful and create a story. For instance, FILL (Phyllis) the CAN (Ken) on the COURT (Courtney) with a MAT (Matt) and put a SHIELD (Sheila) on top, includes all their names.

Whether it's the family across the street or the nine members of the County School Board, a story can be created. It makes no difference as to what the names are.

#54 **Lying in bed, I got a great idea but had forgotten it in the morning. How could I have remembered?**

Generally, when a "light goes on in our head," the lights are off in our room. Why is it that all our best ideas happen in the middle of the night?

You awake at 3:00 with a brilliant idea that will help your company get off the ground. However, hours later when you get up your company stays down. Your idea never made it through the night.

Keep a large legal pad and an uncapped pen on your nightstand. When an idea hits you, write down in big letters, key points. Speaking of ideas, it's not a bad one to make a practice run. While you're fully awake, close your eyes and write a sentence. If you're having trouble comprehending, try writing again with your eyes closed. The rehearsal may come in handy when a moment of genius hits you in the middle of the night.

To remember ideas, associate it to something in the room. For instance, throwing a crumpled piece of paper or a sock on the floor will jolt your memory when you see it the next morning. If your bedroom is already messy, adding a sock or crumpled paper won't help. Instead, straightening your room is the answer. You can also associate your idea to an open drawer or a lamp that you turn to the side. When you awake and notice these objects askew, you'll be reminded of your idea.

If your idea is so good, get up, turn the lights on, and write it down.

101 Ways for Beating Absent-mindedness

55 **I'd like to learn state and world capitals. Is there an easy way to do this?**

By using your imagination you can easily increase your learning in record time. Understanding a few memory tricks will have you standing at the head of the class.

The word *VIA*, meaning by way of, applies to memory, too.
V = Visualize. I = Imagination. A = Association.

How can we use *VIA* to remember Little Rock is the capital of Arkansas? Visualize, imagine, and associate *little rocks* (Little Rock) being filled into the *ark* (Arkansas). By breaking down the state and capital into a visual, and associating them in a bizarre way, it's hard to forget.

London is the capital of England. The words *London* and *England* need to be visualized and then linked. The word *Laundry* is similar to *London*. The word *Ink* is similar to *England*. Using your imagination, visualize dumping *Ink* into the *Laundry*. The ink is ruining your clothes. *England* reminds us of *Ink*, and that reminds us the capital is *London*, similar to the word *laundry*.

If you can imagine a huge *Otter* in a *Can* you'll know *Ottawa* is the capital of *Canada*.

Imagine *Cauliflower* in a *Sack*, and you'll know the capital of *California* is *Sacramento*.

Visualize *Brussels Sprouts* in a giant *Bell* and you'll know *Brussels* is the capital of *Belgium*.

Once you put *VIA* to action, you can remember the capitals of every state and country.

101 Ways for Beating Absent-mindedness

 # 56 I need to get a coupon I saw in last Sunday's paper. How would I remember?

I remember seeing it, but how was I supposed to know I would need the coupon on ridding fleas? I didn't have a dog last Sunday. Now I do and I need to go into the garage to find that coupon. Could it have been in the Flea Market section?

Before you throw the scrambled newspaper in the recycling bin, spend a few moments to separate it. Take all that colored paper with coupons and put it aside. Do you see any coupons you need? If so, grab the scissors and go after it. Put the coupon in your "coupon file." What? You say you don't have one. Well, create one.

Coupons under the refrigerator magnet or left on counters are savings waiting to be lost. Let's face it. We do a good job of clipping the coupons, but what we do with them afterward is anyone's guess. It's not until we vacuum underneath the cushions when we find a jackpot, usually in expired coupons.

Invest in a coupon organizer and use it. Each time you go shopping, take it and you'll hold onto more money.

Organizing everything in your life, even the Sunday newspaper, will save you time, save you money, and save you headaches. Everything has a place. Make sure you know those places.

57 I can never recall how to pronounce Mr. Weinstein's name. How can I be sure?

Is it Wein*stein*, rhyming with *bean* or Wein*stein* rhyming with *sign*? Hmmm, maybe instead of calling, I'll send him a letter.

We know how to spell it, but aren't sure how to say it. Is it *Clough*, rhyming with *cow*, or *Clough* rhyming with *stuff*? Is it *Weiss* rhyming with *rice* or is *Weiss* rhyming with *peace*?

If it's a name that could go either way, quickly associate a word that rhymes with it, and create a little ditty to it. *"Freddy Fertich has an itch, yes, Freddy Fertich is a witch."*

Write the rhyming or recognizable word down when you hear it on the answering machine or when the secretary says "Barbara Detrick is out." You'll know the correct pronunciation when you write (Debt-rick) the next time you call.

Remembering a name and calling it correctly are the first steps in making a good first impression. Rewrite the name in a way you'll know how to pronounce it.

If your name is difficult to pronounce, help others and tell them memorable ways to remember. It's *Mollisee*, like *Policy*. It's *Hyatt*, like the hotel. It's *Gautreaux*, pronounced *Go Tro*.

Names are important. Take the time to get them right.

58 How can I keep my train of thought?

Losing our train of thought is not uncommon. For instance, just the other day .... I'm sorry, what was I talking about?

Our minds, without our permission, can jump from one thought to another in a fraction of a second. We have thoughts coming in, thoughts going out, and thoughts just not happening.

You can keep your thought on track by giving away the ending first. For example, *"Brian and Wendy are getting married next Saturday. Last summer, while living in Winnipeg, Brian had met this wonderful girl ..."*

Tell your listener, *"Remind me to tell you about the circus incident."* If your listener isn't bored after your boating incident, she'll remind you of the circus story.

Slow your rate of speech and look at your listener. Who can remember anything when you notice the waiter with the tray full of shrimp or the ice sculpture of a horse?

When talking on the phone, jot down topics you want to discuss and points you want to make. Cross them off as you go into them.

59 It's late at night and I can't remember where we pitched the tent. Help!

The campground is huge and you realize the folks from Michigan, Maryland, and Massachusetts have bought the same tent you did at Walmart. You happily pitch the tent, not realizing that you'll be doing it again Tuesday on trash day. Because the bugs are biting and the fish aren't, you take the family to the Kountry Korral Kafe down the road.

On your way back through the gates, you're not exactly sure which road to take. You don't remember it being this dark when you left for supper. You keep asking yourself, *"Where did I go wrong?"*

There's a reason why you were given a map of the campsite when you checked in. Become acquainted with it. Your site is #54, around the first curve and past the restrooms on the right. Study the map. This is your new neighborhood for the next 48 hours.

Set your odometer and measure the distance from your lot to the campground's entrance when you leave for the night. You'll be glad you did when you re-enter the grounds.

Make a mental note that you're two sites past the family with the converted school bus and there's an open field across from yours.

Make certain where the road or trail is if you're camping in the woods. This way, you can easily find your way back after tomorrow's hike. Who knows? With proper planning your wife and kids may want to stay another day.

60 I locked my keys in the car (again). How can I prevent this?

You own a car that gets 45 miles to the gallon. However, yesterday you lost a half of a tank of fuel while your car was idling in the driveway. You know you never should have gotten out to scrape your windshield.

There's something about closing doors with keys left behind. We know instantly what we've done. As soon as the door shuts we tell ourselves, "*I don't think I should have done that.*" Yet, we do it. In fact, before this day is out someone on your block will have locked himself out of his house or out of his car. Hopefully, it's not you. By following these key steps you'll always keep track of your keys.

Photographers know how to bring two subjects into focus. We need to do it, too. When closing doors, make certain you're looking at both the door and the key.

When leaving your home keep your keys in your hand.

Please, trust me on this one. Never leave your vehicle with the engine running. I know, you're only going to step out to get the paper or mail a letter, but don't do it. You may be walking from here to eternity, because your automatic lock automatically locked.

Go to the hardware store and spend a few dollars for a spare key. Keep it in your wallet or purse, and may you never have to use it.

101 Ways for Beating Absent-mindedness

 # 61 **I keep forgetting to mail those bills. How can I remember to go to the post office?**

When your A/C won't run, your ice won't freeze, and your lights don't turn on anymore, you'll remember to head to the post office.

Keep a place on your desk or counter top specifically for mail. Buy a small container or box for your mail. Remove the top. You'll want to make sure the envelopes are always visible. You know the old saying when it comes to forgetting to pay bills, "Out of sight, out of light."

Keep a roll of stamps. If your mortgage lender provides you with envelopes, put stamps on them ahead of time. Hopefully, the stamps will be used before the post office raises the rate.

Before leaving the house, stick the mail in the door jam or put them on top of your purse. It will be impossible to forget the mail when it's right in front of your eyes.

Put a rubber band around the mail to eliminate the chance a letter escapes. Your writing class may reward you for dropping a *y*, but when it comes to your mail you don't want any letters to fall.

Put the mail on your dashboard when you're driving away. It will be a constant reminder to go to the post office. Avoid putting the mail under the sun visor. It may be days before you remember; especially if you live in Seattle.

If it's in the budget, write bills as soon as they come in and get them out of the house. It's a nice feeling to know that your cable is paid up for the next month and a half. Now, if I could only find a pen...

Of course, there is online bill paying.

101 Ways for Beating Absent-mindedness

 # 62 I'd like to remember the floor to my doctor's office without checking the big board in the lobby. How can I accomplish this?

You're already running late. The traffic was heavier than usual. The parking deck was full and now you're looking up at a menu board like you're ready to order a Quarter Pounder. But instead, you want to find the floor to get to Dr. Brunansky's office. Whatever happened to house calls?

Associate the floor to an action that makes it memorable. If it's the second floor, think about your visit *2* see the doctor.

If it's the 3rd floor, associate the floor to the three very important people involved; you, the receptionist, and the Doctor.

If it's the 4th floor, remind yourself you're going *4* a check-up.

Is it the 5th floor? It's going to take your whole hand, four fingers, and one thumb, to open the door to the office.

Is it the 16th floor? Visualize driving up to it, like any 16- year-old would do on the first day of getting a driver's license.

If it's the 11th floor, imagine your legs, shaped like the number 11, walking to the elevator.

Find a combination that links the floor to the purpose of your visit. The phonetic alphabet (page 197) will help.

#63 How can I remember keys points I want to make on a job interview?

The voice coming from behind the mahogany desk says, "*Why should I hire you?*" The voice on the other side says, "*Well, if you give me a moment and allow me to make a phone call, I'll tell you.*" Better luck tomorrow.

Write down points you want to make, such as projects you have carried through, awards you have won, and experiences you've had. Keep the points to a sentence. Then, reduce each sentence to a key word that will trigger your memory.

You want to mention your work on the Parks & Rec project, your 3.5 grade average at Penn State and your volunteer work with Habitat for Humanity. In your "mind's eye" visualize a playground with a huge pencil coming down the slide falling into a house. The playground represents Parks & Rec, the pencil represents Penn State and the house reminds you of your community service. Each topic is connected to another and you'll remember.

Make it memorable to the interviewer by saying upfront that your experience at the corporate, college, and community level qualifies you for the position. Then go into each one.

Do your homework on the company you're interviewing with. Link the information the same way, and not only will you remember, but you'll be remembered, too.

You don't want to feel rushed on your big day, so decide early what you're going to wear. Get that decision out of your way. Take a practice run to the building you're going to so you won't get lost come Tuesday. Allow extra time for traffic. Now, you're free to organize your thoughts for the new position.

64 How can I remember to record my mileage each day?

The Pasadena Tournament of Roses has just concluded and you're determined to begin the year keeping accurate records. All goes well until January 3rd when you forget to record your miles.

Drive to the office supply store and buy a booklet with entries to record mileage. While you're at it, buy two pens. When the ink runs out in June, the other will carry you the rest of the year. Make your first entry be the drive to the office supply store.

Keep the book in the glove compartment with a sheet of paper marked *mileage* in plain view. Fold the paper until you can slip it inside the handle of your door. You'll put your hand on it each time you exit your car. This will remind you to record your mileage. As you're stepping out of your car, leave the paper on your car seat. When you come back to your car you'll automatically pick up the paper. What do you do with it? You slip it inside the door handle.

Keeping track of your business mileage can be tough. Some of your miles are business related, other miles aren't. In the car, out of the car, the pattern continues throughout the day. Forgetting to record the mileage is easy.

The act of slipping the paper inside the door handle cannot escape you. It's a constant reminder as you get out of the car to reach for the mileage book. The IRS will have to audit someone else.

#65 **I wish I could remember how Gladys likes her tea. How can I remember if it's sweetened or unsweetened?**

You need not be employed as a waitress to want to know how a friend or client likes their tea. Demonstrating you know the likes and dislikes of your acquaintances' taste buds shows you care. It also shows you paid attention the last time the two of you met.

Listen when your friend places an order at the restaurant. She may be an invited guest at your home later in the year and you'll want to know her likes. For instance, if she prefers chicken only fried, visualize a huge chicken dancing in a frying pan on her head. Don't tell her what you're thinking, unless you don't want to see her again.

If your lunch partner likes tea, visualize a golf ball sitting atop a tee on her head. See yourself pouring sugar on the ball if she likes her tea sweetened. Hold the sugar if the preference is unsweetened.

If the drink of choice is Mr. Pibb, associate pebbles in the glass. Root Beer? Visualize a tree with roots in the glass. Diet Pepsi? Visualize popping (Pepsi) a balloon. The balloon dies (Diet). Any dish or drink can be visualized in a funny and memorable way. Try it the next time you take a friend to lunch.

After meeting a client or prospect for lunch, record the date, restaurant, and your business associate's order on the back of their business card. The next time you meet for a bite, she'll be impressed when you slide the three packets of sweetener her way.

66   How can I remember to stay awake while in meetings?

This is for the thousands of people out there who just can't keep their eyes open in meetings. Who can blame them? Half the meetings we go to aren't worth remembering.

Some meetings last 20 minutes, others a full day. It doesn't matter, we still fall asleep.

Before going to a meeting, grab change from your desk drawer and drop it into a vending machine. Press the drink that you believe contains the most caffeine. Pour the contents into a plain mug. It looks more professional than drinking out of the can. Sip each time a yawn is coming on.

Choose a seat with a window view. You don't think it makes a difference? Who would you rather look at? That boring speaker you're made to look at each week or the redwing blackbirds that frequent your office park?

Bring a pen and notepad with you. Even if you do nod off, your manager will assume you're taking notes.

From a nearby wall, remove the pushpin which holds the information on Amy's bridal shower. No one will miss it. There are 42 others around the 7th floor. Use the pin to gently poke yourself during times you think you're losing it. Be careful not to push too hard.

If you're only interested in getting an answer to one question, ask early. When you finally do fall asleep, at least you'll be informed.

#67 I keep meaning to take my clothes to the dry cleaners, but I forget. Any advice?

It's an awful feeling. The banquet is tomorrow night and the dress should have been at the cleaners. How did I forget? Maybe if I wear that huge scarf no one will notice the chocolate ice cream stain.

Get a separate laundry basket for dry clean only. If you put your clothes meant for dry cleaning into the usual basket, they get lost. More importantly, it's forgotten. If you throw your clothes in the corner of the room, that's not going to work either. It's just like any other day around your house. You don't know if they're clean, dirty, or ready to be sent to the Salvation Army.

Plan on taking your clothes to the dry cleaners on a specific day. Some businesses offer midweek savings if you bring laundry in on a Wednesday. If the store near you offers a deal find out when that day is and stick with it.

Put your clothes in a bag or basket in the front seat of your car. If you lock them in the truck to be dropped off after work you may forget about them. You may not find them until the first nice Saturday in May when you grab your golf clubs.

Attach the copy to the dry cleaning order to your laundry basket. This will remind you that there are clothes to be picked up. It's a terrible feeling to see the old guy downtown wearing your blue blazer because you failed to get your clothes after 30 days.

101 Ways for Beating Absent-mindedness

 # 68 **On my new job I have to know color patterns. How can I remember which color goes to which project?**

Colors just don't add splash in our life, they add meaning. White means "I surrender," black means "I made a profit," and yellow means "Hurry, drive faster." If your job depends on color coding you need to be bright.

Let's say these five objects have to be color-coded. Picnic Table=Green; Phone=Blue; Lamp=Violet; Bicycle=Red; Computer=Brown.

Colors aren't tangibles because they're difficult to remember. Now, let's change them. Green becomes Green Beans, Blue becomes a Blue Diamond, Violet is a Velvet Robe, Red is Blood, and Brown means Brownie.

Colors transformed to objects make them memorable. Imagine a picnic table covered with a heaping pile of green beans. Visualize blue diamonds pouring out of the phone. Imagine that your lamp is wrapped in a velvet robe, your bike is bleeding, and a brownie is wedged between computer keys. Test yourself. It works.

Color-coding works in every situation, such as remembering subway lines. In Boston, visualize blood spilling all over Mass General and you'll know the hospital is on the Red Line.

In London, pretend that the tennis racquet is strung with Green Beans, and you'll know that the Green Line goes to Wimbledon.

In Chicago, visualize smuggling Blue Diamonds through O'Hare Airport, and you'll know that the Blue Line gets you to the plane in time. That's providing you only visualize.

69 I'm getting older and I'm afraid I'm losing my memory? What can I do?

It's a question I hear often. Am I getting Alzheimer's disease? Losing your keys or forgetting someone's name is not a sign of the disease. It would be a concern not knowing what to do with your keys while you're in your car, or if you're unsure which goes on first, shoes or socks.

Alzheimer's is a serious disease and can only be diagnosed by a physician. It's important to get check-ups, eat a well-balanced diet, and to exercise regularly to help maintain good health.

The mind can be exercised, as well. Get in the habit of doing crossword puzzles or the *Jumble* word game found in most newspapers. Check out a book at the library and read. Reading helps keep our mind alert and our imagination on edge. Whether it's suspenseful novels or short stories, books are the calisthenics for our brains.

Practice remembering when the pressure is off. When you watch the evening news, ask yourself how you could remember the reporter's name and try to remember the last three commercials.

While waiting in line at the bank, read the names of the tellers and try to find hidden words. Seeing the name, *Barbara Rosewall*, you can find the words, *bar*, *rose*, *sew*, and *wall*. If all the names are *Next Teller*, play the game at another bank.

Maintain a positive attitude. Stop telling yourself that your memory is awful and you can never remember anything. We become what we believe. Accentuate the positive Say "*I'll remember*," instead of "*I won't forget.*"

70 Is there a fast way to increase my vocabulary?

You storm out of your boss's office to clean out your desk, upset at the words Mr. Williams said, *"You're a salient, perspicacious employee whom I eminently regard."* Don't quit yet. Brush up on your vocabulary. I think he likes you.

The best way to increase your vocabulary is to read. Get a library card, go to a bookstore, and fill your shelves. However, there's one book that doesn't belong on the shelf - the dictionary. Keep your dictionary on your desk and refer to it each time you meet a word you don't know. Like a smoke alarm, keep a dictionary on every floor of your home. You'll never know when you'll need it.

Use your imagination and associate the word to its meaning.

plenary ... complete, full. The PLANE was full.
baleful ... causing harm. Pitching a BALE FULL of hay is harmful.
campanile ... a bell tower. CAMPING by the bell tower is fun.
trumpery ... worthless, junk. Every TRUMPET is worthless.
torpid ... sluggish. The TORPEDO was very sluggish.

Like two graceful dancers, this system brings the two words together. They become inseparable. It's that connection that embeds the meaning into our mind.

The next time you meet a word you don't know, embrace it and welcome it to your increasing, magnifying, enhancing, and proliferating vocabulary.

71 **My 10-year-old keeps forgetting to zip his pants. What can I do to help him remember?**

If you don't have a 10-year old, and the question is from you, that's okay. By the way, why did you sign this letter, '*Name withheld by request?*' Don't worry, my lips are sealed, which brings us to your important question.

Zip before you button. If you button first, the zipper is hidden and you'll walk out of the convenience store thinking you're good to go. It won't be, until you have to go again when you realize your memory lapse. And let's hope it's you who realizes it first.

Teach your son to say, "*Zip to the bathroom,*" instead of "*Have to go to the bathroom.*" That will instill in his mind to 'zip up' after he zips down.

Show your lad discretion on how to check his zipper. A hand on the belt, while the middle finger slips under, works in any public setting. So I've been told. Next question, please...

101 Ways for Beating Absent-mindedness

 # 72 How can I avoid the embarrassment of forgetting a name when I have to make introductions?

You see it coming and there's no escape. You're hoping for the store alarm to sound or for an opportunity to run. It's no use. It's not going to happen, because here she comes. It's the woman from work whose name you can't remember and she's coming your way. Good luck on this one buddy. I'm outta here.

This is the time when you need a friend. You're expected to make an introduction very soon and you have a little anxiety built up. You know this person, but can't think of her name. Quickly whisper to Sandy *"Help me please. Introduce yourself to this lady fast."*

Your friend - we all need friends like this - will take the lead and say, *"Hi, I'm Sandy and you are?"* After you hear, *"Madeline,"* say, *"Madeline, how are you?"* acting as if you knew her name all along.

You could always pretend you're about to sneeze, giving your friend time to introduce herself. Pretending you have laryngitis works, too.

Did someone mention honesty? There's nothing wrong with that. Simply say *"I'm sorry, your name is giving me a mental block."*

So you forgot. Big deal. Get over it and continue shopping, but don't ever forget her name again. If you do, go with the laryngitis.

#\ *73* **I have trouble concentrating on the telephone. How can I do a better job of this?**

The telephone is a wonderful tool. Where else can you present yourself in a professional manner without the listener knowing you're standing on your head smoking a pipe? The drawback is that it takes you awhile to get to the call.

As convenient as the telephone is, it can be challenging when we can't see the person we're talking to. Instead, we're fumbling through papers, doodling on a scratch pad, or watching the fire on television.

Keep a pad and pen nearby so you can write down important information, such as times and dates. Get rid of clutter and distractions. Turn off the radio or TV. If you can't prevent the noisy environment, plug your exposed ear with a finger or fork, or tell the person you'll call back when you can think straight.

Ask questions and reiterate what you've heard to avoid misunderstandings. Use fewer contractions than you would in a face to face meeting. Saying, "*I cannot go to the opera,*" is better understood than saying "*...can't...*" and eliminates the possibility of Richard honking his car horn in front of your condo Saturday night.

Close your eyes so you're able to fully concentrate on the words.

Pull off to the side of the road when on a cell phone. You can never give the listener your full attention when you're speeding down I-95 while the 18-wheeler carrying hogs is running you off the road.

101 Ways for Beating Absent-mindedness

 # 74 On my way home from work I needed to get a few items at the store but forgotten some things when I pulled into the lot. How could I have remembered?

You're speeding down the highway when you realize there are a few things you need at the store. Bread, baking powder, eggs, laundry detergent, and toothpaste are a must. Unfortunately, when you get to the store you only remember the baking powder. Well, at least you can brush your teeth.

Think of a story that strings the items together. Baking Bread in the Laundry room with an Egg stuck in my Tooth is a memorable scene.

You can also remember by linking the items together in a crazy way. Picture a loaf of bread stuffed with a huge egg. Then, imagine breaking an egg and toothpaste oozes out. Now, imagine brushing your teeth with laundry detergent and then, instead of using detergent, you're using baking powder to wash your clothes. It doesn't make sense, but it makes you get everything you need at the store.

Associate the items you need to parts of your car. Pick out five objects inside your car as you're driving. Associate an object to an item. Imagine the steering wheel is a huge loaf of bread. See yourself squeezing the bread as you're turning the wheel. Imagine the dashboard is covered in toothpaste. Visualize egg yolk dripping from the rearview mirror. Imagine the gear shift sprinkled with baking powder, and visualize a full box of laundry detergent spilled onto the passenger seat.

When you get to the store a quick glance to the wheel, dashboard, mirror, gear shift, and seat will remind you what to buy.

101 Ways for Beating Absent-mindedness

75 **I forgot to send Aunt Mabel a postcard. How could I have remembered?**

You could have taken her with you. She kept saying how much she wanted to see Niagara Falls. Now your trip is over, and you're feeling all wet because the postcard your dear aunt patiently waited for never arrived. Of course, you could always mail one of your extra cards, hoping that she doesn't notice the Omaha postmark.

Buy postcard stamps before your trip. You don't want to cut short your visit to the California vineyards, because you need to go to the post office.

Write down names of the people you plan on sending postcards. Write clearly. You don't want your card to Uncle Luke going to 511 Maplewood Lane in Marietta, Georgia, when he lives on 511 Maplewood Lane in Marietta, Ohio.

Choose a time to write and send cards. Are mornings better for you? How about right before going to bed? Don't fret about not finding the post office. Leave the mail at the hotel desk or campground office. They'll be sure it's mailed.

Make a quick notation as to which card you sent to whom. If you sent Grampa a picture of a grizzly bear from Yellowstone, you'll know to send him another type of picture next time. A postcard of Denver's skyline would be better than the one of that city's zoo with a bear pictured.

Never begin a postcard with, "How are you?" For once, it's not about them. This is all about you and the people you've met and the places you've seen. So brag a little. Tell them what you've done. That's what postcards are for.

 # 76   Why do they give me an appointment card six months before my next dental visit? Don't they know I'll forget?

They figure you will. That's why they'll call you a few days before. They don't want any cavities sitting in their appointment book.

Appointments are like mud thrown on a wall. Some will stick while others will be washed away.

Keep an appointment book by the telephone at work and at home. Refer to it before you say *"Yes."* Use a pocket size calendar book when you're out or invest in a smart phone.

It's equally important to make sure that the other party knows about the scheduled meeting. Always confirm appointments. Call a day or two ahead of time to make sure the "green light" is still on. Sending a postcard or text is a great idea when you can add, *"Looking forward to meeting you Monday at 9:00 to discuss your financial future."*

77 How can I remember to take my medication?

Some prescriptions come with a handy memory aid, a dial, or compartment labeled with dates. For the medication without these devices, a sharp memory is needed.

Always leave the pill bottle in the same place in the cabinet or counter top. Having it in a familiar location will be one less thing you have to worry about. Leave the bathroom cabinet door open before going to bed. The next morning when you brush your teeth the pills will be looking right back at you. You could also put your toothbrush on top of the pill bottle.

Tape a small calendar inside the bathroom cabinet or near the pills. Place a checkmark on the date each time you take a pill.

Get rid of old pill bottles. A quick phone call to the doctor's office will let you know which bottles to discard if you're unsure of their longevity. Clutter around the house transforms to clutter in the head.

78 **The overdue library fee now exceeds the cost of the book. How can I remember to go to the library?**

The librarian gives you a slip of paper with the date September 20th on it. That day means something. It's the day she wants her book back. Use the paper as a bookmark or clip it to the book's jacket.

On your calendar, make a notation as to when the book is due. The day before, put the book in front of your door so you will remember. Laying the book on the table near the door isn't enough. The book must be in the direct path to the door. Do you think you'd forget if you stepped on Tom Clancy's name before leaving for work? You won't.

Lay the book on the dashboard. I know. The reflection is awful. Well then, take it to the library and get rid of it.

#79 **How can I remember to turn off the coffee maker when I leave the office?**

You've had a long day. You've made calls, been out on appointments, and filed reports. You're also the last person to leave the office. Tonight, it's your job to make sure computers are off, lights are out, and doors locked. And oh yes, the coffee maker, that needs to be off, too.

Put your coffee mug or Styrofoam cup on top of your computer while you're working. The coffee cup will remind you to turn off the machine before you leave.

Associate the C's before you leave. Computer off? Check! Calendar turned? Check! Counter cleaned? Check! Coffee maker off? Check! Now, time to go home. Coat? Check!

It will only take one week with a sign posted by the lights reading *"Coffee maker off?"* to remind you.

#80 How can I remember what to pack?

A hockey player needs his skates, a track runner needs his shoes, and a moviegoer needs his ticket. There are some things we just can't do without, and we must make sure they're packed.

Stand by your bags or luggage and visualize yourself naked after you've finished packing. Now, start getting dressed. Did you pack your underwear? Your socks? T-shirt? Shoes? Think about what you'll be wearing and needing on your excursion, making sure you have them packed.

The night before your trip, make a list of everything you'll need, including items you know you'll never forget. Check off items on the list as you're stuffing them into the suitcase.

Clear an area around your bags for what you need to pack. You may accidentally pack something you don't want because it was near your socks when you threw them in. You don't want a can of dog food dropping from your blanket when you're on the Florida beach.

Always leave a plastic bag and clothes pins inside your luggage. The bag is for dirty laundry, and the pins are an excellent way to keep those hotel drapes closed.

Double-check essentials leaving nothing to chance, such as tickets, documents, and yes, skates.

81 **I keep forgetting to remove my rings when I do dishes. How can I remember?**

When a Vegas casino dealer comes to work, she will *High Ten* her replacement. It's standard practice so cameras can capture if dealers have money in their hands. A dishwasher needs to do the same.

High Ten the wall, above the sink, before turning on the faucet. Extended hands on the wall provide your eyes to check for rings. Why not just look down on your hands? You may forget to do that. It's not as memorable as a prewash slap to the wallpaper. If the day comes when you do lose your rings, it will be the day when you didn't *High Ten* the wall.

Another idea is to run water over your hands before you fill the sink. As the water hits your fingers, you can remove the rings.

The action of hitting the wall or running your hand underneath the faucet is a procedure giving you a final check to remove rings.

 # 82 **How can I remember to pick up my child at school?**

Your child is a regular on school bus #324; however on this day, little Emma is working with a science tutor. She's depending upon you to be there at 3pm.

Set your watch alarm or any other gadget you own that comes with a buzzing noise. When the alarm sounds, grab your car keys and go. Allow for extra time if you're at work, shopping, or a long way from the school.

Put a photo of your child near the front door or by the stairs to remind you she needs to be driven home. If you're at work, tape the photo to your computer or phone.

Of course, you love your daughter. Her picture is already in every room. However, moving the photo to a site that is out of the ordinary will trigger your memory. A picture of a bus will accomplish the same result, but who wants to explain that?

Do your best to arrive on time. She's ready to come home. You'll treasure those drive home moments long after she's grown up and moved away.

83 I keep forgetting to do the wash. How can I remember?

When your pants start walking down the stairs, it's time to get the *Tide*. Let's hope no one needs to remind you on this one. But, hey, sometimes we ... well ... forget.

Soon after you come home from work, you'll be going out for the evening. It's important to do a load of laundry, because tomorrow morning is the piano recital. Call your house while you're at work. Leave a message on the answering machine that the laundry needs to be done. What's the first thing we do when we come home from work? That's right. We look for the blinking light.

Visualize a huge washing machine blocking your front door. It's gigantic and suds are going everywhere. When you pull into your driveway and walk toward the door, you'll be reminded of the blockade. That image will remind you to do the laundry.

Keep a dirty sock by the door or wrap it around a table or chair. This simple procedure will remind you as to what to do when you come home from work. Come to think of it, a clean sock will have the same effect. Let's go with that.

84 Twice last week I've forgotten to wear a belt. How can I prevent this from happening?

Leaning back in your chair, with arms at your hips, you've just concluded you have forgotten something. How did this happen?

In the closet, drape your belts over the hanger holding your pants. The belt will be in your hands before you know it. Somehow, get the belt touching your pants when they're in the closet. You needn't tell anyone.

Another reminder is making sure your tie, after you put it on, touches your belt buckle.

When you hold your belt, don't let go. Put your pants on with belt in hand. It's when you let go of it your mind does the same.

85 I can't remember the last time I changed the battery to the smoke alarm. How can I remember?

Grill those hamburgers in the den. Wait four seconds.

It has been well publicized that we should change the smoke alarm battery on the days we turn the clocks. Why is that so? It's a simple memory aid reminding us to do it twice a year; the same number of times we change the clocks. One action reminds us of another.

The local news suggest that we change the battery when we 'Spring Forward' and 'Fall Back' the hour. Still, many people forget. Usually, it's the people who are an hour late to church that day.

Since we get reminders, this question relates to more than changing the battery. It's about all those times we get reminded of doing things, but don't carry them through. We put them off.

Whenever possible, capture the moment now. When you think of something to do, to get, to send, do it now. When others remind you to "don't forget" or "you need to remember," do it then. Putting it off puts too much pressure on our mind to remember.

Procrastination is poison. Just ask the 45-year old man who never left home. His mother said, "*Marvin, you'll never amount to anything because you procrastinate.*" Marvin looked at his mother and said, "*I'll show you. You just wait.*"

When you're reminded to do something ... DO IT NOW.

#86 I can never remember the order of downtown streets. How can I fix this to memory?

Okay, ready? Downtown San Diego: 1st, 2nd, 3rd, 4th, 5th, 6th, and 7th Street. Got that? Oh, you say you're visiting San Francisco. That's not so easy. When you know the series of streets in a city you're visiting, you'll never get lost. That's a feeling every traveler wants.

Let's go back to San Francisco and look at the order of 10 downtown streets; *Chestnut, Lombard, Greenwich, Filbert, Union, Green, Vallejo, Broadway, Pacific*, and *Jackson*.

See any patterns? Other than a Green Valle(y) it's going to take some work. The street names need to be nudged to make them memorable. The new word will remind us of the street.

Chestnut to Chest, Lombard to Lamb, Greenwich to Sandwich, Filbert to Film, Union to Onion, Green to Grin, Vallejo to Veil, Broadway to Board, Pacific to Pacifier and Jackson to Jack in the Box. Now we can create a story.

A CHEST falls on a LAMB, which falls on a SANDWICH. Inside the Sandwich is a roll of FILM tied around an ONION. A man takes a bite and GRINS. Hiding his grin with a VEIL, he walks into a big BOARD. The board becomes a PACIFIER in his mouth. He begins to jump up and down like a JACK IN THE BOX.

It takes only a minute to become familiar with the street names. The SANDWICH will remind you of GREENWICH and FILM reminds you of FILBERT. Use your imagination and you'll remember.

Visit a city soon. There's a story waiting for you.

#*87* **How do I remember to flip the mattress prolonging its life?**

It's always a good idea to turn your mattress over every few months to extend its durability. Families with teenagers always have the best mattress. (Mothers have been known to flip mattresses quite frequently). Although, they would save their back muscles if they waited until Junior got off it first.

Here are six times during the year reminding you to flip the bed.

January 1. A new beginning. A time to TURN OVER a new leaf.
March 1. *MA*rch and *MA*ttress go together.
May 1. *MA*y and *MA*ttress go together.
July 4th. Did someone lay a firecracker underneath my bed?
Labor Day. The labor of turning the mattress over.
October 31. I know a good place to stash the candy.

You could also put a small dot on the calendar to remind you. Only you will know what it means. Therefore, when it comes to knowing when to turn the mattress, you'll always be on top of it.

#88 **My checkbook hasn't turned up in days. I can't remember where I put it. Any suggestions?**

If you want to keep a check on your checkbook, leave it in one place. Each time you move it, the odds work against you with finding it. Keep it in the drawer on the desk where you write checks. Put it in the same spot after each use.

If the checkbook stays in your purse or wallet, then set aside a specific place for it and leave it there. Keep the checks and the register together by putting a rubber band around them. Toss the check covers out if you don't use them. Less is best, of course, not if you're referring to your balance.

Immediately record the amount in the register after you write the check. The wise guy behind you at the grocery store may grumble because you're taking too much time but go ahead and do it now. It's a matter of checks and balances.

89   **I forgot to water the lawn last night. How can I remember?**

If the grass is greener on the other side of the fence, your neighbor remembers to water the lawn.

Remember many years ago while pulling into the gas station the 'ding, ding' sound you heard while riding over the black tube? It signaled to the attendant for him to "fill 'er up." That 'ding, ding' sound is seldom heard now, but the principle applies when needing to remember to water the lawn.

Stretch your hose over the driveway. When you come home from work, it's impossible for you to forget to turn the hose on. But, I know, you'll do it after dinner or after the football game and before you go to bed. You won't forget, will you?

Reach down and pluck a couple of blades of grass on your way to the front door. Tape them to the remote control. After the game you'll be reminded to tend to your lawn.

Watch football games that are played only on natural grass. Any game played on artificial surface is not going to help you remember.

Suggest to your wife that she serve French style green beans. They look a lot like grass, and that will remind you to water the lawn.

Wives can play a major role, too. Pull the hose into the house and tie two loops around his neck. You might be headed for divorce court, but at least you'll have nice grass.

#*90* **I often forget to turn my car's turn signal off. How can I remember?**

You think you're the most popular person in town. Everyone waves and makes interesting gestures to you. Of course, it only happens when you're behind the wheel of your car. Usually, it comes after you change lanes, turn corners, or go back the other way.

If you don't think this happens to you, would you know? Take this short quiz to see if you're one of those drivers who forget to turn off the turn signal.

Question #1. Do you keep hearing an irritating sound in your car that goes on for miles, thinking it's a truck backing up?

Question #2. Do you keep your eyes on the road, but never look at your control panel?

Question #3. Do you think you're sexy, because those two blondes in the red sports car keep honking the horn and mouthing words to you?

Keep your hand on the turn signal until you turn it off, especially on the Interstates when you're changing lanes.

Get in the habit of periodically checking the controls, making sure the turn signal is off.

Be gracious when your wife says, *"You idiot, turn that thing off."*

If the turn signal doesn't turn off after you make a turn, it's time to buy a new car. Yours is very outdated.

101 Ways for Beating Absent-mindedness

91 How do I remember to put the gas cap on after a fill up?

Moments after you pull up to the Shell station, you realize your gas cap is at Exxon, 423 miles back.

Some cars are equipped with gas caps that are connected by cord to the car. We hope our next car is like that. In the meantime, we have to rely on our memory. It's easy to place the cap on top of the pump while we're filling the tank. It's out of the way, but unfortunately, out of our mind.

Try keeping one hand on the door of the gas tank while you're filling up. This action is a constant reminder to get the cap.

Try wedging the cap in the empty slot where the pump is housed. It's impossible to forget, because the pump is blocked from going back in. It's when you only remove the cap that you can return the pump to its original position. Now, the cap is in your hand.

As you're filling the tank, fill your free hand with the cap. If possible, slip on one of those flimsy plastic mitts to keep your hand clean. Later in the day, you don't want to be drinking unsweetened tea while smelling unleaded gas. There are some things you don't want to remember after you fill your tank.

Apply the verbal "IN / ON" method when refueling. When you return the hose back to the pump, say "*IN*." This will prompt you to say "*ON*" as you reach for the cap.

92 How can I remember an author's book?

A friend asks if you've read any good books lately. You tell her the new one by Patricia Cornwell, but you can't remember the title.

You call the bookstore asking if they have the James Thurber book. When asked, "Which one?" You say, "The blue cover."

Nine down in Sunday's crossword puzzle reads, *Author of Wuthering Heights*. All you know is that it has six letters.

Authors need for you to remember their work. That's why their name stands three inches high in bold letters on the front cover. Like the authors themselves, you need to write a story to remember. Here are five bestselling books for 2017.

Autumn, Ali Smith. *Autumn* leaves fall in the town of *Smithfield.*

Exit West, Mohsin Hamid. A canned *Ham* is *Exiting West.*

Pachinko, Min Jin Lee. *Pa's Chin* is *Lee*-king (leaking).

The Power, Naomi Alderson. *Power* to *All.*

Sing, Unburied, Sing, Jesmyn Ward. In the emergency *Ward* they *Sing, Unbury* you, and *Sing* again.

Any book title can easily be associated with its author, including *Finding the Keys* in a *Melon (Mellor).*

93 How can I remember to wear a different dress the next time we get with the Johnson's?

You recall the wonderful compliments you got, but you're uncertain as to which dress you were wearing. Now, the party is Saturday night and you want to make sure you're wearing a different outfit.

Does your husband remember? Oh well, it was worth asking. Is there anyone you can call who was at the party? Of course, it would be terribly embarrassing to find out she wasn't invited to this one. Maybe you can borrow her dress.

Save the literature from the functions you attend. Write on the back of the wedding program, ticket stub, or recital flyer what you were wearing. When you get the handout during your monthly club meeting, jot down on the back what you have on. This way, you won't be wearing the pink flowery dress with matching heels to next month's function.

Of course, you could always spill the contents of your glass on your lap. You might get a lot more stares, but at least you'll know not to wear the stained dress to next year's 3rd Annual Wine Festival.

 # 94 **This morning I realized I was out of coffee filters. How could I have remembered to get some?**

Say it ain't so. You can't go through the day without your coffee. How will you cope? How will you function? How will you survive? What do you have to say for yourself?

We need to get you some coffee.

When you have only a few filters, leave the box by the door so you'll remember to get more. Tearing off the box top may be the only reminder you'll need. Also, clean out the old filter after each use, so you'll know immediately if you need to buy more later in the day.

If you've already discarded the box, bring another mug with you on your way to work. The empty coffee mug is a reminder to get filters.

95 How can I remember which way to turn the key when locking the door?

Okay, if you're wrong you'll just turn it the other way. But wait, you've just wasted one second of your life. Multiply that by 5, then multiply it by 15. Add 3 and multiply it by 21. Wow! You've could have gone to Med School with all the time you squandered.

Do you turn the key to the *Left* to *Leave* or to the *Left* to *Lock*? Do you turn the key to the *Right* to *Return* or to the *Right* to *Ride away*?

Do you turn the key to the *Left* to *Let in* or to the *Right* to *Restrict* others from getting in?

Which way does the key fit? If grooves up, visualize raising the roof. If grooves down, visualize my home is a foundation.

For safety purposes, grasp the key you're going to use before you walk outside or before you leave your vehicle. There are some seconds you don't want to waste.

96 By the time I walk upstairs I've forgotten what I was supposed to do. How can I remember?

Whether you live in a mansion in the mountains or a boarding house in the burbs, walking from one room to another does something to our memory. There's something about that ninth step leading to the bedroom when we ask ourselves, *"Why am I going upstairs?"*

You may be on the phone, washing your hands, or putting the leftovers in the microwave, when the thought hits you of retrieving the file from upstairs. Moments later you forget.

Once the idea hits you, latch on to it. Are you on your way upstairs to fold clothes? Then say it. *"I'm on my way upstairs to fold the clothes."* It's like snapping your fingers in front of your face forcing you to remember. Sing a song about what you're supposed to do. *"Folding clothes, folding clothes, I'm on my way to folding clothes."*

Use the body peg method to remember. Visualize your *head* covered in towels, *elbowing* your computer, having your *waist* wrapped with plants, and *kicking* toilet paper.

You may forget once you're upstairs, but you'll quickly remember when you think of those five body parts. Each one reminds you. Your head reminds you to fold towels, your elbow reminds you to turn off the computer, your waist reminds you to water the plants, and your foot reminds you to put a new roll in the bathroom.

Attaching new information (Computer) to what we already know (Elbow). That's how we remember.

97 The milk spoiled again. How do I train my kids to put the milk in the refrigerator?

Don't be too hard on your kids. They were only following directions. They simply misunderstood the date printed on the container. They thought they had 10 days left to put it away.

Telling them not to close the refrig won't help either. Not only will your milk spoil, but your electric bill will go through the roof.

Associate the milk to their favorite sport. *"Billy, taking the milk out is like playing catch. You have to return it quickly."*

"Billy, the milk is like a big soccer ball (be careful with this one). *The refrigerator is the goal."*

"Billy, you get two points for pouring it into the glass, providing you return the milk in under 24 seconds."

"Billy, before you can play, everything must be put away."

If all else fails, *"Billy, put the $%@*& milk away!"*

98 I can't remember when the movie is playing. How can I remember?

It was sad to hear about the Minnesota couple who froze to death at the drive-in theatre. Too bad they misunderstood the sign by the entrance; *"Closed for the Season."*

The movie you want to see is playing 5 times today. However, you remember only one of those times and that was 15 minutes ago, about the same time you tossed the movie section away. What time's the next showing?

Write down the time of that show when you call the theatre. It will come in handy if you notice the waitress is going too slowly, or if the cops notice you going too fast. Always have Plan B ready. Who knows? Your date may have trouble with the curling iron and the delay could cut into the movie.

Program your car radio dials to the times of the movie. If you ever forget, just hit the buttons. Your date will be very impressed.

101 Ways for Beating Absent-mindedness

99 How can I remember to cover the plants on cold nights?

You spent an entire weekend last autumn designing the landscape around your home. The payoff has been worth it. You've also taught the neighborhood kids to kick the ball in someone else's yard. However, tonight another enemy is lurching - lower temperatures. It's time to cover the plants.

While you're in your stocking feet and about to sit for dinner, you hear Irv, channel 11's meteorologist, warning that temperatures will drop overnight. Right now you'd rather tend to the greens on your plate than the ones outside in the cold. So enjoy your meal.

Before you eat, pull the plant stand out from its present spot. Place the greenery in front of the television or slide it near the banister leading upstairs. This maneuver will remind you about the plants that need to be covered before you go to bed.

If the inside plants are too heavy to shift, leave them. Instead, find the empty plant holder in the back hall closet and put it in full view on the kitchen counter, on top of the TV, or on the stairs. Putting the object where you eventually have to move it reminds you to cover the plants.

Don't freeze when you hear about the frost warning. By taking some action now, you'll remember to take some action later.

If you do forget, tell the neighborhood kids to return to your yard. Planting season will be back before you know it.

 # 100 **On the few mornings I find a great parking space at work, I walk to my usual spot in the back. How can I remember?**

You've parked in this lot each morning for years. It's automatic the front rows are always taken. By habit you go to the back of the lot. This morning is different. There's an opening up front.

Stop and look back to your car before you enter your building. See it? It's over there, instead of way over there. That short pause will come in handy after you hear the 5:00 bell.

Don't fret if you forget and walk to your usual space. Remain calm and pretend you're taking a late afternoon walk. Walk to the red Porsche and fumble for your keys. Your co-workers will think you've gotten a raise. Hustle back to your car when you're sure no one is looking. Park in your usual place the next day. The walk will do you good.

101 Ways for Beating Absent-mindedness

#101 **How can I remember the words inscribed at the base of the Statue of Liberty?**

Imagine the excitement for those who came before you on your visit to the Statue of Liberty; of immigrants wanting a better way of life. In Emma Lazarus' sonnet, "The New Colossus", she writes what the great statue represents, concluding with ...

Give me your tired, your poor, your huddled masses yearning to breathe free. The wretched refuse of your teaming shore. Send these, the homeless, the tempest-tost to me, I lift my lamp beside the golden door!

To remember the first line, visualize Lady Liberty yelling for you to give her your *tie* (tired). She'll use that tie to *pour* (poor) water down to the *huddled masses*. Another example that *tired* comes before *poor*, is there are more letters in *tired* than *poor*. The longer word goes first.

Note the patterns of the letter *y*. There's *your, your, your,* and *yearn*. Imagine breathing free. Imagine *wrestlers* (wretched) *refusing* (refuse) to *team* up by the *shore*, and you'll remember the next line.

From *shore* it's *Send*. Both words begin with the letter *s*. Imagine the *homeless* have *tempers* (tempest-tost) as you lift *my lamp beside the golden door!* Note all those letter *t*'s, as in *the tempest-tost to...*

Make it a point to visit the *Statue of Liberty*. It's a destination every American should make.

ADVANCED SECTION

Step into this next section to take your memory to a higher level

(Chapter 6 - 12)

CHAPTER 6

Phonetic Alphabet

The phonetic alphabet has been around for centuries and is the best way for remembering numbers. It's a system that codes numbers to letters to form a word.

In the English language, there are ten consonant sounds. Coincidently, ten is also the number of digits (0-9).

Since numbers are difficult to remember, they will be replaced with words. Those words will help us remember any number.

To start, we must know which letters correspond to which number.

0 = *s*, *z*, and *soft c*. You'll notice that your teeth, tongue, and lips are in the same position when you utter the words **S**ay, **Z**oo, and i**C**e. As a reminder...Zer**O** ends with *O*.

1 = *t/d*. These two letters produce the same sound. Notice the position of your tongue when you begin to say the words **T**ea and **D**ew. As a reminder...the letters *t/d* stand on 1 leg.

2 = *n*. There's no sound like the *N*. Words such as **N**o, **N**ew and k**N**ee begin with your tongue pressed to the roof of your mouth. As a reminder...the letter *n* stands on 2 legs.

3 = *m*. Your lips are together when you begin to say **M**a, **M**ow, and **M**e. As a reminder...the letter *m* stands on 3 legs.

4 = *r*. Note the position of your lips and tongue when you pronounce words such as, **R**ye, **R**ay, and **R**ah. As a reminder...the number fou**R** ends with *R*.

5 = *L*. The words **L**ay, **L**ow, and **L**aw produce the same sound. Your tongue touches the roof of your mouth. As a reminder...Roman numeral **5**0 is *L*.

Phonetic Alphabet

6 = *ch, sh, j*, and *soft g*. Words, such as **_Ch_**ew, **_SH_**oe **_J_**oy, **_G_**ee and all start with your lips puckered. As a reminder...mirror image of 6 resembles *j*.

7 = *k, q, hard c/g*. The *KA* sound equals the number 7. Words, such as **_K_**ey, **_Q_**ue, **_C_**ard, **_G_**o begin with the same sound. As a reminder...a backward 7 makes up k.

8 = *f/v, ph*. Lips are close together when you utter the letters *f/v* and *ph*, such as i**_F_**, **_V_**ie, and **_PH_**onetic. As a reminder...a cursive *f* resembles an 8.

9 = *p/b*. The popping sounds of **_P_**ea, **_P_**a, **_B_**ee, and **_B_**oo equals the number 9. As a reminder...a mirror image of *P* resembles 9.

A recap of the Phonetic Alphabet.

0 = s, z, soft c,
1 = t, d
2 = n
3 = m
4 = r
5 = L
6 = sh, ch, j, soft g
7 = k, q, hard c/g
8 = f, v, ph
9 = p, b

Phonetic Alphabet

The Rules

Like everything in life, there are rules to follow. Here are a dozen to stay on course for remembering numbers:

- Ten digits are replaced by ten consonant sounds to make words.

- The vowels, *a, e, i, o, u,* as well as *w, h, y* are not coded to any letter. They're used as fillers.

- The letters *th*, when together, have no value, such as **th**ou, and **th**e. The sound is slightly different than the *t* and *d* sound.

- You need not be a good speller. It's the sound that matters. Therefore, the word, *k**nif**e* translates to only 2 and 8, instead of 7 2 8, because the letter *k* is silent.

- The letter **x** equals the number 70. **X** is pronounced e**KS**, because *k* equals 7 and *s* equals 0.

- Double letters count as one. **Su**mm**er** codes to 034, not 0334. **Bu**tt**er** is 914, not 9114. However, the word, *accent* is 7021, because it's pronounced a**K**-**C**e**NT**.

- *Tion* equals 62, as in opera**tion** (opera-**shun**), na**tion** (na-**shun**), and ova**tion** (o-va-**shun**).

- *Tch* equals 6 because it's a quick *ch* sound, such as i**tch**, ha**tch**, wi**tch**, and wa**tch**.

- *Dg* equals 6, as in fu**dg**e, ju**dg**e, and e**dg**e.

- *Ck* equals 7, not 77. Words such as wha**ck**, hi**ck**, and ho**ck**ey have the *ak* sound. A hard *k* represents the number 7.

- Tough equals 18, because it's pronounced **t**u**f**. **R**ou**gh** is 48, whereas **D**ough is 1, because it's pronounced **d**oe.

- Learn this system. It will change your life.

194

Phonetic Alphabet

Warmup Round

(Match word with its corresponding number)

TABLE	148
DESK	27
OMAHA	58
TROPHY	2972
NAPKIN	027
POTATO	195
SING	071
I LOVE YOU	55
BASEBALL	911
SKATE	9095
ALBUQUERQUE, NEW MEXICO	107
DANCE	120
TENNIS	852
INK	045
CEREAL	5974723707
PAPER	120
VIOLIN	994
LILY	3

100 Anchors

1 – hooD	26 - NaCHo	51 - waLLeT	76 - CouCH
2 – hoNey	27 - NeCK	52 - LioN	77 - CaKe
3 - haM	28 - kNiFe	53 - LiMe	78 - CoFFee
4 - haiR	29 - kNoB	54 - LawyeR	79 - CaPe
5 - wheeL	30 - MouSe	55 - LiLy	80 - VaSe
6 - SHoe	31 - MuD	56 - LeaSH	81 - FeeT
7 - Key	32 - MoNey	57 - LoG	82 - PHoNe
8 - iVy	33 - MuMMy	58 - LaVa	83 - FoaM
9 - hooP	34 - haMMeR	59 - LiP	84 - FiRe
10 - ToSS	35 - MaiL	60 - CHeeSe	85 - FiLe
11 - ToaD	36 - MatCH	61 - JeT	86 - FiSH
12 - TuNa	37 - haMMoCK	62 - CHaiN	87 - FiG
13 - DiMe	38 - MoVie	63 - ChiMe	88 - FiFe
14 - DooR	39 - MaP	64 - CHaiR	89 - FBI
15 - DoLL	40 - hoRSe	65 - JaiL	90 - BuS
16 - DiSH	41 - RoD	66 - JuDGe	91 - BaT
17 - DuCK	42 - RaiN	67 - ShaKe	92 - PiaNo
18 - TV	43 - RaM	68 - CheF	93 - BoMb
19 - TuB	44 - ReaR	69 - ShiP	94 - BeaR
20 - NoSe	45 - RaiL	70 - CaSe	95 - PaiL
21 - wiNDow	46 - RoaCH	71 - CaT	96 - BuSH
22 - oNioN	47 - RoCK	72 - waGoN	97 - BiKe
23 - gNoMe	48 - RooF	73 - GuM	98 - BeehiVe
24 - wieNeR	49 - RoBe	74 - CaR	99 - PiPe
25 - NaiL	50 - LaSSo	75 - eaGLe	100 - DaiSieS

Phonetic Alphabet

Learn these anchors. Practice by reviewing them in tens. Note the words from numbers 10-19 have a beginning consonant letter *t* or *d*; words from 20-29 have a beginning consonant *n*; and words from 30-39 all have the *m* sound.

Pay attention to the capitalized letter in **bold**. These are the letters that code to a number and note that some of these words begin with a vowel which have no value.

For each number, visualize where you've seen this object. Make that object your anchor. For instance, for 92, imagine a particular piano you have seen. Do this with each number.

For number 10, visualize tossing a particular ball; for number 5, imagine a specific wheel, whether it's the wheel from television's Wheel of Fortune or a bicycle wheel. If it's the latter, don't confuse this with the bike for number 97.

Personalize these objects. Find the best word that works for you. These are your anchors. For instance, here are examples from numbers 70-79.

70 - **gas**, **keys**, **kiss**
71 - **cat**, **coat**, **kite**
72 - wa**gon**, gu**n**, **can**
73 - **comb** (*b* is silent), **gum**, **Guam**
74 - **car**, **core**, **choir** (pronounced *kwire*)
75 - **gal**, ea**gle**, **coil**
76 - **cash**, **couch**, **quiche**
77 - **cake**, **kick**, **quake**
78 - **coffee**, **cough**, **cave**
79 - **cape**, **cup**, **cube**

It may seem like a daunting task to memorize 100 objects for 100 numbers, but you'll be able to accomplish this easily. There are plenty of moments to practice. When you're on the highway, glance at license plate numbers and convert numbers to your anchor word.

197

Phonetic Alphabet

Look at your digital clock and code the last two numbers to an object. For numbers 00-09, you'll be able to mentally see a *seesaw*, *seed*, *sun*, *swim*, *soar*, *sail*, *switch*, *sock*, *safe*, and *soap*.

Anytime you need to recall a list of items, or recall a number from 1-100, associate that object to what you want remembered.

Here are some examples ...

You want to remember your car gets *37* mpg. Visualize your car swinging on a *hammock*.

You want to remember the Disney Channel is on channel *48*. Imagine Disney characters dancing atop your *roof*.

You want to remember Joe DiMaggio's *56*-game hitting streak. Imagine the Yankee Clipper hitting the ball with a *leash*.

Image Chris Evert playing Martina Navratilova with a *vase* and you'll know they competed against each other *80* times.

Can't recall where to set the thermostat? You will when you associate it with a *chef*'s hat (68).

When you learn the phonetic alphabet like the 'back of your hand', your memory will vastly improve.

Phonetic Alphabet

ANSWERS (from page 201)

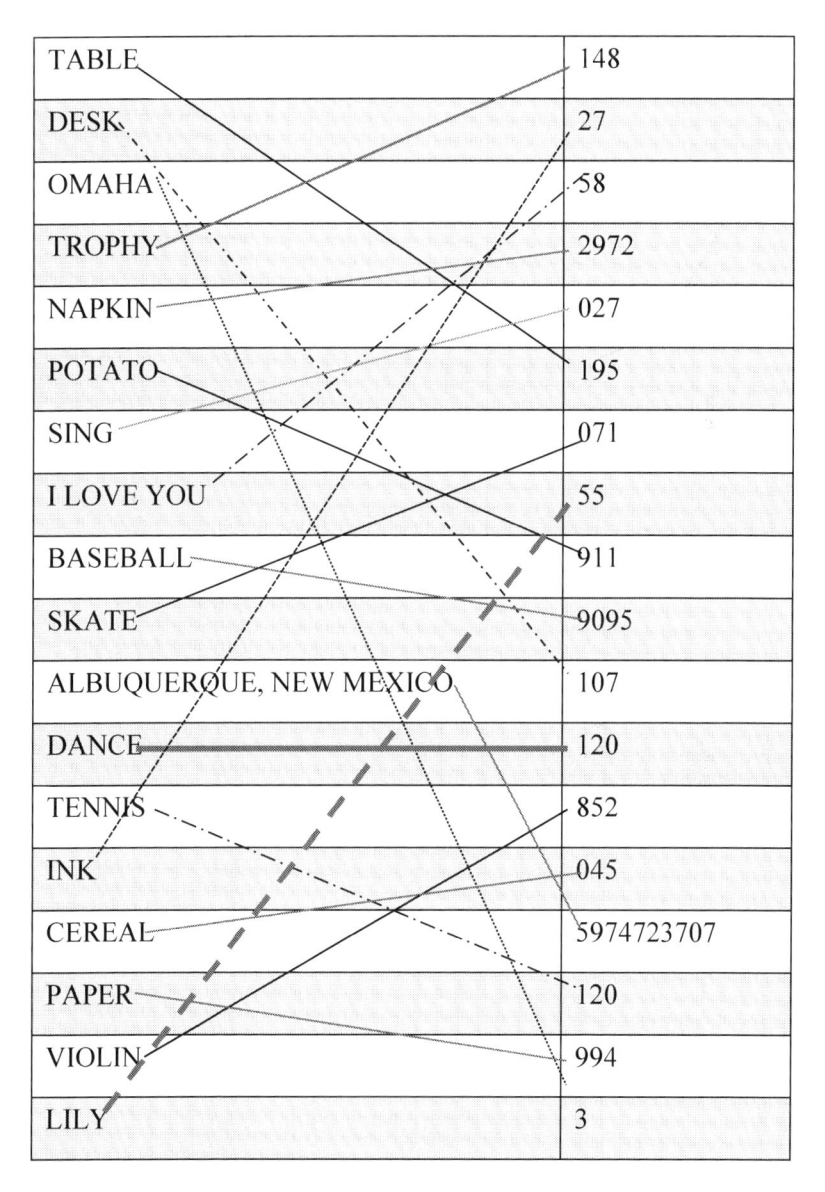

TABLE	148
DESK	27
OMAHA	58
TROPHY	2972
NAPKIN	027
POTATO	195
SING	071
I LOVE YOU	55
BASEBALL	911
SKATE	9095
ALBUQUERQUE, NEW MEXICO	107
DANCE	120
TENNIS	852
INK	045
CEREAL	5974723707
PAPER	120
VIOLIN	994
LILY	3

199

CHAPTER 7

How to
Remember Numbers

How to Remember Numbers

The process begins in the beginning. Shortly after our parents name us, we're numbered. Through the years, we sort through all sorts of numbers.

We carry a social security number, a locker number, a grade point average number, a uniform number, a telephone number, a credit card number, a house number, a license number, and an IQ number, which would be very low if we had to remember all these numbers.

Everywhere we turn numbers are numbing us. Until now...

Numbers come at us from different directions. However, when you analyze them, you realize there are only ten of them.

0 1 2 3 4 5 6 7 8 9

Ten digits. That's it! By themselves they're not so hard to remember. However, when they're strung together and rearranged, numbers are downright difficult to deal with.

Numbers clog our mind because they create no memorable picture. All they do is get in our way causing us to forget.

Utilizing the Phonetic Alphabet (see page 196) changes any boring, humdrum number into a colorful, electrifying object or phrase. It has no boundaries. Your memory power will soar once you learn this approach. In fact, after I mastered this system, I chose to speak on *Memory Skills* full time.

Learning this method takes effort but achieving anything of importance takes time. Becoming skilled at the phonetic alphabet is similar to learning a foreign language, but easier. With a foreign language, there are multiple words, phrases, and accents you need to master. With the phonetic alphabet, you have to know only the letter codes for each of the ten individual numbers.

Here's a review.

0 = s, z, soft c
1 = t/d
2 = n
3 = m
4 = r
5 = L
6 = ch, sh, j, soft g
7 = k, q, hard c/g
8 = f/v
9 = p/b

Examples

The number 12 is coded to *t/d* for the 1; and *n* for the 2. By placing vowels around these two consonant letters, the following words are created: t**u**n**a**, t**u**n**e**, t**ee**n, t**a**n, t**o**n, t**o**n**e**, t**i**n, **d**e**n**, **d**i**n**e, **d**o**n**e, **t**wi**n**e, **t**wi**n**, and **t**i**n**y.

Some of these words produce more visuals and movement than others. For instance, a *tuna* can swim, it can be caught in a fishing line, and it can produce a scent. Open a can of tuna and your cat will be at your feet in seconds.

To remember the Dallas Cowboys won Super Bowl XII, we can imagine a cowboy *tuna* throwing a football.

Visualize a *tuna* in a voting booth and you're reminded that the 12th Amendment is about the process for electing the President and Vice President.

Imagine a *tuna*, dressed in long *tails*, delivering the State of the Union Address, and you'll always be reminded that Zachary *Tailor* was the 12th President.

How to Remember Numbers

Mentally see a *tuna* hitchhiking because it has *no car*, and you'll know *No*rth *Car*olina was the 12th state to join the union.

Oh, what joy it would be to see a *tuna* drumming under the Christmas tree. It would also stick in your mind what your true love gave you on the 12th day of Christmas.

Imagine a *tuna* drinking wine and you're reminded that Highway 12 cuts through wine country in Northern California.

I have nothing against the number 12. It's never caused me any harm, but I would rather do away with it. A tuna is more fun to be around than plain old 12. I've fished for tuna, I've eaten tuna, and I've seen tuna on the National Geographic channel. I can remember *tuna* a lot easier than the number 12, only because there's life in it.

The phonetic alphabet can add life to any number. Here's another example using the number 21. With 2 coding to *n*, and 1 coding to either *t/d*, we get the following words: **n**e**t**, k**n**ea**d**, **n**ee**d**, **n**o**d**, **n**ea**t**, **n**u**d**e, wi**nd**ow, we**nt**, wa**nt**, and k**n**o**t**.

*Wi**nd**ow* is a good choice because it produces action as it's being opened or closed.

Visualize former astronaut John Glenn using a *window* to put out candles on his birthday cake. That bizarre image also tells us he was born in 19**21**. Taking it a step farther, we can "see" him dumping we**t p**ai**nt** on the cake. We**t p**ai**nt** translates to 1921.

The birthday cake is the anchor reminding us that it's his birthday we want remembered.

Imagine an *artist* painting all the *windows* in the White House, and you'll remember that Chester A. *Arthur* was the 21st President.

Imagine a *window* that's *ill*, and you'll be reminded that *Illinois* is the 21st state.

How to Remember Numbers

To remember that the cholesterol count of a slice of cheese pizza is 12mg, imagine throwing the slice through the *wi**nd**ow*.

To remember that an egg has about 212mg of cholesterol, visualize a spinning giant *egg* wearing a *collar* (a word similar to *cholesterol*) attached to an a***nt**e**nn**a* (212).

Note the ingredients in that picture. Visualization: egg, collar, and antenna. Action: spinning. Exaggeration and Association: collar around egg connected to an antenna.

Antenna isn't the only option for 212. The word *I**nd**ia**n*** can also be used, as well as the words ***n**ot **n**ow*, wa***nt*** ho***n**ey*, and *u**nd**o**n**e*.

When I moved to Richmond, Virginia, I opened a checking account at *Crestar Bank*. While others were struggling to remember their PIN number, I simply looked at the big, red sign in front, reading *Crestar*. My PIN number was 7401, the first four consonant sounds in ***Cr**e**st**a**r***. (Don't bother, the bank is no longer around).

We live in a world of letters and numbers, yet we've been schooled in reading letters, not numbers. A quick glance at the following letters ... C A R D I N A L S ... and you have them memorized. You didn't remember the *C* and then memorize the *A*, and then tried to remember the *R*. Instead, you were able to take all those letters and remember them because you read them as one.

You can do the same with numbers. With a little practice, you'll be able see the numbers ... 7 4 1 2 5 0 ... as easily and quickly as you read C A R D I N A L S.

Anytime you need to remember a number, change it into a word and link it to what you want remembered. The phonetic alphabet will help with remembering historical dates, measurements, codes, and more.

Visualize sitting in the ***b**a**ck*** ***s**ea**t*** of a plane flying over Mount *McKinley*, and you'll know that William *McKinley* served as President from 18***97***-19***01*** (***b**a**ck*** ***s**ea**t***).

How to Remember Numbers

Imagine Neil Armstrong pulling *wa**gons*** on the *****ch**opp**y*** moon, and you'll know that the first moon landing was *7-20-69*.

Visualize placing a phone call to a Vegas casino, and you'll know the area code to Sin City is *702* (*****c**a**s**i**n**o***).

Mentally see slices of *****b**ac**o**n*** passing through airport security, and you always remember 1*972* was the first year it became mandatory to screen passengers and luggage at U.S. airports.

Imagine a double-decker bus in the *ou**tf**ie**l**d*, and you'll know that the two-story bus was invented in *1851*.

When you imagine a huge *****d**og b**o**n**e*** wedged at the door of the New York Stock Exchange, you'll know that it was *1792* when the trading first began.

Visualize taking a *****ch**i**s**el*** to Seattle's Space Needle, and you'll be reminded that the structure's height is 605 feet.

Imagine a *****r**oa**ch*** crawling down the nose of the Statue of Liberty, and you'll remember that the length of Lady Liberty's nose is **4 feet, 6 inches**.

Imagine Charles Lindbergh *****L**a**ND**i**NG*** in Paris, and you'll know that the date he touched down from his trans-Atlantic flight was *5-21-27*. Plus, the first three consonant sounds in *****L**i**nd***burgh are 5-21.

CHAPTER 8

How to Remember Appointments

How to Remember Appointments

Time is money. Not remembering a dental appointment, business meeting, or luncheon can cost us. If we had only remembered to write it on the calendar or put the information into our phones, everything would had been right. Unfortunately, we forgot. The upside is we still have our brains. The brain will bail us out.

The key is to bring the day, the time, and the event into one visual. This is how it's accomplished using anchors of the phonetic alphabet (see page 196).

Each day of the week will be coded to a number, beginning with Monday.

Monday = 1 (t/d)
Tuesday = 2 (n)
Wednesday = 3 (m)
Thursday = 4 (r)
Friday = 5 (L)
Saturday = 6 (sh/ch,j, soft g)
Sunday = 7 (k/q, hard c/g)

You want to remember a dental appointment for Thursday at 3 pm. Those are three things you need to remember.

What Day?	Thursday
What Time?	3:00 pm
What's It For?	Dental

Thursday is the 4th day of the week. Four = r. The appointment is for 3 pm. Three = m. The anchor for a combined 4 and 3 is *ram*.

The first consonant sound is the day of the week; the second sound is the time. Therefore, *ram* can only be Thursday at 3. Now, let's bring the day, time, and appointment into one ridiculous picture.

How to Remember Appointments

Imagine a *ram* working on your teeth. It's a talented animal, so don't worry. However, it is unusual.

As you mentally review your anchors for each day, you'll be reminded of the 3:00 dental appointment when you get to *ram*.

Match the visual with the day and time of the week.

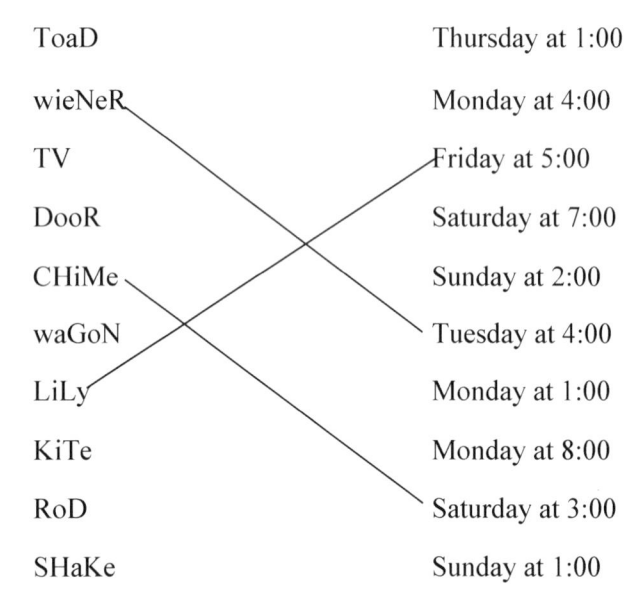

ToaD	Thursday at 1:00
wieNeR	Monday at 4:00
TV	Friday at 5:00
DooR	Saturday at 7:00
CHiMe	Sunday at 2:00
waGoN	Tuesday at 4:00
LiLy	Monday at 1:00
KiTe	Monday at 8:00
RoD	Saturday at 3:00
SHaKe	Sunday at 1:00

For 10:00, since it's the only time with a 0 present, we can drop the 1. For example, Thursday at 10 is *rose*; Tuesday at 10 is *nose*; and Saturday at 10 is *cheese*.

What day is …

keys? _____   **l**asso? _____   **m**ouse? _____   **d**aisy? _____

A) Wednesday at 10:00   C) Sunday at 10:00

B) Friday at 10:00   D) Monday at 10:00

How to Remember Appointments

For 11:00, Monday is *dotted*; Tuesday is *knotted*; Wednesday is *matted*; Thursday is *rotted*; Friday is *loaded*; Saturday is *cheated*; and Sunday is *cadet*.

For 12:00, Monday is *Titan*; Tuesday is *antenna*; Wednesday is *mitten*; Thursday is *red wine*; Friday is *Aladdin*; Saturday is *showtune*; and Sunday is *kitten*.

Think of quarters for quarter after the hour; a grapefruit half for half past the hour; and an old, vinyl 45 rpm record or a Colt 45 pistol for 45 minutes past the hour.

For specific times, consult the number directory beginning on page 236.

There should be no confusion with morning or evening times. You'll know not to show up at the dentist on Monday at 8:00 *pm* when you visualize a TV. You'll also know the soccer banquet on Friday doesn't begin at 7:00 *am* when you visualize kicking a log.

Before bed, quickly go over the next day's anchors in your mind. When one of your objects is doing something, you'll be reminded of the appointment. With passing days, there's no confusion that the dance recital is at 4:00 on Friday, when last week it was 1:00 on Tuesday. Incorporating association and exaggeration overrides previous image.

ANSWERS from previous page.

Toad	Monday at 1:00	Wagon	Sunday at 2:00
Wiener	Tuesday at 4:00	Lily	Friday at 5:00
TV	Monday at 8:00	Kite	Sunday at 1:00
Door	Monday at 4:00	Rod	Thursday at 1:00
Chime	Saturday at 3:00	Shake	Saturday at 7:00

Keys (C)   Lasso (B)   Mouse (A)   Daisy (D)

CHAPTER 9

How to Remember Important Dates

How to Remember Important Dates

Every day someone is celebrating a birthday. Today could be that special day for a friend, a relative, or co-worker. If it were, would you know?

Birthdays and anniversaries come and go. The problem is, trying to remember them is difficult, because our memory comes and goes, too. September 9th, August 9th, or was it March 29th? Who remembers? Months and days run together, making it difficult to tell them apart.

This section makes each one of your schoolmates', co-workers', cousins', kids', and anyone else's special day, memorable.

Each day of the year will have a unique meaning for you. But first, you must familiarize yourself with the phonetic alphabet.

<u>Recap of The Phonetic Alphabet</u>
(from pages 197-199)

0 = s/z, soft c
1 = t/d
2 = n
3 = m
4 = r
5 = L
6 = ch/sh/j, soft g
7 = k/q, hard c/g
8 = f/v
9 = p/b

How to Remember Important Dates

January is the 1ˢᵗ month, therefore every visual for January will begin with the consonant sound *t/d*. The second consonant sound represents the day of that month. For instance, the word ***denim*** can only mean January 23 (*d* codes to *1*; *n* codes to *2*; *m* codes to *3*).

February is the 2ⁿᵈ month; therefore, each visual for that month begins with the consonant sound *n*. The next sound will be the day of that month. The word ***onion*** translates to February 2.

When someone tells you their birthday, visual that person cutting into a birthday cake, and imagine the object coming out. Visualizing a ***monkey*** can only mean the birthday is March 27. The first sound is the month. The second sound is the day.

If it's a wedding anniversary you want to remember, visualize the couple getting married. However, instead of exchanging rings, they exchange a ***piano*** (September, 2); an ***old shoe*** (May, 16); or a ***fish*** (August, 6).

NOTE: October is the 10ᵗʰ month, but each object in that month begins with a *z/s* or *soft c*, instead of a *t/d*. It's the only month with a 0 present, and therefore we don't have to recall up to four digits. For instance, October 18 translates to 018 (***stove***), instead of 1018.

The days in January will not be confused with those in November. For instance, January 14 transposes to 114, while November 4 transposes to 1104. Single digits for the 11ᵗʰ month include a 0.

Each date represents a visual or phrase which makes it memorable. Associate the image to the person who is celebrating the special day and you'll hold that connection.

How to Remember Important Dates

Do you know...

The day in 1706 Benjamin Franklin was born? If you connect *hotdog* to him, you'll know it was January 17th.

The day in 1932 actress Elizabeth Taylor was born? Think of her *yawning*, and you'll know it was February 27th.

The day in 1877 Alexander Bell uttered "Mr. Watson. Come here."? If you *fiddle* with your phone, you'll know it was August 15th.

The day in 1953 John F. Kennedy married Jacqueline Bouvier? If you imagine the couple exchanging a *button*, you'll know it was September 12th.

The day in 1973 Secretariat won the Triple Crown? If you imagine the racehorse on a *ship*, you'll know it was June 9th.

After centuries of lying dormant, the calendar has now come alive. Each day is a living, breathing organism waiting to attach itself to the event you want remembered. Get to know it and put it to work today.

How to Remember Important Dates

JANUARY (t/d)	FEBRUARY (n)	MARCH (m)
1 toad	1 net	1 maid
2 tuna	2 Nun	2 money
3 tomb	3 gnome	3 mummy
4 tire	4 wiener	4 hammer
5 doll	5 nail	5 mail
6 dish	6 nacho	6 match
7 dog	7 neck	7 hammock
8 TV	8 knife	8 movie
9 tub	9 knob	9 map
10 dates	10 windows	10 mitts
11 dated	11 knotted	11 matted
12 Titan	12 antenna	12 mitten
13 tea time	13 anatomy	13 medium
14 detour	14 winter	14 motor
15 title	15 needle	15 medal
16 hot dish	16 untouch	16 muddy shoe
17 hotdog	17 antique	17 medic
18 white dove	18 nod off	18 midwife
19 hot tub	19 no tip	19 made up
20 twins	20 onions	20 moons
21 tent	21 unwind	21 mint
22 white onion	22 no, no, no	22 mean hen
23 denim	23 no name	23 my name
24 diner	24 no winner	24 minor
25 toenail	25 new nail	25 manly
26 teenage	26 an inch	26 munch
27 tongue	27 yawning	27 monkey
28 wet knife	28 new knife	28 mean wave
29 tune-up	29 onion pie	29 mean boy
30 dimes		30 Moms
31 timid		31 mimed

How to Remember Important Dates

APRIL (r)	MAY (L)	JUNE (sh, ch, j, soft g)
1 road	1 wallet	1 shed
2 rain	2 lion	2 chain
3 ram	3 lime	3 jam
4 rail	4 lawyer	4 cherry
5 rail	5 lily	5 jail
6 roach	6 leash	6 judge
7 rock	7 lock	7 shake
8 roof	8 leaf	8 chef
9 robe	9 lip	9 ship
10 radios	10 lettuce	10 jets
11 rotted	11 low tide	11 cheated
12 red wine	12 Aladdin	12 showtune
13 redeem	13 yell time	13 huge dome
14 radar	14 ladder	14 chowder
15 rattle	15 ladle	15 shuttle
16 radish	16 old shoe	16 huge dish
17 red wig	17 old wig	17 huge dog
18 write off	18 lead off	18 shut off
19 read up	19 laid up	19 chewed up
20 rinse	20 lines	20 jeans
21 rent	21 walnut	21 giant
22 reunion	22 linen	22 John Wayne
23 rename	23 yell enemy	23 shiny ham
24 runner	24 liner	24 shiner
25 renewal	25 lonely	25 channel
26 wrench	26 lunch	26 change
27 ring	27 lingo	27 junk
28 runoff	28 lean off	28 huge Navy
29 rainbow	29 line-up	29 chin up
30 rooms	30 limbs	30 chimes
	31 helmet	

How to Remember Important Dates

JULY (hard c/g, q, k)	AUGUST (f/v, ph)	SEPTEMBER (p/ b)
1 coyote	1 photo	1 bat
2 wagon	2 phone	2 piano
3 gum	3 foam	3 bomb
4 car	4 fire	4 bear
5 eagle	5 file	5 pillow
6 couch	6 fish	6 peach
7 cake	7 fog	7 bike
8 coffee	8 fife	8 beehive
9 cape	9 FBI	9 pipe
10 goats	10 fits	10 beets
11 cadet	11 faded	11 potato
12 kitten	12 futon	12 button
13 academy	13 feed me	13 bottom
14 guitar	14 fighter	14 butter
15 cattle	15 fiddle	15 paddle
16 cottage	16 fetish	16 paid wage
17 aquatic	17 fatigue	17 boutique
18 get off	18 vote off	18 bit off
19 giddy up	19 fed up	19 paid up
20 canes	20 vans	20 bones
21 candy	21 faint	21 paint
22 cannon	22 funny one	22 banana
23 can ham	23 phone home	23 Panama
24 canary	24 funnier	24 pioneer
25 canal	25 vinyl	25 panel
26 gun show	26 finish	26 bench
27 king	27 funky	27 bank
28 go Navy	28 funny wife	28 pen wife
29 canopy	29 heavy nap	29 pin-up
30 combs	30 fumes	30 poems
31 comedy	31 vomit	

How to Remember Important Dates

OCTOBER (s, z)	NOVEMBER (t/d)	DECEMBER (t/d, n)
1 sod	1 hot toast	1 twin city
2 sun	2 too, too soon	2 tiny son
3 zoom	3 dates him	3 tiny sum
4 soar	4 dates her	4 dinosaur
5 seal	5 wet tassel	5 tonsil
6 switch	6 Dad's shoe	6 tan switch
7 sock	7 today is okay	7 tiny sock
8 sofa	8 date is off	8 twin sofa
9 soap	9 heated soup	9 tones up
10 seeds	10 eat toads	10 doughnuts
11 seated	11 toot, toot	11 height and weight
12 stone	12 hit Titan	12 downtown
13 sodium	13 dotted ham	13 Tiny Tim
14 star	14 dated her	14 twin tower
15 steel	15 do detail	15 tiny hotel
16 stash	16 heated dish	16 tiny dish
17 stick	17 heated deck	17 tan dog
18 stove	18 dead dove	18 tune TV
19 step	19 dotted pie	19 don't buy
20 swans	20 Titans	20 eat onions
21 sand	21 dead end	21 tenant
22 icy onion	22 heated onion	22 tiny onion
23 sunny home	23 titanium	23 tiny gnome
24 sonar	24 eat dinner	24 tiny honor
25 snail	25 hit toenail	25 down the Nile
26 snowshoe	26 heated nacho	26 twin nacho
27 sink	27 Titanic	27 tanning
28 sniff	28 diet on/off	28 tan knife
29 snap	29 heated knob	29 tiny knob
30 swims	30 dead mouse	30 tan moose
31 summit		31 dynamite

Remembering Birthdays of the Rich and Famous

Elvis Presley	See Elvis on **TV**	Jan 8
Kate Middleton	Kate in the **TuB**	Jan 9
Justin Timberlake	Timberlake is **TiMiD**	Jan 31
Jane Seymour	See Jane carrying big **NeeDLe**	Feb 15
Charles Barkley	Sir Charles dribbling o**NioNS**	Feb 20
Patricia Heaton	Ms. Heaton swings ha**MMeR**	Mar 4
Eva Mendes	In the eve, Eva will **MaiL** letter	Mar 5
Mariah Carey	Mariah singing with **MoNKey**	Mar 27
Claire Danes	Actress drinking **ReD** wi**Ne**	Apr 12
Mark Zuckerberg	Facebook CEO climbs **LaDDeR**	May 14
Brooke Shields	Shields her head with he**LMeT**	May 31
Prince William	William turns into Gia**NT**	Jun 21
Will Ferrell	Comedian in **CoTTaGe**	Jul 16
Tom Brady	Brady throws **FoaM** football	Aug 3
Meghan Markle	The Duchess on **FiRe**	Aug 4
Raquel Welch	**PiLL**ow talk with Raquel	Sep 5
Serena Williams	Tennis star sits on **BeNCH**	Sep 6
Katy Perry	**SNaiL** crawling on Ms. Perry	Oct 25
Bruce Lee	Bruce Lee kicks **TiTaNiC**	Nov 27
Jay-Z	Jay-Z climbs onto **DiNoSauR**	Dec 04
Taylor Swift	**TiNy TiM** attends Taylor's party	Dec 13

How to Remember Important Dates

Match the Birthdate with the Person

She's on FIRE (8/4)   Raquel Welch

Dribbling ONIONS (2/20)   Bruce Lee

Sitting on the BENCH (9/26)   Will Farrell

PILLOW talk (9/5)   Meghan Markle

Carrying a big NEEDLE (2/15)   Claire Danes

He's in the COTTAGE (7/16)   Charles Barkley

Kicks in TITANIC (Nov 27)   Serena Williams

Drinking RED WINE (4/12)   Jane Seymour

Climbs the LADDER (5/14)   Jay-Z

Head shielded by HELMET (5/31)   Mark Zuckerberg

On top of DINOSAUR (12/04)   Tom Brady

TINY TIM attends her party (12/13)   Brooke Shields

Off to MAIL a letter (3/5)   Taylor Swift

He's a GIANT (6/21)   Mariah Carey

Sings with a MONKEY (3/27)   Prince William

FOAM football thrower (8/3)   Eva Mendes

CHAPTER 10

How to Remember Playing Cards

How to Remember Playing Cards

*G*o Fish isn't just a popular card game; it's what we ask our brains to do when we try to remember information. Often it pulls up the line with nothing on the hook. Let's face it, we just plain forget.

The same is true when playing cards. Cards flash by us and we can't remember if the 3 of Clubs or the 5 of Spades was played. They all look the same. Think of the advantage you'd have if you could remember.

No matter what game you're playing, a powerful memory gives you an advantage and a leg up on the competition. Even if you're not holding all the cards, your mind will be.

If you're not a card player, you'll be an instant hit at parties by demonstrating your incredible memory card trick. All it takes is learning a few simple rules, a creative imagination, and a deck of cards.

What are you waiting for? It's your move.

Linking Pictures to Pictures

So many cards, so many numbers and shapes. How can we remember them? We remember them by making each one of the 52 cards memorable, by creating one vivid image that separates it from the next.

Numbers are boring. They're just a collection of some vertical lines, horizontal lines, and some loops. Since numbers are not lifelike, we'll make them so by utilizing a variation of the phonetic alphabet (see page 197).

Phonetic Alphabet for Playing Cards

0 = s   Reminder ... send help... SOS

2 = n   Reminder ... n stands on 2 legs

3 = m   Reminder ... m stands on 3 legs

4 = r   Reminder ... four ends with r

5 = L   Reminder ... Roman Numeral 50 is L

6 = ch   Reminder ... ahCHoo, I'm 6 (sick)

7 = c   Reminder ... sail the 7 c's

8 = v   Reminder ... V8 Juice

9 = b   Reminder ... upside b resembles 9

How to Remember Important Dates

By using the phonetic alphabet, numbers are turned into words. The letters, *w, h, a, e, i, o, u,* and *y* do not transpose to any number. They are used to set up words.

For example, the *4 of Spades* does not make for a memorable image, therefore, we need to create one.

The number *4* equals an *R* sound. Spades begin with the letter *S*. The word **R**o**S**e is the *4* of Spades. The *R* and *S* sounds are heard.

**The first sound is the number,
the second sound is the suit.**

The *4 of Spades* has become memorable because it can be visualized. It's a **R**o**S**e. You can plant it, smell it, or give it to someone you like. When you want to recall the *4 of Spades* visualize a *ROSE*. That's memorable!

Forgetful   Memorable

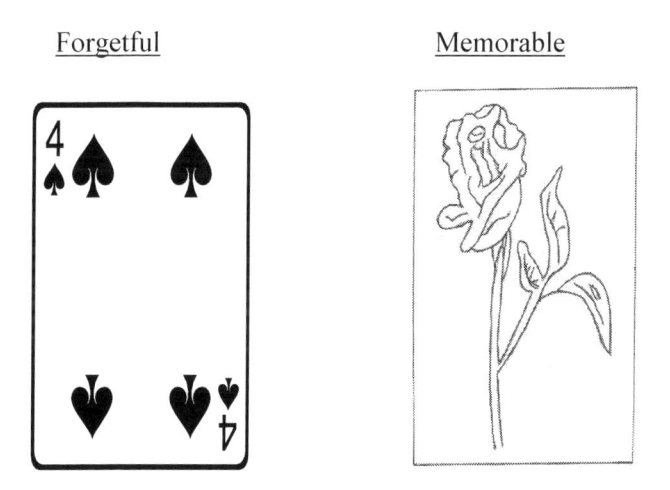

223

How to Remember Important Dates

Diamonds	**Hearts**	**Clubs**	**Spades**
AD / Diamond	AH / Heart	AC / Club	AS / Shovel
2D / Noodle	2H / Neigh	2C / Knocker	2S / Nose
3D / Mud	3H / Mouth	3C / Microphone	3S / Mouse
4D / Rod	4H / Reach	4C / Rock	4S / Rose
5D / Lid	5H / Leash	5C / Lock	5S / Lasso
6D / Chowder	6H / Shiloh	6C / Chick	6S / Cheese
7D / Cud (cow)	7H / Cough	7C / Cone	7S / Case
8D / Video	8H / Van Gogh	8C / Vacuum	8S / Vase
9D / Bed	9H / Bath	9C / Bike	9S / Bus
10D / Sod	10H / Sleigh	10C / Sock	10S / Seesaw
JD / Jackpot	JH / Jackhammer	JC / J. Nicholas	JS / Jacks
QD / Quads	QH / Q. Elizabeth	QC / Quack	QS / 'Q' Stick
KD / Kid	KH / Khakis	KC / Kick	KS / Keys

The cards have now taken on a new life. Study the pictures, then close your eyes and visualize each card. For instance, the 3 of Diamonds translates to MuD (first sound is number; second sound is suit). See in your "mind's eye" jumping into a mud puddle. The mud puddle will always represent the 3 of Diamonds.

The pictures are memorable because they are action-oriented. The duck quacks, the dog bites, the vacuum runs, and the bike rolls. They're more memorable than the cards they replace.

For the 2C, visualize a door knocker. For the JC, visualize Jack Nicklaus swinging a golf club or simply, imagine a golf club. For the AC, imagine a caveman's club. For the QC, imagine a duck quacking, or mentally see a duck. For KC, visualize kicking a football, or just imagine a football.

For the 2N, imagine a horse. For the 4H, imagine reaching for something, such as an apple. For the 6H, imagine a rifle or cannon at the Battle of Shiloh. For the 8H, imagine the artist Van Gogh, or simply think of a van. Make certain you have one standard visual for each card. Since the visual for 3H and 7H are similar, imagine a tissue for the latter.

How to Remember Important Dates

For the 4D, imagine a fishing rod. For the QD, visualize working your quads at the gym, or just picture any piece of workout equipment.

Why do all the 10's begin with an S? It's the only card with a zero. Therefore, *Sod*, *Sock*, *Seesaw*, and *Sleigh* can mean only the 10 of Diamonds, Clubs, Spades, and Hearts, respectively.

To help you associate each visual, get a deck of playing cards and write the object onto the card it represents. Therefore, when you're looking at the card, you're also looking at the object. Spend an evening studying each suit. Before the week is out, you'll automatically "see" a slice of cheese pizza when you're looking at the 6 of Spades, a jackhammer when you see a Jack of Hearts, and an ice cream cone will be dripping off the 7 of Clubs.

WHAT'S THE PURPOSE OF THIS AGAIN?
We've taken 52 ordinary cards and associated each one with a visual. We remember in pictures. Pictures leave an impression. It's easier to imagine a horse sitting atop a bicycle than it is to picture the 2 of Hearts, followed by the 9 of Clubs.

I NOTICED A PATTERN WITH THE ACES.
The Aces represent the suit. Nothing complicated there.

HOW CAN I REMEMBER CARDS THAT WERE PLAYED?
You must go on the attack. Use a baseball bat and destroy the image of the card that's been played. For example, see yourself whacking a *Leash* (5H), a *Sleigh* (10H), a *Van* (8H), *Football* (KC), a *Rose* (4S), a *Mouse* (3S), and a fishing *Rod* (4D). When you mentally go through each card, you'll know which cards were played and which cards weren't.

WON'T THIS CONFUSE ME WHEN I PLAY ANOTHER GAME?
It could if you play back to back, so it's best to use another weapon. In the next game, visualize pouring hot coffee on the cards that were played. A hockey stick or grenade would work, too.

How to Remember Important Dates

WHY SO VIOLENT?
You want to win the game, don't you?

WHAT WEAPONS SHOULDN'T I USE?
A club, a fishing rod, and a cue stick, to name a few. All those represent certain cards. You want to use a weapon that won't confuse you with any of the 52 cards.

I REALLY LIKE THE PEOPLE I PLAY BRIDGE WITH, SO IS THERE A NON- VIOLENT METHOD TO REMEMBERING?
Yes. It's called the Link System. It's simple. Mentally place the first card into the environment of the following card and continue the pattern. Here's an example: The cards that were played are the *8 of Hearts, 5 of Clubs, King of Spades, 2 of Diamonds, 4 of Clubs,* and the *10 of Diamonds.*

Visualize a *Van* full of thousands of *Locks*. Now, imagine a giant lock and you're using it to lock up a huge *Key*. Imagine putting hundreds of keys into a plate full of *Noodles*. Now, visualize a pile of noodles, instead of *Rocks*, in your yard. Finally, imagine mowing your *Sod* with a giant rock or mowing thousands of rocks. Exaggerate the image. Make the mental images bizarre and ridiculous and you'll remember.

ISN'T THAT A LOT TO REMEMBER?
No, because we are remembering only two objects at a time. Once we get to *Rock* we are no longer thinking of *Van* or *Lock* or *Key*. One image automatically brought us to the next. As soon as a card is played, change it to a visual image and wait until the next card is put down to see the environment it's going to enter.

IT'S GOING TO TAKE SOME PRACTICE, ISN'T IT?
Yes, but here's the good part: There are only 52 cards. Devote a week to one suit. Learn the 13 pictures until you master it. Use the Link System to practice remembering the cards in random order, then move on to the next suit.

How to Remember Important Dates

HOW CAN I AMAZE MY FRIENDS AND MEMORIZE 52 CARDS IN LESS THAN FIVE MINUTES?
Mentally link each one of the 52 cards to each one of your 52 Loci (see page 20).

Here's an example, using ten objects in your home, and ten cards you want to recall in order.

Objects	Cards
Couch	2D / noodles
Television	4D / rod
Ceiling Fan	2S / nose
Lamp	QK / quack
Recliner	2H / neigh
Fireplace	AH / heart
Table	7S / case
Light Switch	9D / bed
Bookshelf	4H / reach
Plant Stand	5S / lasso

How to Remember Important Dates

Associate *Noodles* to *Couch*. Visualize the *Couch* is covered with *Noodles*.

In your "mind's eye" imagine the next object, *Television*. Link it with the next card, 4D. Imagine hooking the *Television* with a *Fishing Rod*. See the rod bend and feel the weight as it's being tested.

Next, visualize your *Ceiling Fan* and associate it with the next card, 2S. Imagine sticking your *Nose* between the blades of the fan. That smarts, but smart you are because you'll recall what the third card is when you go back to your objects.

The next object is *Lamp*. The next card is a *Duck Quacking*. Imagine a *Duck* is sitting atop a lamp, while another duck is trying to turn the lamp on.

Continue associating each object with each playing card. Then, visualize the first place in your home. In this example, it's the couch. When you "see" the couch, you'll automatically see the noodles. Noodles equals the 2 of Diamonds.

Like picking up breadcrumbs, you'll remember each card when you go back and visualize each object of your home.

Spend time drawing up 52 additional objects in another locale. Once the list is complete, visualize each object. This way, once you memorize one deck, you can quickly memorize another, by associating them with these new 52 objects. It eliminates any confusion with cards you previously memorized.

CHAPTER 11

Have some Pi (60 slices)

How to Remember Important Dates

The average person could never memorize over 60 numbers of Pi. You can, but then, you're not average.

3.14159265358979323846264338327950288419716939937510 58209749445923 07...

MY TURTLE plays the PIANO in a CHILLY MALL with a HEAVY PACK and people PAY MONEY. I'M VERY happy!

But, GINGER, my MOM, is FUMING he PLAYS ON, especially with a FEVER.

Get him a TOPCOAT, a CHEAP MAP, and BUY HIM a COLD CELL PHONE so he can leave in a ZIPPY CAR.

Oh BROTHER, HELP. NOW I'M SICK.

The uses of the phonetic alphabet are endless.

CHAPTER 12

Beginning on page 240 is a directory. Each double, triple, and quadruple number is coded into a word or phrase.

When you need to remember ANY number, locate the number in the directory and link it with what you want to remember.

Note that the **BOLD** letter represents the corresponding number.

CAUTION:

Before proceeding ...

Pages 197 - 199 must have been fully understood

Directory

00 seesaw	38 movie	76 coach	014 steer
01 seed	39 map	77 cake	015 steel
02 sun	40 rose	78 coffee	016 stash
03 sum	41 rod	79 cup	017 stick
04 soar	42 rain	80 face	018 stove
05 soil	43 ram	81 feet	019 stop
06 switch	44 rear	82 phone	020 suns
07 sock	45 rail	83 foam	021 sand
08 safe	46 roach	84 fire	022 use a noun
09 soup	47 rug	85 file	023 use a name
10 toss	48 roof	86 fish	024 snare
11 Dad	49 rope	87 fog	025 snail
12 tin	50 lasso	88 fife	026 snatch
13 dime	51 wallet	89 FBI	027 sink
14 door	52 lion	90 bus	028 sniff
15 tail	53 lamb	91 bat	029 snap
16 dish	54 lawyer	92 bone	030 swims
17 dog	55 lily	93 bomb	031 summit
18 TV	56 leash	94 bear	032 summon
19 tub	57 leg	95 ball	033 swim home
20 nose	58 leaf	96 beach	034 smear
21 window	59 elbow	97 bike	035 smile
22 onion	60 cheese	98 puff	036 smooch
23 enemy	61 shed	99 pipe	037 smoke
24 owner	62 chain	000 soy sauce	038 swim off
25 nail	63 gym	001 housesit	039 swamp
26 nacho	64 chair	002 season	040 soars
27 neck	65 jail	003 says me	041 sword
28 knife	66 judge	004 Caesar	042 siren
29 knob	67 shake	005 sizzle	043 swarm
30 mouse	68 chef	006 sausage	044 sore ear
31 mat	69 ship	007 seasick	045 cereal
32 money	70 keys	008 seize half	046 search
33 mummy	71 cat	009 icy soup	047 icy - rocky
34 hammer	72 gun	010 seeds	048 serve
35 mail	73 gum	011 seated	049 syrup
36 match	74 car	012 stone	050 sails
37 hammock	75 eagle	013 sodium	051 sled

Directory

052 saloon	093 so balmy	134 timer	175 tackle
053 slim	094 spur	135 oatmeal	176 dog show
054 slower	095 spill	136 dumb show	177 hot cocoa
055 slowly	096 speech	137 atomic	178 hot coffee
056 slash	097 ice pack	138 time off	179 teacup
057 slug	098 so puffy	139 tempo	180 TV's
058 sleeve	099 see the Pope	140 tires	181 tough hit
059 slip	100 disease	141 tired	182 dive in
060 switches	101 test	142 train	183 white foam
061 switched	102 tow away zone	143 drum	184 diver
062 switch on	103 days home	144 terrier	185 hateful
063 switch them	104 dizzier	145 trail	186 TV show
064 switcher	105 tassel	146 trash	187 tough guy
065 satchel	106 dosage	147 truck	188 TV off
066 switch shoe	107 desk	148 driveway	189 tough boy
067 switch week	108 dizzy wife	149 trap	190 tips
068 switch off	109 day spa	150 dolls	191 top hat
069 switch pie	110 toads	151 toilet	192 white pen
070 socks	111 deadwood	152 ate alone	193 tip him
071 socket	112 hot town	153 tell me	194 diaper
072 skin	113 daytime	154 taller	195 table
073 skim	114 detour	155 tell-all	196 hot beach
074 scar	115 title	156 wet leash	197 tea bag
075 scale	116 hot dish	157 wet log	198 top off
076 sickish	117 hot dog	158 tea leaf	199 wet baby
077 icy Coke	118 white dove	159 tulip	200 noses
078 ice coffee	119 hot tip	160 dishes	201 nest
079 ice cap	120 tennis	161 touched	202 unseen
080 saves	121 tent	162 wet chin	203 enzyme
081 seafood	122 white onion	163 teach me	204 answer
082 use phone	123 denim	164 teacher	205 nozzle
083 save me	124 toner	165 touch wall	206 wins show
084 safer	125 tunnel	166 touch shoe	207 nice guy
085 swivel	126 teenage	167 touch wig	208 unsafe
086 savage	127 tank	168 deja vu	209 nice boy
087 so foggy	128 hide knife	169 touch up	210 nets
088 safe wave	129 tune-up	170 dogs	211 knotted
089 safe hop	130 dimes	171 ticket	212 Indian
090 space	131 tomato	172 token	213 anatomy
091 spit	132 time in	173 Tacoma	214 winter
092 spin	133 time me	174 taker	215 needle

Directory

216 window wash	257 unlucky	298 now behave	339 my map
217 antique	258 only half	299 new baby	340 hammers
218 handoff	259 no help	300 misses	341 mart
219 no tip	260 nachos	301 mist	342 homerun
220 onions	261 inched	302 Amazon	343 my room
221 new window	262 nation	303 museum	344 mirror
222 an onion	263 no shame	304 miser	345 moral
223 no name	264 injury	305 muzzle	346 march
224 no winner	265 angel	306 massage	347 mark
225 ninth hole	266 enjoy the show	307 music	348 I'm rough
226 an inch	267 unshake	308 massive	349 more pie
227 winning	268 inch off	309 mess up	350 malice
228 new knife	269 inch by	310 mitts	351 melt
229 onion pie	270 knocks	311 matted	352 melon
230 names	271 naked	312 mitten	353 I'm lame
231 inmate	272 noggin	313 medium	354 mailer
232 honeymoon	273 honeycomb	314 motor	355 mail all
233 No Mom	274 anchor	315 motel	356 mulch
234 no more	275 nickel	316 my dish	357 milk
235 animal	276 hang wash	317 medic	358 mail off
236 no match	277 young guy	318 motive	359 my lip
237 anemic	278 young wife	319 made-up	360 matches
238 new movie	279 hang up	320 mayonnaise	361 machete
239 new map	280 knives	321 mint	362 machine
240 honors	281 unfit	322 ham, onion	363 my shame
241 honored	282 no phone	323 my name	364 major
242 no rain	283 new fame	324 minor	365 match well
243 no room	284 unfair	325 thumbnail	366 I'm the judge
244 in her hair	285 navel	326 munch	367 magic
245 unreal	286 no fish	327 monkey	368 I'm the chef
246 energy	287 no fog	328 mean wife	369 matchup
247 New York	288 Navy wife	329 mean boy	370 mugs
248 nerve	289 new VP	330 Moms	371 mugged
249 unwrap	290 on the bus	331 homemade	372 mahogany
250 nails	291 unpaid	332 my man	373 home game
251 knelt	292 now open	333 my Mom	374 my car
252 nylon	293 no bomb	334 memory	375 my gal
253 only me	294 neighbor	335 home meal	376 make a wish
254 only her	295 noble	336 my match	377 my cookie
255 Honolulu	296 on the beach	337 mimic	378 make off
256 unleash	297 unpack	338 home movie	379 make-up

Directory

380 movies	421 warrant	462 Russian	503 wholesome
381 moved	422 reunion	463 regime	504 loser
382 muffin	423 uranium	464 richer	505 loosely
383 move him	424 runner	465 hair gel	506 lose watch
384 mover	425 renewal	466 reach show	507 Alaska
385 muffle	426 ranch	467 a rush week	508 illusive
386 move the show	427 ring	468 rush off	509 yells up
387 I'm vague	428 runoff	469 worship	510 lettuce
388 move off	429 rainbow	470 rocks	511 low tide
389 move up	430 rooms	471 rocket	512 Aladdin
390 mops	431 roomed	472 raccoon	513 yell time
391 mopped	432 Roman	473 rock 'em	514 ladder
392 hambone	433 our Mom	474 rocker	515 ladle
393 my poem	434 rumor	475 regal	516 late show
394 hamper	435 airmail	476 ricochet	517 late walk
395 maple	436 rematch	477 your kick	518 loud wife
396 ambush	437 remake	478 rake off	519 let up
397 I'm back	438 war movie	479 your cup	520 lions
398 I'm above you	439 ramp	480 reviews	521 walnut
399 my baby	440 roars	481 horrified	522 linen
400 roses	441 reread	482 raven	523 yell enemy
401 rest	442 rerun	483 our fame	524 liner
402 raisin	443 war room	484 river	525 lonely
403 resume	444 hear the roar	485 raffle	526 lunch
404 razor	445 hear her yell	486 raw fish	527 long
405 wrestle	446 you're rich	487 you're vague	528 yellow knife
406 horseshoe	447 rework	488 rough wave	529 lineup
407 rescue	448 rearview	489 rough up	530 limes
408 receive	449 rare buy	490 ribs	531 helmet
409 recipe	450 rolls	491 robot	532 lemon
410 roads	451 world	492 ribbon	533 hello Mom
411 rooted	452 hairline	493 hear poem	534 yell more
412 red wine	453 realm	494 rubber	535 lame wheel
413 redeem	454 roller	495 ripple	536 I'll match you
414 radar	455 really yell	496 rubbish	537 yellow mug
415 rattle	456 relish	497 air bag	538 I'll move
416 radish	457 relic	498 rip off	539 lamp
417 red wig	458 relief	499 rip up	540 walrus
418 write-off	459 roll up	500 laces	541 Lord
419 wiretap	460 riches	501 lost	542 learn
420 rinse	461 reached	502 loosen	543 alarm

Directory

544 layer hair	585 level	626 change	667 huge check
545 laurel	586 lavish	627 junk	668 huge chef
546 allergy	587 yell fake	628 huge knife	669 huge ship
547 oil rig	588 leave off	629 chin up	670 Jacuzzi
548 lower half	589 leave up	630 jams	671 jacket
549 yellow robe	590 lips	631 chimed	672 chicken
550 yellow wheels	591 leaped	632 chimney	673 chew gum
551 loyalty	592 whale bone	633 show Mom	674 sugar
552 all alone	593 album	634 wash my hair	675 juggle
553 hollow limb	594 helper	635 huge mall	676 huge catch
554 yell lawyer	595 lapel	636 huge match	677 Chicago
555 yell, yell, yell	596 I'll push	637 jam key	678 shake off
556 yellow leash	597 yellow bike	638 show movie	679 checkup
557 lilac	598 I'll pay half	639 shampoo	680 shaves
558 lowlife	599 yellow pipe	640 chairs	681 shoved
559 yell help	600 chases	641 shirt	682 huge van
560 leashes	601 chest	642 journey	683 shave him
561 lash out	602 chosen	643 germ	684 chauffeur
562 lotion	603 chase him	644 huge rear	685 shovel
563 I'll show him	604 chase her	645 cheer - yell	686 huge fish
564 wheelchair	605 chisel	646 church	687 JFK
565 leash law	606 Jazz show	647 shark	688 shove off
566 yellow judge	607 choose a week	648 sheriff	689 show off pie
567 logic	608 chase off	649 cherry pie	690 jobs
568 he'll show off	609 choose up	650 shoelace	691 chipped
569 hollow ship	610 jets	651 child	692 wishbone
570 locks	611 cheated	652 huge lion	693 huge bomb
571 locket	612 showtune	653 huge lime	694 chipper
572 log on	613 showtime	654 jewelry	695 chapel
573 welcome	614 ashtray	655 huge lily	696 huge push
574 locker	615 huge tail	656 geology	697 hatchback
575 legal	616 huge dish	657 chilly week	698 chip off
576 luggage	617 watchdog	658 shelf	699 shape up
577 yellow cake	618 showed off	659 huge lip	700 gases
578 lake view	619 showed up	660 judges	701 guest
579 lockup	620 Chinese	661 judged	702 casino
580 leaves	621 giant	662 huge ocean	703 cosmo
581 loved	622 John Wayne	663 judge him	704 kisser
582 leave on	623 huge name	664 wash ashore	705 castle
583 leave home	624 January	665 huge jail	706 weak switch
584 lover	625 channel	666 show judge	707 kiosk

Directory

708 ex-wife	749 grape	790 cups	831 foamed
709 gazebo	750 calls	791 Cupid	832 famine
710 cats	751 colt	792 cabin	833 I have Mom
711 cadet	752 clown	793 keep them	834 foamier
712 kitten	753 clam	794 copper	835 family
713 academy	754 color	795 cable	836 heavy match
714 guitar	755 ukulele	796 cabbage	837 heavy mug
715 cattle	756 clash	797 go back	838 have my half
716 cottage	757 clock	798 keep off	839 have my pie
717 catwalk	758 glove	799 keep up	840 fires
718 get off	759 clip	800 faces	841 fried
719 get up	760 coaches	801 faucet	842 frown
720 wagons	761 cashed	802 fasten	843 farm
721 Canada	762 cushion	803 face me	844 fire her
722 cannon	763 catch me	804 VCR	845 farewell
723 economy	764 catcher	805 vessel	846 fresh
724 canary	765 catch well	806 heavy switch	847 frog
725 canal	766 catch show	807 physique	848 very heavy
726 gun show	767 hockey check	808 face-off	849 frappe
727 king	768 catch a wave	809 faceup	850 falls
728 weak Navy	769 ketchup	810 fads	851 flat
729 canopy	770 cookies	811 photo ID	852 violin
730 combs	771 kicked	812 half ton	853 flame
731 comet	772 cocoon	813 feed me	854 flower
732 common	773 kick me	814 fatter	855 follow all
733 come home	774 Quaker	815 fiddle	856 village
734 comb hair	775 giggle	816 fetish	857 flag
735 camel	776 quick show	817 vodka	858 fluff
736 game show	777 cakewalk	818 feet off	859 flip
737 comic	778 kickoff	819 fed up	860 fishes
738 game off	779 cake, pie	820 fence	861 fished
739 camp	780 caves	821 faint	862 fashion
740 cars	781 coughed	822 heavy onion	863 fetch him
741 karate	782 coffin	823 venom	864 voyager
742 green	783 give me	824 funny hair	865 facial
743 cream	784 caviar	825 vinyl	866 a heavy judge
744 career	785 gavel	826 finish	867 heavy check
745 grill	786 go fish	827 funky	868 heavy chef
746 crash	787 hockey fake	828 funny wife	869 heavy job
747 crack	788 give off	829 phone booth	870 fakes
748 grave	789 give up	830 famous	871 faked

Directory

872 heavy gun	913 bottom	954 player	995 bubble
873 vacuum	914 butter	955 pool hall	996 baby shoe
874 faker	915 battle	956 blush	997 pay back
875 vehicle	916 paid wage	957 black	998 pop off
876 fake show	917 paddock	958 bluff	999 pop up
877 heavy cake	918 paid off	959 apple pie	0000 sees a seesaw
878 heavy cough	919 bathtub	960 bushes	0001 he says stay
879 have a cup	920 bones	961 pushed	0002 sassy son
880 heavy vase	921 paint	962 passion	0003 house is same
881 heavy food	922 banana	963 push him	0004 seesaw soar
882 have fun	923 Panama	964 pusher	0005 icehouse sale
883 half of me	924 pioneer	965 bushel	0006 seize switch
884 fever	925 pinwheel	966 pay the judge	0007 Swiss sock
885 half full	926 punch	967 paycheck	0008 Swiss sofa
886 heavy fish	927 hopping	968 push off	0009 seize sub
887 heavy fog	928 bowie knife	969 push up	0010 suicides
888 off, off, off	929 pinup	970 pucks	0011 US state
889 half off pie	930 poems	971 bucket	0012 sustain
890 heavy bus	931 bombed	972 bacon	0013 system
891 heavy bat	932 pay money	973 back home	0014 sister
892 heavy piano	933 pay Mom	974 biker	0015 see Seattle
893 heavy bomb	934 balmy weather	975 buckle	0016 sauce dish
894 fiber	935 pay me well	976 package	0017 sassy dog
895 fable	936 pay my wage	977 peacock	0018 Swiss TV
896 off the beach	937 pay my week	978 back off	0019 sized up
897 halfback	938 pay me half	979 back up	0020 seasons
898 off by half	939 pump	980 beehives	0021 icy, sandy
899 heavy baby	940 press	981 buffed	0022 Swiss Nun
900 passes	941 bird	982 buffoon	0023 season ham
901 pest	942 brown	983 above me	0024 see icy Norway
902 poison	943 broom	984 beaver	0025 seasonal
903 opossum	944 barrier	985 buffalo	0026 sauce on watch
904 busier	945 barrel	986 buff shoe	0027 his song
905 puzzle	946 brush	987 pay off week	0028 Swiss knife
906 passage	947 brick	988 pay off half	0029 he's snappy
907 bask	948 proof	989 behave boy	0030 sees a mouse
908 passive	949 bathrobe	990 babies	0031 icy summit
909 pea soup	950 pillows	991 beeped	0032 seize money
910 boathouse	951 plate	992 baboon	0033 says Mom
911 potato	952 plane	993 baby him	0034 hazy summer
912 button	953 bloom	994 paper	0035 he's smelly

Directory

0036 sees my watch	0077 Swiss cake	0118 used TV	0159 saddle up
0037 hazy, smoky	0078 Swiss coffee	0119 stayed up	0160 stitches
0038 Swiss movie	0079 sauce cap	0120 stones	0161 stitched
0039 Swiss map	0080 sassy face	0121 stand	0162 station
0040 scissors	0081 sees food	0122 sweet onion	0163 city gym
0041 sees red	0082 sees phone	0123 sit on him	0164 wise teacher
0042 Caesar won	0083 sees fame	0124 stunner	0165 city jail
0043 Swiss Army	0084 cease fire	0125 stone wall	0166 city judge
0044 seas roar	0085 sees fuel	0126 stingy	0167 sad joke
0045 seize roll	0086 sees fish	0127 stung	0168 city chief
0046 so so rich	0087 sees fog	0128 used knife	0169 sweatshop
0047 Swiss rug	0088 saws half off	0129 side knob	0170 steakhouse
0048 saucer heavy	0089 sues FBI	0130 stems	0171 stakeout
0049 Swiss Air up	0090 icy subways	0131 icy tomato	0172 used wagon
0050 sizzles	0091 icy houseboat	0132 stamina	0173 used comb
0051 house salad	0092 saucepan	0133 sweet Mom	0174 used car
0052 house salon	0093 sees a bomb	0134 steamer	0175 sad eagle
0053 see Salem	0094 icy supper	0135 icy oatmeal	0176 side coach
0054 wise sailor	0095 cesspool	0136 sweat much	0177 sidekick
0055 Swiss lily	0096 he's so peachy	0137 stomach	0178 yes, hot coffee
0056 weighs sludge	0097 use icepack	0138 sweet movie	0179 stock up
0057 wise slug	0098 seize beehive	0139 stamp	0180 soda fizz
0058 house slave	0099 sues the Pope	0140 stars	0181 stay fit
0059 wise slap	0100 seduces	0141 straw-hat	0182 stove on
0060 sausages	0101 sawdust	0142 acid rain	0183 sweet fame
0061 Swiss jet	0102 citizen	0143 storm	0184 city fire
0062 uses the john	0103 stays home	0144 his terrier	0185 stifle
0063 sees a chum	0104 soda, sir	0145 stroll	0186 see TV show
0064 icy, icy chair	0105 icy tassel	0146 starch	0187 this TV week
0065 Swiss jail	0106 set switch	0147 strike	0188 has TV off
0066 sees the judge	0107 stays awake	0148 strife	0189 has TV up
0067 house is shaky	0108 satisfy	0149 strap	0190 steps
0068 Swiss chef	0109 side swipe	0150 stalls	0191 stopped
0069 sea was choppy	0110 statehouse	0151 satellite	0192 step in
0070 Swiss kiss	0111 statehood	0152 stallion	0193 sweaty palm
0071 ice skate	0112 sit down	0153 stall him	0194 stopper
0072 seize the gun	0113 stadium	0154 stole her	0195 staple
0073 I say sick'em	0114 soda water	0155 sweet lily	0196 stopwatch
0074 his cigar	0115 state law	0156 stylish	0197 stay back
0075 his skull	0116 side dish	0157 city look	0198 step off
0076 Swiss coach	0117 static	0158 stay alive	0199 soda pop

Directory

0200 sneezes	0241 snort	0282 sun fun	0323 same name
0201 snowsuit	0242 sunny, rainy	0283 sign of him	0324 seminar
0202 sun - sun	0243 I see an Army	0284 sign waiver	0325 Seminole
0203 suns me	0244 sunnier here	0285 sniffle	0326 same nacho
0204 sincere	0245 snarl	0286 sunfish	0327 swimming
0205 suns oil	0246 synergy	0287 sunny, foggy	0328 see men off
0206 sneeze - achu	0247 see New York	0288 sniff half	0329 salmon up
0207 sun soak	0248 sunroof	0289 sniff pie	0330 wise Moms
0208 snow is heavy	0249 sun ripe	0290 snow peas	0331 swim meet
0209 sun's up	0250 snails	0291 snapped	0332 swim men
0210 sunny days	0251 sunlight	0292 snow bunny	0333 swim Mom
0211 sunny today	0252 sign loan	0293 sunbeam	0334 swim more
0212 suntan	0253 ice on limb	0294 sniper	0335 swim a mile
0213 sandy home	0254 ozone layer	0295 snowball	0336 swim much
0214 snow tire	0255 see Honolulu	0296 sunny beach	0337 use my mug
0215 sundial	0256 ice on eyelash	0297 sign back	0338 same movie
0216 sandwich	0257 swan lake	0298 snap off	0339 use my map
0217 San Diego	0258 I was in love	0299 snap up	0340 summers
0218 Sony TV	0259 snowy, help	0300 wise misses	0341 summer heat
0219 sunny top	0260 snowshoes	0301 swim suit	0342 see home run
0220 use onions	0261 snow shed	0302 wise mason	0343 smear him
0221 sign note	0262 sunshine	0303 see museum	0344 hazy mirror
0222 CNN on	0263 sunny gym	0304 wise miser	0345 is moral
0223 sign name	0264 snow watcher	0305 icy muzzle	0346 see the march
0224 sign in here	0265 snow chilly	0306 same switch	0347 smirk
0225 CNN will	0266 zany judge	0307 hazy mask	0348 summer off
0226 sunny, enjoy	0267 sign check	0308 same sofa	0349 summer boy
0227 sunning	0268 snow chief	0309 his mishap	0350 smells
0228 a sane Navy	0269 snatch up	0310 housemates	0351 he smiled
0229 sun on the bay	0270 snacks	0311 swim to it	0352 swim alone
0230 wise names	0271 sneaked	0312 his hometown	0353 smell them
0231 sun made	0272 sunken	0313 same time	0354 smaller
232 snowman	0273 sink him	0314 cemetery	0355 smelly hallway
0233 zany Mom	0274 sneaker	0315 icy metal	0356 smallish
0234 sun more	0275 snake oil	0316 use my dish	0357 ice milk
0235 sign my will	0276 sink wash	0317 use my deck	0358 see him leave
0236 sign my shoe	0277 synagogue	0318 zoom TV	0359 small pie
0237 ice on mug	0278 sneak off	0319 swim to boy	0360 smooches
0238 seen a movie	0279 sneak up	0320 summons	0361 smudged
0239 sign me up	0280 sunny face	0321 cement	0362 ice machine
0240 snores	0281 snow fed	0322 iceman won	0363 smooch me

Directory

0364 swim ashore	0405 yes, wrestle	0446 sorry Archie	0487 serve, OK
0365 see my shell	0406 sores age	0447 sorry Iraq	0488 survive
0366 some judge	0407 his rescue	0448 sorry roof	0489 serve pie
0367 same joke	0408 see her sofa	0449 see-thru robe	0490 sour puss
0368 same chef	0409 his hour is up	0450 cereals	0491 is Aruba hot
0369 smash up	0410 house riots	0451 his world	0492 icy ribbon
0370 smokehouse	0411 serrated	0452 sirloin	0493 sore bum
0371 smoked	0412 sardine	0453 his realm	0494 sour pear
0372 smoke on	0413 his red home	0454 sorry lawyer	0495 sewer bill
0373 same game	0414 icy radar	0455 cereal all	0496 has rubbish
0374 smoker	0415 sore tail	0456 use relish	0497 sore back
0375 smuggle	0416 sour dish	0457 cereal, OK	0498 soar above
0376 swim coach	0417 icy, red key	0458 see her leave	0499 sorry, Papa
0377 swim - kick	0418 see her TV	0459 see her lip	0500 slices
0378 some cough	0419 he's read up	0460 has riches	0501 he's lost
0379 same cup	0420 sirens	0461 surge ahead	0502 slow zone
0380 see movies	0421 serenade	0462 sore chin	0503 a seal swam
0381 same food	0422 sour onion	0463 sorry Jimmy	0504 sells hair
0382 symphony	0423 see her name	0464 he's richer	0505 sells oil
0383 swim off me	0424 see runner	0465 a sorry jail	0506 sells shoe
0384 swim far	0425 ice, rain, hail	0466 a sorry judge	0507 see Alaska
0385 some fail	0426 his ranch	0467 sorry Jack	0508 sails off
0386 swim fish	0427 soaring	0468 a sorry chef	0509 slows up
0387 some fog	0428 sour enough	0469 serge by	0510 slides
0388 swim half off	0429 he's run by	0470 circus	0511 sold it
0389 some VP	0430 icy rooms	0471 a sorry cat	0512 slow down
0390 same bus	0431 sorry mate	0472 saw a raccoon	0513 sold home
0391 swamped	0432 ceremony	0473 sour gum	0514 salute her
0392 swim pony	0433 sorry Mom	0474 a sorry car	0515 salad oil
0393 swim by him	0434 house warmer	0475 circle	0516 slide show
0394 swim by her	0435 sorry meal	0476 sorry, Coach	0517 sell dog
0395 symbol	0436 sorry match	0477 sour cake	0518 sold off
0396 some beach	0437 ceramic	0478 a sorry cough	0519 seal it up
0397 swim back	0438 sour movie	0479 has wreck up	0520 saloons
0398 swim above	0439 icy ramp	0480 sour face	0521 Iceland
0399 some baby	0440 a sorry rose	0481 sore feet	0522 swollen knee
0400 psoriasis	0441 sore throat	0482 icy ravine	0523 slain him
0401 house arrest	0442 see a rerun	0483 serve me	0524 slain her
0402 hazy Arizona	0443 sour aroma	0484 icy river	0525 salon oil
0403 his resume	0444 sore rear	0485 serve all	0526 icy lunch
0404 sorry sir	0445 has her role	0486 serve hash	0527 sailing

Directory

0528 sell knife	0569 sail ship	0610 see jets	0651 switch wallet
0529 has line-up	0570 slugs	0611 switched tea	0652 switch lane
0530 slams	0571 silk tie	0612 switched on	0653 switch lime
0531 soulmate	0572 slogan	0613 switch team	0654 switch lawyer
0532 silly man	0573 slug him	0614 switch hitter	0655 was she loyal
0533 sell my home	0574 sell car	0615 switch towel	0656 switch leash
0534 silly hammer	0575 he's legal	0616 switch dish	0657 switch lock
0535 seal mail	0576 sluggish	0617 switch dog	0658 icy shelf
0536 sell my shoe	0577 sell cookie	0618 switched off	0659 switch help
0537 slam week	0578 slack off	0619 switched pie	0660 switch cheese
0538 silly movie	0579 silly cowboy	0620 icy chains	0661 was she shot
0539 slump	0580 slaves	0621 switch hand	0662 association
0540 sellers	0581 slow feet	0622 switch onion	0663 switch gym
0541 sleigh ride	0582 cell phone	0623 switch name	0664 switch chair
0542 silly run	0583 slow foam	0624 switch owner	0665 switch jail
0543 sell rum	0584 silver	0625 switch nail	0666 switch judge
0544 silly roar	0585 sea level	0626 see a change	0667 switch joke
0545 slower whale	0586 selfish	0627 switching	0668 sushi chef
0546 slow reach	0587 slave walk	0628 switch knife	0669 switch job
0547 slower walk	0588 sleeve off	0629 switch knob	0670 switch keys
0548 slower half	0589 sell off pie	0630 saw chimes	0671 icy jacket
0549 seal - wrap	0590 silly boys	0631 was she mad	0672 switch gun
0550 slow lasso	0591 slipped	0632 switch money	0673 switch comb
0551 sell wallet	0592 sleep in	0633 switch Mom	0674 switch gear
0552 sell lion	0593 sell poem	0634 switch hammer	0675 switch call
0553 slalom	0594 slipper	0635 switch mail	0676 switch coach
0554 cellular	0595 sleigh bell	0636 switch match	0677 see Chicago
0555 silly lily	0596 azalea bush	0637 switch mug	0678 switch coffee
0556 silly eyelash	0597 sleepwalk	0638 switch movie	0679 was shut off
0557 silly league	0598 slip off	0639 switch map	0680 switch wives
0558 slow lava	0599 slip up	0640 his jersey	0681 switch food
0559 seal lip	0600 switches house	0641 his shirt	0682 switch phone
0560 sell shoes	0601 ice chest	0642 his journey	0683 switch fame
0561 slashed	0602 switch is on	0643 his germ	0684 switch over
0562 solution	0603 switches ham	0644 switch rower	0685 such a fool
0563 slash him	0604 switches hour	0645 switch rail	0686 switch fish
0564 slasher	0605 ice chisel	0646 his church	0687 saw JFK
0565 sell Jello	0606 switches shoe	0647 see a shark	0688 switch half off
0566 slow choo-choo	0607 switch sock	0648 see the sheriff	0689 switch VP
0567 slow check	0608 switch is off	0649 his cherry pie	0690 switch bus
0568 silly chef	0609 switch soap	0650 seashells	0691 switch bait

242

Directory

0692 switch pen
0693 switch bomb
0694 switch bar
0695 switch ball
0696 was she pushy
0697 switchback
0698 switch above
0699 sewage pipe
0700 squeezes
0701 squeezed
0702 his cousin
0703 skis home
0704 whiskey sour
0705 ski icy hill
0706 soaks wash
0707 zig zag
0708 squeeze wife
0709 sky is up
0710 skits
0711 skated
0712 ski down
0713 sick time
0714 skater
0715 skate well
0716 soak dish
0717 sick dog
0718 skydive
0719 skate by
0720 skins
0721 scant
0722 skin knee
0723 skinny Ma
0724 scanner
0725 signal
0726 skinny shoe
0727 skiing
0728 skinny half
0729 ski on by
0730 skims
0731 soak meat
0732 sick man

0733 sick Mom
0734 sycamore
0735 see camel
0736 sick match
0737 soggy, muggy
0738 sick movie
0739 skimpy
0740 cigars
0741 cigarette
0742 screen
0743 ice cream
0744 soak her hair
0745 squirrel
0746 scratch
0747 scary walk
0748 scarf
0749 scrub
0750 sea gulls
0751 skillet
0752 cyclone
0753 icy clam
0754 scholar
0755 scale wall
0756 psychology
0757 sickly wig
0758 icy cliff
0759 scallop
0760 soggy shoes
0761 sketched
0762 suction
0763 so catch me
0764 he's a catcher
0765 sick jail
0766 sick judge
0767 sick joke
0768 sick chef
0769 sick job
0770 ice cakes
0771 sick cat
0772 soggy wagon
0773 so kick him

0774 he's a kicker
0775 sick eagle
0776 soggy cash
0777 soggy cake
0778 see kickoff
0779 sick cub
0780 suck face
0781 sock fight
0782 soggy van
0783 sick of him
0784 sick of her
0785 scuffle
0786 sick fish
0787 sick of the guy
0788 sick of ivy
0789 scuff up
0790 skips
0791 ice capped
0792 sick pony
0793 skip him
0794 zookeeper
0795 scapple
0796 skip wash
0797 skip walk
0798 the sky above
0799 sick baby
0800 see faces
0801 save seat
0802 save the sun
0803 safe sum
0804 saves her
0805 see fossil
0806 saves wash
0807 saves wig
0808 safe, safe
0809 saves up
0810 see videos
0811 soft head
0812 save a ton
0813 save time
0814 software

0815 soft wheel
0816 soft shoe
0817 Soviet guy
0818 save the TV
0819 he's fed up
0820 use fins
0821 safe night
0822 save the union
0823 safe name
0824 souvenir
0825 use vinyl
0826 see the finish
0827 saving
0828 save the Navy
0829 see funny boy
0830 he's famous
0831 savvy maid
0832 save money
0833 savvy Mom
0834 sophomore
0835 save mail
0836 safe match
0837 safe mug
0838 safe move
0839 save the map
0840 sapphires
0841 severed
0842 sovereign
0843 ice farm
0844 save your hair
0845 several
0846 he's fresh
0847 he's freaky
0848 safe roof
0849 save our boy
0850 save whales
0851 asphalt
0852 use a violin
0853 swivel him
0854 Civil War
0855 swivel wheel

243

Directory

0856 his flesh	0897 save a buck	0938 sub movie	0979 use a backup
0857 U.S. Flag	0898 icy half above	0939 use a pump	0980 swap vase
0858 save a life	0899 safe pipe	0940 zippers	0981 soapy feet
0859 has a flap	0900 use passes	0941 subway ride	0982 soapy phone
0860 ice fishes	0901 he's a pest	0942 aspirin	0983 soapy, foamy
0861 has fished	0902 soup's on	0943 supreme	0984 zap the fire
0862 save the ocean	0903 sub swim	0944 whisperer	0985 swipe file
0863 save Jimmy	0904 he's busier	0945 subway rail	0986 zap fish
0864 safe highchair	0905 subs awhile	0946 use a brush	0987 zap the fog
0865 safe jail	0906 see boys itch	0947 iceberg	0988 sip half off
0866 savvy judge	0907 see boys walk	0948 has proof	0989 zap the FBI
0867 safe joke	0908 see boys off	0949 use a prop	0990 soapy bus
0868 safe shave	0909 soaps up	0950 say please	0991 swipe bat
0869 safe ship	0910 spits	0951 split	0992 swipe pen
0870 save gas	0911 spit out	0952 spleen	0993 zap! bam!
0871 save the cat	0912 sew button	0953 spoil ham	0994 soap opera
0872 safe gun	0913 sip it Ma	0954 spoiler	0995 soapy pail
0873 save the gum	0914 spider	0955 spill oil	0996 swap beach
0874 safe car	0915 hospital	0956 splash	0997 swap back
0875 safe call	0916 soap dish	0957 ice block	0998 see Pope off
0876 save cash	0917 sip tea, OK	0958 spill half	0999 swap pipe
0877 safe kick	0918 was paid off	0959 he's a playboy	1000 diseases
0878 save coffee	0919 speed up	0960 speeches	1001 deceased
0879 save the cub	0920 spins	0961 soapy sheet	1002 wet season
0880 save face	0921 spend	0962 has passion	1003 it's so homey
0881 safe food	0922 spin wine	0963 so push him	1004 it was sorry
0882 safe haven	0923 spy on him	0964 he's a pusher	1005 it's so oily
0883 save the foam	0924 spin hair	0965 special	1006 it's so chewy
0884 safe fire	0925 spin wool	0966 a sub judge	1007 it's sick
0885 save fuel	0926 spinach	0967 sip, choke	1008 it's so heavy
0886 safe fish	0927 sipping	0968 so push off	1009 tosses up
0887 save half, OK	0928 spinoff	0969 soapy ship	1010 wet seeds
0888 save, half off	0929 spun by	0970 swap keys	1011 tested
0889 save FBI	0930 has bombs	0971 spaghetti	1012 Dizzy Dean
0890 safe bus	0931 sip my tea	0972 soup can	1013 toast him
0891 use heavy bat	0932 spy man	0973 soapy comb	1014 hot cider
0892 save a penny	0933 spy Mom	0974 subway car	1015 wet saddle
0893 safe bomb	0934 sip more	0975 speckle	1016 toast a wish
0894 save par	0935 use up my oil	0976 icy backwash	1017 wet sidewalk
0895 use heavy pail	0936 swap wash	0977 sip cocoa	1018 wood stove
0896 safe beach	0937 use up my egg	0978 sip coffee	1019 heats it up

Directory

1020 it's noisy	1061 it's shoddy	1102 die too soon	1143 daydream
1021 disowned	1062 it's shiny	1103 dates me	1144 what a terror
1022 it's neon	1063 it's a huge home	1104 today is here	1145 hot trail
1023 it's on me	1064 it's cheery	1105 wet tassel	1146 out with trash
1024 designer	1065 it's jolly	1106 Dad's watch	1147 tow truck
1025 wet snail	1066 dizzy Judge	1107 today is OK	1148 hot driveway
1026 it's in wash	1067 it's shaky	1108 date is off	1149 tightrope
1027 tossing	1068 eats huge half	1109 heated soup	1150 details
1028 it's in the ivy	1069 toss ship	1110 eat toads	1151 detailed
1029 it's in the pie	1070 disguise	1111 outdated	1152 dateline
1030 dismiss	1071 wet socket	1112 hit titan	1153 dead limb
1031 eats meat	1072 it's gone	1113 dead time	1154 weed tiller
1032 that's a man	1073 it's a game	1114 dated her	1155 dead lily
1033 that's mom	1074 disagree	1115 do detail	1156 detail wash
1034 eats more	1075 it's ugly	1116 hot, hot dish	1157 deadlock
1035 decimal	1076 it's catchy	1117 dead duck	1158 tidal wave
1036 ate so much	1077 eats cake	1118 dead dove	1159 Dad, help
1037 that's my guy	1078 it's coffee	1119 heat hot tub	1160 hot dishes
1038 that's my wife	1079 it's a wake-up	1120 titans	1161 detached
1039 wet swamp	1080 it's fuzzy	1121 dead end	1162 dietician
1040 tweezers	1081 too soft	1122 hot, hot onion	1163 head to gym
1041 dessert	1082 it was fun	1123 titanium	1164 heated chair
1042 it's rainy	1083 it's foamy	1124 eat dinner	1165 heated jail
1043 disarm	1084 it's fire	1125 wet toenail	1166 did huge wash
1044 it's a horror	1085 it's awful	1126 tighten shoe	1167 do that joke
1045 eat cereal	1086 it's fishy	1127 Titanic	1168 had to shave
1046 it's rich	1087 it's foggy	1128 date on/off	1169 had touch up
1047 it's rocky	1088 day's half off	1129 had a tune-up	1170 hot dogs
1048 it's rough	1089 it's halfway up	1130 dead mouse	1171 dedicate
1049 disrobe	1090 dispose	1131 dead meat	1172 hit Tokyo now
1050 tassels	1091 dispute	1132 dead man	1173 heated comb
1051 disallowed	1092 teaspoon	1133 dead mummy	1174 white tiger
1052 twice alone	1093 it's a bomb	1134 hit timer	1175 hit the tackle
1053 hot salami	1094 disappear	1135 eat oatmeal	1176 wet dog wash
1054 eat celery	1095 toss ball	1136 too, too much	1177 Diet Coke
1055 disloyal	1096 hit icy patch	1137 today muggy	1178 eat at the cafe
1056 hit, slash	1097 toss back	1138 do eat my half	1179 heated cup
1057 dislike	1098 it's up a half	1139 hot Tampa	1180 heed advice
1058 heats loaf	1099 it's a baby	1140 detours	1181 hot, hot, food
1059 had a slip	1100 eat daises	1141 dehydrate	1182 had TV on
1060 hot switches	1101 dead city	1142 wide turn	1183 wet, wet foam

Directory

1184 wet diver	1225 down the Nile	1266 tiny Judge	1307 tummy sick
1185 hot devil	1226 tiny notch	1267 tiny check	1308 hide my safe
1186 dead fish	1227 tanning	1268 tiny chef	1309 eat my soup
1187 today foggy	1228 twin knife	1269 township	1310 timeouts
1188 had TV off	1229 tiny knob	1270 tanks	1311 demoted
1189 hit TV up	1230 tan moose	1271 hoodwinked	1312 wet mitten
1190 hot tubs	1231 dynamite	1272 tin can	1313 dumb dumb
1191 deadbeat	1232 tinman	1273 tiny comb	1314 diameter
1192 dead pony	1233 tiny mummy	1274 tanker	1315 timidly
1193 do tip him	1234 Den Mother	1275 heating oil	1316 heat my dish
1194 teddy bear	1235 hit animal	1276 do hang wash	1317 automatic
1195 heated pool	1236 twin match	1277 tiny cake	1318 hit my TV
1196 eat at beach	1237 dynamic	1278 wedding vow	1319 timid boy
1197 tote bag	1238 twin movie	1279 tin cup	1320 demons
1198 do the tipoff	1239 tone me up	1280 tiny office	1321 diamond
1199 today be happy	1240 dinners	1281 tiny feet	1322 dominion
1200 downsize	1241 Tony Award	1282 tiny phone	1323 hate my name
1201 twin city	1242 tune her in	1283 tiny foam	1324 demeanor
1202 tunes in	1243 tiny room	1284 Denver	1325 too menial
1203 a tiny sum	1244 dinnerware	1285 downfall	1326 diminish
1204 dinosaur	1245 wooden rail	1286 tuna fish	1327 timing
1205 tonsil	1246 tiny rash	1287 head in fog	1328 dummy knife
1206 twins age	1247 tiny rug	1288 tiny fife	1329 do men obey
1207 tiny sock	1248 tin roof	1289 tiny ivy hoop	1330 hid my mouse
1208 what a nice wife	1249 tiny rope	1290 twin boys	1331 teammate
1209 tunes up	1250 tunnels	1291 wooden bat	1332 dumb man
1210 doughnuts	1251 tiny wallet	1292 tune piano	1333 time Mom
1211 dented	1252 tan line	1293 tiny palm	1334 tame my hair
1212 downtown	1253 tiny limb	1294 downpour	1335 hid my mail
1213 Tiny Tim	1254 tan lawyer	1295 downplay	1336 time my wash
1214 twin tower	1255 tiny lily	1296 tiny beach	1337 time my walk
1215 hot handle	1256 tiny leash	1297 dune buggy	1338 dumb movie
1216 tiny dish	1257 wooden leg	1298 twin beehive	1339 dim my hope
1217 tan dog	1258 tiny leaf	1299 tiny baby	1340 timers
1218 attentive	1259 tiny lip	1300 hit / misses	1341 demerit
1219 don't buy	1260 wooden shoes	1301 die, homicide	1342 time the run
1220 eat onions	1261 tiny shed	1302 time is now	1343 heat my room
1221 tenant	1262 tension	1303 hit museum	1344 admirer
1222 tiny nun	1263 tiny gym	1304 I do miss her	1345 admiral
1223 tiny name	1264 teenager	1305 hid the missile	1346 hot mirage
1224 tuna on rye	1265 tiny jail	1306 time his wash	1347 hit the mark

Directory

1348 dome roof	1389 eat my half up	1430 drums	1471 target
1349 hid my ruby	1390 dumps	1431 doormat	1472 dragon
1350 dumb laws	1391 dump it	1432 doorman	1473 drug him
1351 dim light	1392 hid my pony	1433 Dear Mom	1474 trucker
1352 tame lion	1393 atom bomb	1434 drummer	1475 terry cloth
1353 oatmeal, yum	1394 damper	1435 dry meal	1476 tire gauge
1354 hit molar	1395 temple	1436 dry match	1477 dry cake
1355 dumb oil well	1396 dump wash	1437 dream/awake	1478 drag off
1356 hid my eyelash	1397 dime back	1438 dream off	1479 trek by
1357 time log	1398 tempo off	1439 tramp	1480 drives
1358 dumb love	1399 Tampa Bay	1440 terrors	1481 drift
1359 oatmeal pie	1400 white roses	1441 try hard	1482 drive in
1360 wet matches	1401 trust	1442 dry run	1483 dry foam
1361 damaged	1402 treason	1443 to your room	1484 driver
1362 admission	1403 dries him	1444 dry your hair	1485 travel
1363 dumb gym	1404 dresser	1445 true, really	1486 try fudge
1364 hot Major	1405 drizzle	1446 terror watch	1487 terrific
1365 dumb jail	1406 dressage	1447 tire wreck	1488 drive off
1366 dumb judge	1407 to the rescue	1448 dry her off	1489 drive up
1367 dumb joke	1408 dries off	1449 tore, rip	1490 troops
1368 dumb chef	1409 tree sap	1450 trials	1491 tribute
1369 dime shop	1410 treats	1451 derailed	1492 turban
1370 tomahawks	1411 traded	1452 water lawn	1493 drop me
1371 tame cat	1412 trade-in	1453 tree limb	1494 drapery
1372 hide my gun	1413 Dartmouth	1454 trailer	1495 doorbell
1373 dumb game	1414 trader	1455 eat really well	1496 wet rubbish
1374 hate my car	1415 turtle	1456 door latch	1497 drawback
1375 he had me call	1416 tradeshow	1457 hydraulic	1498 drop off
1376 hide my cash	1417 dry dock	1458 true love	1499 drop by
1377 demagogue	1418 trade off	1459 wet ear lobe	1500 white laces
1378 heat my coffee	1419 tree top	1460 trashes	1501 deal set
1379 do makeup	1420 trains	1461 watershed	1502 dials in
1380 at the movies	1421 Toronto	1462 Trojan	1503 tails him
1381 hide my fat	1422 dry onion	1463 doorjamb	1504 Dolly's here
1382 hide my phone	1423 train them	1464 dry chair	1505 till soil
1383 hate my fame	1424 trainer	1465 dry jail	1506 dials shoe
1384 time over	1425 drain well	1466 Dear Judge	1507 white Alaska
1385 hide my file	1426 drench	1467 try a shake	1508 tells off
1386 eat my fish	1427 drink	1468 true chef	1509 dials up
1387 dummy, fake	1428 lawyer fee	1469 trash up	1510 toilets
1388 eat my half off	1429 doorknob	1470 tear gas	1511 diluted

Directory

1512 dial tone	1553 tall lamb	1594 had a helper	1635 touch the mail
1513 tell it, Ma	1554 tell a lawyer	1595 white label	1636 touch match
1514 tall door	1555 tall oil well	1596 daily push	1637 teach my guy
1515 tall tale	1556 it will latch	1597 tailback	1638 touch him off
1516 tall dish	1557 daily log	1598 it will pay off	1639 hide shampoo
1517 tall dog	1558 tall leaf	1599 tell Papa	1640 teachers
1518 tall TV	1559 hotel lobby	1600 hot chases	1641 T-shirt
1519 teletype	1560 delicious	1601 digest	1642 hot journey
1520 daily news	1561 tool shed	1602 touch the sun	1643 had a germ
1521 talent	1562 hotel chain	1603 touches him	1644 touch rear
1522 wet linen	1563 tall chum	1604 touches her	1645 teach her well
1523 tell on him	1564 daily chore	1605 teach us well	1646 white church
1524 tell on her	1565 daily chili	1606 touches shoe	1647 dishrag
1525 tall nail	1566 tell the judge	1607 teach us, OK	1648 hit sheriff
1526 eat lunch	1567 tell a joke	1608 touch sofa	1649 hot cherry pie
1527 dialing	1568 tell the chef	1609 touches up	1650 wet shells
1528 hotel knife	1569 tall ship	1610 wet sheets	1651 touch wallet
1529 hot line-up	1570 delicacy	1611 dish it out	1652 eat chili now
1530 tell him so	1571 tailgate	1612 touchdown	1653 touch limb
1531 deli meat	1572 tall can	1613 it shot him	1654 teach lawyer
1532 tall man	1573 daily game	1614 white shutter	1655 touch lily
1533 tell Mom	1574 teal car	1615 dish towel	1656 touch eyelash
1534 tall hammer	1575 tall gal	1616 touch dish	1657 touch leg
1535 it will mellow	1576 tell the coach	1617 touch dog	1658 touch lava
1536 it will match	1577 tall cake	1618 touch TV	1659 touch lip
1537 tall mic	1578 tall coffee	1619 touch it up	1660 touch shoes
1538 dull match	1579 tell a cop	1620 touch nose	1661 touch a jet
1539 hot lamp	1580 hotel office	1621 hid giant	1662 teach Johnny
1540 tellers	1581 hotel food	1622 touch onion	1663 touch a chime
1541 tall award	1582 telephone	1623 teach in home	1664 dishwasher
1542 it will rain	1583 do u love me	1624 teach in Rio	1665 touch a shell
1543 hotel room	1584 deliver	1625 teach in L.A.	1666 teach judge
1544 taller oar	1585 tall fellow	1626 wet change	1667 teach Shag
1545 it will roll	1586 tall fudge	1627 touching	1668 teach the chef
1546 it will reach	1587 daily fog	1628 touch knife	1669 touch ship
1547 it will rock	1588 Tel Aviv	1629 touch knob	1670 hot checks
1548 tell her off	1589 hotel phobia	1630 touch a moose	1671 teach a kid
1549 Delaware Bay	1590 tall boys	1631 touch mud	1672 touch a gun
1550 it will lose	1591 hotel patio	1632 teach me now	1673 touch comb
1551 tall load	1592 tailbone	1633 teach Mom	1674 touch car
1552 tall lion	1593 tell the poem	1634 touch my hair	1675 teach a gal

Directory

1676 teach coach	1717 tick tock	1758 white glove	1799 dog puppy
1677 touch cookie	1718 talkative	1759 yacht club	1800 wet faces
1678 touch the cave	1719 take it up	1760 dog chews	1801 TV set
1679 dish, cup	1720 Dickens	1761 tuck sheet	1802 TV is on
1680 touch face	1721 eat candy	1762 education	1803 TV zoom
1681 hot itchy feet	1722 take onion	1763 attack the jam	1804 tough sir
1682 touch phone	1723 attack on home	1764 head cashier	1805 hide fossil
1683 touch fame	1724 attack owner	1765 attack the jail	1806 TV switch
1684 touch fire	1725 wet canal	1766 attack judge	1807 TV is wacky
1685 white shovel	1726 attack Nashua	1767 dog show, OK	1808 TV is off
1686 touch a fish	1727 digging	1768 dog showoff	1809 tough soap
1687 touch fog	1728 attack Navy	1769 dock ship	1810 divots
1688 to shove off	1729 take a nap	1770 dog wags	1811 divided
1689 teach FBI	1730 take my house	1771 take coat	1812 out of town
1690 odd jobs	1731 take me out	1772 attack wagon	1813 dive team
1691 touch bat	1732 take me in	1773 dog comb	1814 tough tire
1692 touch pen	1733 take me home	1774 take care	1815 daffodil
1693 touch a bomb	1734 tug my hair	1775 attack! kill!	1816 divide wash
1694 touch a bear	1735 take the mail	1776 take cash	1817 Daffy Duck
1695 teachable	1736 take match	1777 duck - quack	1818 tough, tough
1696 touch up shoe	1737 take mug	1778 dog cough	1819 divide by
1697 touchback	1738 take me off	1779 attack cop	1820 advance
1698 touch above	1739 take me up	1780 dog face	1821 defined
1699 teach baby	1740 degrees	1781 dog food	1822 tough nun
1700 Texas	1741 ID card	1782 dog heaven	1823 dive on him
1701 tuxedo	1742 take a run	1783 dog fame	1824 divine hair
1702 hit casino	1743 diagram	1784 takeover	1825 tough nail
1703 decks him	1744 tag rear	1785 dig - fill	1826 divine witch
1704 dogs her	1745 heat grill	1786 take fudge	1827 diving
1705 white castle	1746 at car show	1787 attack fog	1828 TV on/off
1706 dog switch	1747 wet creek	1788 take half off	1829 divine hope
1707 toxic	1748 autograph	1789 take off pie	1830 white foams
1708 takes off	1749 take her up	1790 whitecaps	1831 tough meat
1709 duck soup	1750 tackles	1791 tugboat	1832 tough man
1710 tickets	1751 white cloud	1792 dog bone	1833 tough Mom
1711 dictate	1752 hide clown	1793 attack by him	1834 dive more
1712 take down	1753 eat a clam	1794 dog breath	1835 day of mail
1713 dog team	1754 tickler	1795 duckbill	1836 tough match
1714 doctor	1755 tickle all	1796 dog patch	1837 tough mug
1715 dog-tail	1756 dog leash	1797 take back	1838 TV movie
1716 dog dish	1757 white cloak	1798 dig up ivy	1839 tough map

Directory

1840 divorce	1881 tough feet	1922 eat banana	1963 tip jam
1841 too afraid	1882 day of fun	1923 top name	1964 tip chair
1842 tavern	1883 day of fame	1924 top owner	1965 eat a bushel
1843 deform	1884 tough fire	1925 wet pinwheel	1966 top judge
1844 tough roar	1885 dove flew	1926 hit - punch	1967 tip the shake
1845 dive - roll	1886 tough fish	1927 tipping	1968 top chef
1846 hot, fresh	1887 tough fog	1928 tip knife	1969 top shape
1847 wet frog	1888 dove half off	1929 top knob	1970 tea bags
1848 tougher half	1889 TV phobia	1930 wet palms	1971 topcoat
1849 eat free pie	1890 tough boss	1931 tie up meat	1972 toboggan
1850 devils	1891 dive boat	1932 tie up man	1973 top game
1851 outfield	1892 day of pain	1933 tie up Mom	1974 woodpecker
1852 Teflon	1893 dive bomb	1934 dip more	1975 white buckle
1853 hot flame	1894 tough bear	1935 tie up mail	1976 top coach
1854 white flower	1895 tough pill	1936 top match	1977 dab cookie
1855 tough lily	1896 tough beach	1937 tip mug	1978 tip coffee
1856 hot flash	1897 dive back	1938 top movie	1979 tip cup
1857 out of luck	1898 dive above	1939 heat pump	1980 dab face
1858 tough love	1899 tough baby	1940 depress	1981 top video
1859 develop	1900 day passes	1941 tea party	1982 heat up oven
1860 TV shows	1901 toothpaste	1942 white - brown	1983 tape foam
1861 TV watched	1902 eat poison	1943 tapeworm	1984 tip over
1862 devotion	1903 tips him	1944 hit barrier	1985 top of hill
1863 tough jam	1904 tips her	1945 top rail	1986 dopey fish
1864 TV chair	1905 topsoil	1946 toothbrush	1987 top half, OK
1865 tough jail	1906 tips a witch	1947 wet park	1988 hit above ivy
1866 tough judge	1907 toupee is wig	1948 deprive	1989 tip the FBI
1867 ate a fish egg	1908 tipsy wife	1949 eat - burp	1990 tip bus
1868 tough shave	1909 hit the busboy	1950 tables	1991 tip boat
1869 tough job	1910 diabetes	1951 tablet	1992 tip piano
1870 tough guys	1911 hot potato	1952 Dublin	1993 dip palm
1871 TV Guide	1912 deep down	1953 diploma	1994 white paper
1872 TV gone	1913 top team	1954 dip lower	1995 wet bubble
1873 tough game	1914 tap water	1955 hit blue whale	1996 tip bush
1874 hot figure	1915 top hotel	1956 hot blush	1997 tip bike
1875 tough gal	1916 top dish	1957 diabolic	1998 tip above
1876 tough cashew	1917 tape deck	1958 double off	1999 hit a pop-up
1877 tough cookie	1918 deep dive	1959 hot apple pie	2000 nice oasis
1878 day of coffee	1919 tiptop	1960 wet bushes	2001 nice sod
1879 tough cabby	1920 head pains	1961 head pushed	2002 nice son
1880 tough face	1921 wet paint	1962 hot passion	2003 nice swim

250

Directory

2004 necessary
2005 nice sale
2006 nice switch
2007 niece is weak
2008 nice sofa
2009 noisy subway
2010 nice days
2011 nice Dad
2012 nice tan
2013 nice time
2014 insider
2015 nice deal
2016 nice touch
2017 nest egg
2018 nose dive
2019 instep
2020 nuisance
2021 nice window
2022 on CNN
2023 nice name
2024 nice honor
2025 knees kneel
2026 nice nacho
2027 unsung
2028 niece nephew
2029 nice nap
2030 noisy mouse
2031 noisy maid
2032 insomnia
2033 nosy Mom
2034 owns more
2035 nice meal
2036 nice match
2037 no smog
2038 nice movie
2039 in a swamp
2040 nice raise
2041 nice hairdo
2042 nice rain
2043 newsroom
2044 answer her

2045 newsreel
2046 nicer age
2047 Noah's ark
2048 nice roof
2049 nice robe
2050 noose loose
2051 new sled
2052 new salon
2053 in slime
2054 wine cellar
2055 noisy oil well
2056 in sludge
2057 knees - leg
2058 no sleeve
2059 no sleep
2060 nice choice
2061 nice shot
2062 nice shine
2063 nice gym
2064 nice chair
2065 nice jewel
2066 nice judge
2067 no such guy
2068 nice shave
2069 nice job
2070 nice guys
2071 nice kitty
2072 noisy gun
2073 NCAA game
2074 nice car
2075 unicycle
2076 nice coach
2077 nice kick
2078 nice cough
2079 nice cop
2080 nice office
2081 nice photo
2082 nice van
2083 wins fame
2084 henhouse fire
2085 nice veil

2086 wins a fish
2087 nice fog
2088 unsafe wife
2089 unsafe boy
2090 no subs
2091 nice bat
2092 nice pen
2093 no soap, Ma
2094 inspire
2095 nice pal
2096 nosy, pushy
2097 nice bag
2098 noisy beehive
2099 nice baby
2100 notices
2101 window seat
2102 end zone
2103 handsome
2104 needs her
2105 window sill
2106 window sash
2107 new desk
2108 need a sofa
2109 hand soap
2110 haunted house
2111 knitted hat
2112 hunt down
2113 night time
2114 anteater
2115 need a hotel
2116 need a dish
2117 hound dog
2118 nodded off
2119 knotted up
2120 Indians
2121 night, night
2122 Indiana won
2123 need a name
2124 no dinner
2125 in denial
2126 Indian shoe

2127 knitting
2128 need a knife
2129 antenna up
2130 need my hose
2131 handmade
2132 handyman
2133 I need Mom
2134 nightmare
2135 windmill
2136 need much
2137 nutmeg
2138 no time off
2139 in Tampa
2140 undress
2141 under head
2142 on a train
2143 new drum
2144 underwear
2145 new trial
2146 no trash
2147 network
2148 interview
2149 on a trip
2150 night owls
2151 night light
2152 a night alone
2153 needle him
2154 antler
2155 needle well
2156 indulge
2157 night league
2158 need love
2159 antelope
2160 need cheese
2161 window washed
2162 window shine
2163 wind chime
2164 window washer
2165 wind chill
2166 need a judge
2167 handshake

Directory

2168 need a chef	2209 onion soup	2250 no nails	2291 own new boat
2169 window shop	2210 no windows	2251 neon light	2292 neon piano
2170 index	2211 in and out	2252 new nylon	2293 non bomb
2171 no ticket	2212 no antenna	2253 on any limb	2294 new neighbor
2172 nightgown	2213 on a new time	2254 onion layer	2295 in Nepal
2173 night game	2214 non odor	2255 in Honolulu	2296 non bushy
2174 need a car	2215 no night owl	2256 neon leash	2297 non baggy
2175 nautical	2216 onion dish	2257 neon leg	2298 neon beehive
2176 need cash	2217 no, no doggy	2258 neon leaf	2299 neon baby
2177 need a kick	2218 on and off	2259 neon lip	2300 no misses
2178 handcuff	2219 onion dip	2260 no nachos	2301 no mist
2179 handicap	2220 no onions	2261 on new sheet	2302 no my son
2180 window office	2221 no one knew it	2262 own a nation	2303 new museum
2181 need food	2222 no, no, no, no	2263 neon gym	2304 no miser
2182 need a phone	2223 no one name	2264 knee injury	2305 no missile
2183 want fame	2224 non owner	2265 neon jail	2306 name switch
2184 need a fire	2225 onion on hill	2266 neon judge	2307 no mask
2185 nightfall	2226 new neon show	2267 Union Jack	2308 in my safe
2186 want fish	2227 no yawning	2268 non chef	2309 no mess up
2187 hand vac	2228 own new knife	2269 union job	2310 unmade house
2188 want half off	2229 onion knob	2270 winnings	2311 animated
2189 hand off pie	2230 no names	2271 union coat	2312 new mitten
2190 no tips	2231 new one made	2272 union gun	2313 new medium
2191 notepad	2232 union man	2273 owning me	2314 new motor
2192 window pane	2233 Nun, Mom	2274 neon car	2315 win medal
2193 hunt bomb	2234 union hammer	2275 a winning yell	2316 enemy touch
2194 hunt berry	2235 any new mail	2276 winning wage	2317 name tag
2195 handball	2236 onion match	2277 winning guy	2318 own my TV
2196 need a push	2237 union mug	2278 non coffee	2319 in my tub
2197 notebook	2238 neon movie	2279 owning up	2320 no mayonnaise
2198 no tipoff	2239 union map	2280 in a new office	2321 new mint
2199 naughty baby	2240 win honors	2281 own new food	2322 in my union
2200 in nice house	2241 non road	2282 union phone	2323 in my name
2201 nuns eat	2242 the union ran	2283 non foamy	2324 in my honor
2202 no, no son	2243 Union Army	2284 union free	2325 name on wall
2203 in a nice home	2244 neon rear	2285 union file	2326 on my nacho
2204 nuns hair	2245 union railway	2286 non fish	2327 numbing
2205 no nozzle	2246 in any rush	2287 non foggy	2328 on my knife
2206 Nuns age	2247 in New York	2288 onion half off	2329 new moonpie
2207 nun is awake	2248 neon roof	2289 union VP	2330 in my maze
2208 union is off	2249 neon rope	2290 union boss	2331 now I'm mad

Directory

2332 win my man	2373 on my comb	2414 no radar	2455 near oil well
2333 enemy mom	2374 in my car	2415 on your dial	2456 on her eyelash
2334 no memory	2375 on my call	2416 newer dish	2457 on your leg
2335 in my mail	2376 on my couch	2417 newer deck	2458 win her love
2336 enemy match	2377 in my cocoa	2418 unheard of	2459 on your lip
2337 in my mug	2378 in my coffee	2419 on your top	2460 no riches
2338 in my movie	2379 in my cup	2420 no runs	2461 unreached
2339 enemy map	2380 no movies	2421 no rent	2462 Norwegian
2340 no more ice	2381 on my feet	2422 no reunion	2463 newer gym
2341 win my heart	2382 on my phone	2423 own her name	2464 no richer
2342 no maroon	2383 name of him	2424 no rain here	2465 New Rochelle
2343 in my room	2384 enemy fire	2425 no rain, hail	2466 honor Judge
2344 on my rear	2385 in my file	2426 on the range	2467 no rich guy
2345 no moral	2386 on my fudge	2427 honoring	2468 honor chef
2346 in my reach	2387 name vague	2428 no runoff	2469 ownership
2347 in America	2388 now move off	2429 no run up	2470 new rugs
2348 on my roof	2389 win MVP	2430 enormous	2471 new rocket
2349 in my robe	2390 on my bus	2431 in warm heat	2472 in Oregon
2350 animals	2391 on empty	2432 win your man	2473 narrow comb
2351 in my wallet	2392 on my piano	2433 honor Mom	2474 New Yorker
2352 enemy line	2393 enemy bomb	2434 no rumor	2475 on your call
2353 animal home	2394 number	2435 normal	2476 New York wish
2354 name lawyer	2395 honey maple	2436 win her match	2477 New York guy
2355 animal hall	2396 now I'm pushy	2437 in your mug	2478 narrow cave
2356 on my eyelash	2397 on my back	2438 honor movie	2479 New York boy
2357 no milk	2398 enemy above	2439 on ramp	2480 newer office
2358 in my loaf	2399 name the baby	2440 no errors	2481 narrow foot
2359 on my lip	2400 no roses	2441 narrow road	2482 newer van
2360 no matches	2401 unrest	2442 Henry Aaron	2483 newer fame
2361 on my jet	2402 in Arizona	2443 honorarium	2484 in the river
2362 on a mission	2403 honors me	2444 on your rear	2485 won raffle
2363 in my gym	2404 nursery	2445 honor roll	2486 in her fudge
2364 in my chair	2405 no resale	2446 honor the rich	2487 no rough guy
2365 in my shell	2406 owners wish	2447 honor	2488 in rough ivy
2366 numb judge	2407 no rescue	2448 on our roof	2489 honor the VP
2367 no magic	2408 New Year's Eve	2449 honor Rabbi	2490 newer bus
2368 win me a chef	2409 newer soap	2450 win or lose	2491 unripped
2369 enemy ship	2410 no radios	2451 new world	2492 new hairpin
2370 in my gaze	2411 honor the dead	2452 narrow lawn	2493 near a bomb
2371 in my coat	2412 no radio on	2453 no realm	2494 no riper
2372 own my gun	2413 on your dime	2454 new ruler	2495 North Pole

Directory

2496 no rubbish	2537 nail mug	2578 only coffee	2619 now shut up
2497 win her back	2538 only a movie	2579 only a cup	2620 nations
2498 no rip-off	2539 in limbo	2580 no leaves	2621 nationwide
2499 honor baby	2540 no yellow rose	2581 unloved	2622 now shine on
2500 new laces	2541 on alert	2582 only a phone	2623 now join me
2501 win lawsuit	2542 only rain	2583 only fame	2624 engineer
2502 kneel son	2543 in yellow room	2584 unlover	2625 national
2503 nails them	2544 kneel - roar	2585 unlevel	2626 no change
2504 new laser	2545 kneel - roll	2586 unlavish	2627 now showing
2505 nails wall	2546 enlarge	2587 only fog	2628 enjoy Navy
2506 nail switch	2547 nail rug	2588 only half off	2629 enjoy a nap
2507 nails wig	2548 nail roof	2589 only half up	2630 new chums
2508 kneels off	2549 only a robe	2590 no lips	2631 unjammed
2509 nails up	2550 nail walls	2591 only a bat	2632 enjoy money
2510 annual dues	2551 only a wallet	2592 only a pen	2633 enjoy Miami
2511 annihilated	2552 only a loan	2593 only a bomb	2634 enjoy more
2512 nail down	2553 only lamb	2594 only a bear	2635 enjoy meal
2513 annihilate them	2554 only a lawyer	2595 no label	2636 enjoy match
2514 annihilator	2555 only a lily	2596 only a push	2637 enjoy mug
2515 no ladle	2556 only a leash	2597 only a buck	2638 enjoy movie
2516 nailed shoe	2557 nail, lock	2598 only a beehive	2639 no shampoo
2517 an old guy	2558 only lava	2599 only a baby	2640 New Jersey
2518 newlywed wife	2559 nail lip	2600 no choices	2641 injured
2519 no let up	2560 no eyelashes	2601 unjust	2642 on a journey
2520 nylon hose	2561 unleashed	2602 unchosen	2643 inchworm
2521 inland	2562 honey lotion	2603 nachos - yum!	2644 no chair here
2522 new linen	2563 only jam	2604 enjoys her	2645 on a huge rail
2523 only a name	2564 nail chair	2605 new chisel	2646 in church
2524 nylon wire	2565 only jail	2606 enjoys show	2647 knee jerk
2525 noel, noel	2566 only a judge	2607 nachos - OK	2648 no sheriff
2526 no lunch	2567 only a shake	2608 enjoys the eve	2649 no cherry pie
2527 nailing	2568 only a shave	2609 inches up	2650 no jails
2528 nylon half	2569 only a chip	2610 no shots	2651 enchilada
2529 no line-up	2570 no legs	2611 enjoyed day	2652 one huge loan
2530 no limbs	2571 unlocked	2612 new showtune	2653 in chilly home
2531 nail mat	2572 only a gun	2613 new showtime	2654 no chili here
2532 only money	2573 annual game	2614 no chowder	2655 angel well
2533 only Mom	2574 onlooker	2615 new huge toll	2656 on huge leash
2534 nail hammer	2575 unlikely	2616 enjoyed show	2657 no jelly, OK
2535 only a male	2576 only cash	2617 new show dog	2658 enjoy love
2536 only my wish	2577 only a cookie	2618 enjoy TV	2659 no jelly pie

Directory

2660 enjoy shows	2701 no guest	2742 unicorn	2783 Yankee fame
2661 new huge jet	2702 Yankees win	2743 anagram	2784 no caviar
2662 no shoe shine	2703 wings me	2744 new career	2785 no gavel
2663 in huge gym	2704 Yankees hour	2745 uncurl	2786 young fish
2664 enjoy shower	2705 in a castle	2746 Anchorage	2787 yank fig
2665 in a huge jail	2706 new quiz show	2747 new crack	2788 yank off half
2666 hunch Judge	2707 yanks wig	2748 engrave	2789 yank the VP
2667 enjoy shake	2708 knocks off	2749 neck rub	2790 young boys
2668 on edge chef	2709 wings up	2750 wine glass	2791 now keep it
2669 one huge ship	2710 neckties	2751 include	2792 new cabin
2670 when she goes	2711 uncoated	2752 unclean	2793 young bum
2671 no jacket	2712 knock down	2753 unclaim	2794 wing by her
2672 no shakin'	2713 Yankee team	2754 unclear	2795 no cable
2673 enjoy game	2714 knock door	2755 an ugly whale	2796 new cop show
2674 no joker	2715 in kettle	2756 English	2797 hang back
2675 unshackle	2716 Yankee Dutch	2757 an ugly guy	2798 now keep off
2676 enjoy couch	2717 naked guy	2758 no glove	2799 young baby
2677 nacho - Coke	2718 knock it off	2759 unclip	2800 new faces
2678 no shakeoff	2719 hang it up	2760 engages	2801 invest
2679 in a shake up	2720 nick nose	2761 ink jet	2802 naive son
2680 new chefs	2721 knock on wood	2762 yank chain	2803 envies them
2681 enjoy food	2722 hang on now	2763 young chum	2804 no officer
2682 unshaven	2723 nickname	2764 hung jury	2805 Navy Seal
2683 enjoy fame	2724 young winner	2765 yank the shell	2806 on/off switch
2684 inch fire	2725 in the canal	2766 young Judge	2807 envies the guy
2685 Nashville	2726 new gun show	2767 young jockey	2808 new face-off
2686 one huge fish	2727 honking	2768 young chef	2809 Navy soap
2687 I knew JFK	2728 yank on/off	2769 no ketchup	2810 new videos
2688 inch half off	2729 young'in boy	2770 no egg yokes	2811 invaded
2689 inch half up	2730 win games	2771 now kick it	2812 invite in
2690 no chips	2731 weighing meat	2772 young again	2813 invade home
2691 on huge boat	2732 young man	2773 no cake Ma	2814 no food here
2692 in Japan	2733 weighing Mom	2774 new kicker	2815 knife dull
2693 inch by him	2734 weighing more	2775 young gal	2816 navy dish
2694 inch by her	2735 weighing mail	2776 young coach	2817 invade guy
2695 in a chapel	2736 weighing much	2777 yank cookie	2818 unfit wife
2696 enjoy beach	2737 yank mug	2778 yank coffee	2819 navy top
2697 inch back	2738 knock him off	2779 no cake, pie	2820 no finesse
2698 inch above	2739 knock him up	2780 young face	2821 invent
2699 enjoy the baby	2740 new cars	2781 Yankee food	2822 unfunny hen
2700 no guesses	2741 new grad	2782 yank phone	2823 uneven hem

255

Directory

2824 uneven hair	2865 unofficial	2906 unhappy switch	2947 wine break
2825 no vinyl	2866 naive judge	2907 knapsack	2948 NBA ref
2826 unfinish	2867 new fish egg	2908 now pass off	2949 no bribe
2827 knifing	2868 Navaho Chief	2909 no pass up	2950 no apples
2828 on/off, on/off	2869 Navy ship	2910 no pets	2951 an apple a day
2829 now phone up	2870 no fakes	2911 unpadded	2952 no plane
2830 infamous	2871 navigate	2912 unbutton	2953 no blame
2831 knife the meat	2872 knife, gun	2913 nap time	2954 unhappy lawyer
2832 Navaho man	2873 Navy game	2914 no butter	2955 nip lily
2833 Navy Mom	2874 no figure	2915 wine bottle	2956 no bleach
2834 Navy hammer	2875 naïve gal	2916 unpaid wage	2957 unplug
2835 no heavy mail	2876 Navy coach	2917 nip/tuck	2958 now I believe
2836 Navaho match	2877 knife - cake	2918 now pay it off	2959 an apple pie
2837 Navy mug	2878 on/off coffee	2919 now pay it up	2960 in the bushes
2838 Navy movie	2879 Navaho cup	2920 no pens	2961 NBA shot
2839 Navy map	2880 Navaho face	2921 one pint	2962 no passion
2840 universe	2881 Navy food	2922 no opinion	2963 unhappy chum
2841 on Friday	2882 navy van	2923 unhappy gnome	2964 unhappy jury
2842 no frown	2883 in heavy foam	2924 wine opener	2965 one bushel
2843 uniform	2884 no fever	2925 on a bony heel	2966 unhappy Judge
2844 no fire here	2885 in heavy foil	2926 Hawaiian Punch	2967 knobby jug
2845 unfurl	2886 knife a fish	2927 new bank	2968 no push off
2846 unfresh	2887 in heavy fog	2928 NBA, Navy	2969 one push up
2847 no frog	2888 on/off, off, off	2929 nap, nap	2970 unpacks
2848 on heavy roof	2889 Navy VP	2930 no bombs	2971 in a bucket
2849 Navy rope	2890 no fibs	2931 unhappy maid	2972 napkin
2850 no flies	2891 Navy boat	2932 unhappy man	2973 NBA game
2851 inflate	2892 navy pen	2933 NBA Mom	2974 no poker
2852 win a violin	2893 on heavy bomb	2934 unhappy Mayor	2975 unbuckle
2853 no volume	2894 no vapor	2935 unhappy male	2976 unhappy coach
2854 no valor	2895 navy blue	2936 nap much	2977 nab a cake
2855 now fly all	2896 an ivy patch	2937 nap - hammock	2978 win bake-off
2856 no flesh	2897 navy pack	2938 NBA move	2979 now bake pie
2857 no flack	2898 on/off above	2939 no bump	2980 unhappy face
2858 no fluff	2899 naive puppy	2940 neighbors	2981 honeybee food
2859 envelope	2900 no passes	2941 neighborhood	2982 NBA fan
2860 no fishes	2901 no pest	2942 NBA arena	2983 NBA fame
2861 Navy jet	2902 no poison	2943 own a broom	2984 a nap for you
2862 invasion	2903 win a possum	2944 no barrier	2985 Napa Valley
2863 Navaho chum	2904 now busier	2945 neighborly	2986 unhappy fish
2864 in heavy chair	2905 new puzzle	2946 no brush	2987 no beef, guy

256

Directory

2988 nap half off	3029 messin' up	3070 miscues	3111 meditate
2989 unhappy FBI	3030 museums	3071 mosquito	3112 midtown
2990 no babies	3031 mass media	3072 miss again	3113 made it home
2991 nip body	3032 messy woman	3073 miss game	3114 matador
2992 unhappy pony	3033 I miss Mom	3074 mascara	3115 made it well
2993 nip poem	3034 messy Mayor	3075 musical	3116 mad dash
2994 no paper	3035 miss a meal	3076 music show	3117 mad dog
2995 new Bible	3036 mismatch	3077 messy cake	3118 mute TV
2996 nip bush	3037 may I smoke	3078 mask off	3119 made it up
2997 nip book	3038 museum fee	3079 music boy	3120 mittens
2998 nip above	3039 I'm so mopey	3080 messy face	3121 midnight
2999 nap baby	3040 miseries	3081 messy feet	3122 mitten on
3000 misses us	3041 misread	3082 messy van	3123 made a name
3001 misused	3042 miss the rain	3083 I miss fame	3124 hometown hero
3002 Miss USA won	3043 messy room	3084 misfire	3125 my toenail
3003 misses him	3044 mess her hair	3085 misfile	3126 muddy nacho
3004 I'm so sorry	3045 my cereal	3086 miss voyage	3127 mating
3005 misses wheel	3046 I'm so rich	3087 massive ache	3128 muddy knife
3006 misses a shoe	3047 messy work	3088 massive wave	3129 mitten boy
3007 I'm so sick	3048 messy roof	3089 massive boy	3130 Mighty Mouse
3008 I'm so safe	3049 my syrup	3090 mishaps	3131 medium height
3009 Mississippi	3050 missiles	3091 mouse pad	3132 madman
3010 moist eyes	3051 mistletoe	3092 messy pony	3133 meet Mom
3011 misty-eyed	3052 I'm so alone	3093 messy bum	3134 medium hair
3012 messy den	3053 mausoleum	3094 I'm super	3135 medium well
3013 I missed him	3054 I'm slower	3095 mass appeal	3136 medium age
3014 hamster	3055 muzzle well	3096 messy beach	3137 muddy mug
3015 messy doll	3056 I'm a slouch	3097 messy book	3138 meet my wife
3016 mustache	3057 I'm slack	3098 misbehave	3139 muddy map
3017 mystic	3058 myself	3099 messy baby	3140 mattress
3018 my staff	3059 I'm a slob	3100 my disease	3141 maitre d'
3019 messed up	3060 massages	3101 midwest	3142 my train
3020 messy nose	3061 miss shot	3102 medicine	3143 humdrum
3021 Amazon heat	3062 homes join	3103 meets him	3144 motor here
3022 mess no one	3063 massage me	3104 meets her	3145 motor oil
3023 missin' him	3064 massage her	3105 muddy soil	3146 my trash
3024 missin' her	3065 massage oil	3106 made a switch	3147 Amtrak
3025 I'm senile	3066 massage show	3107 I'm too sick	3148 midriff
3026 I'm a snitch	3067 massage wig	3108 met his wife	3149 home tribe
3027 missing	3068 mischief	3109 muddy soup	3150 motels
3028 messy knife	3069 messy job	3110 muddy toes	3151 meddled

Directory

3152 medallion	3193 may I tip him	3234 many more	3275 mink oil
3153 Ma, tell me	3194 may I tip her	3235 main meal	3276 mean coach
3154 I'm taller	3195 mud pile	3236 mean match	3277 maniac guy
3155 metal wheel	3196 I'm at beach	3237 money mug	3278 monkey off
3156 metal watch	3197 mudpack	3238 mean move	3279 monkey boy
3157 motel key	3198 meaty - beefy	3239 men may buy	3280 mean face
3158 made you laugh	3199 meet the baby	3240 minors	3281 many wed
3159 metal hip	3200 a mean sis	3241 human heart	3282 minivan
3160 muddy shoes	3201 Minnesota	3242 man ran	3283 money, fame
3161 he might shed	3202 monsoon	3243 main room	3284 maneuver
3162 I might join	3203 mini swim	3244 I'm in error	3285 many fail
3163 Ma, teach me	3204 menswear	3245 monorail	3286 mean fish
3164 I'm a teacher	3205 mean seal	3246 money rich	3287 my Navy guy
3165 muddy jail	3206 men's watch	3247 monarch	3288 many have wife
3166 mad judge	3207 women's wig	3248 I'm on roof	3289 man half boy
3167 muddy check	3208 man's wife	3249 minor boy	3290 Moon Pies
3168 mad chef	3209 mine sweep	3250 manuals	3291 money pit
3169 I might shop	3210 mints	3251 moon light	3292 mean pony
3170 medics	3211 mandate	3252 mean lion	3293 moonbeam
3171 my ticket	3212 mountain	3253 I'm on a limb	3294 manpower
3172 muddy gun	3213 menu item	3254 mean lawyer	3295 monopoly
3173 muddy game	3214 monitor	3255 men will lie	3296 I'm on beach
3174 Medicare	3215 mantel	3256 monthly wage	3297 money bag
3175 medical	3216 main dish	3257 monologue	3298 men behave
3176 met the coach	3217 mean dog	3258 woman I love	3299 my own baby
3177 made a cake	3218 minute off	3259 monthly pay	3300 I'm a misses
3178 made coffee	3219 Manitoba	3260 munchies	3301 Miami's hot
3179 muddy cape	3220 mean, nosy	3261 munch out	3302 Mom's a honey
3180 motives	3221 manhunt	3262 mansion	3303 Mom's home
3181 made a video	3222 mean Nun	3263 manage him	3304 Mom's here
3182 muddy van	3223 mean name	3264 manager	3305 Mom's well
3183 made fame	3224 mean owner	3265 manage well	3306 Moms age
3184 metaphor	3225 women only	3266 mean judge	3307 Mom's weak
3185 medieval	3226 money in shoe	3267 money choke	3308 Mom is a wife
3186 MTV show	3227 mining	3268 mean shove	3309 Mama's boy
3187 I'm tough guy	3228 man 'n wife	3269 man the ship	3310 my mates
3188 meat, half off	3229 men nap	3270 monkeys	3311 I'm mad at you
3189 muddy VP	3230 Minnie Mouse	3271 mean cat	3312 my hometown
3190 mud pies	3231 woman I met	3272 my own gun	3313 Mom ate ham
3191 made a bet	3232 man / woman	3273 money game	3314 Mommy dear
3192 meaty - bony	3233 mean Mom	3274 manicure	3315 Muhammad Ali

Directory

3316 Mom hid wash	3357 Yum! milk	3398 Mom, behave	3439 humor me up
3317 Miami dog	3358 Mom, love u	3399 Miami baby	3440 more rosy
3318 Mom ate half	3359 Mom, help	3400 my roses	3441 Mayor rode
3319 homemade pie	3360 Miami chase	3401 Mayor's aide	3442 more rain
3320 Mom knows	3361 Mom should	3402 I'm your son	3443 more room
3321 Miami night	3362 my machine	3403 hammers me	3444 hammer rear
3322 my man won	3363 Miami gym	3404 my rosy hair	3445 hammer rail
3323 Mom knew him	3364 Miami shore	3405 morsel	3446 more rich
3324 Miami owner	3365 Miami jail	3406 my horseshoe	3447 hammer rock
3325 Mom knew all	3366 Miami judge	3407 more sick	3448 marry her off
3326 Mom, enjoy	3367 mom shook	3408 marry his wife	3449 hammer, rub
3327 I'm humming	3368 Miami chef	3409 more soap	3450 morals
3328 mummy in half	3369 Miami job	3410 merits	3451 my world
3329 Mom, nap	3370 my mugs	3411 marry today	3452 marlin
3330 Mom messy	3371 Miami cat	3412 martini	3453 more lamb
3331 Mom, may I eat	3372 Mom again	3413 maritime	3454 mere lower
3332 Miami moon	3373 Miami game	3414 murder	3455 moral law
3333 Mom, Mom	3374 homemaker	3415 marital	3456 ham, relish
3334 Mom, more	3375 Miami gal	3416 ham, radish	3457 merrily go
3335 my home meal	3376 Miami coach	3417 married guy	3458 humor, laugh
3336 my home match	3377 Mom, a cook	3418 mortify	3459 more lip
3337 Mom, may I go	3378 mummy cave	3419 married boy	3460 marches
3338 Mom, move	3379 Miami cop	3420 marathons	3461 merged
3339 Miami map	3380 home movies	3421 marinate	3462 martian
3340 memories	3381 Miami food	3422 my reunion	3463 march him
3341 Mom read	3382 may I move in	3423 more numb	3464 merger
3342 my homerun	3383 Miami fame	3424 mariner	3465 marshall
3343 Miami room	3384 Miami fire	3425 hammer nail	3466 humor Judge
3344 my mirror	3385 Mom flew	3426 maroon shoe	3467 march, walk
3345 memorial	3386 Miami fish	3427 hammering	3468 marriage off
3346 memory wish	3387 Miami fog	3428 hammer knife	3469 march by
3347 my mark	3388 Mom half off	3429 may I run by	3470 marks
3348 Miami rough	3389 Miami VIP	3430 homerooms	3471 market
3349 hem may rip	3390 Mom buys	3431 mermaid	3472 American
3350 mammals	3391 memo pad	3432 Mormon	3473 more gum
3351 Mom will eat	3392 me, my, pony	3433 me or Mom	3474 marker
3352 my melon	3393 Miami bum	3434 murmur	3475 miracle
3353 Mom will hum	3394 member	3435 more mail	3476 mortgage
3354 Miami lawyer	3395 mumble	3436 I'm your match	3477 more cake
3355 Mom will yell	3396 Miami Beach	3437 my remake	3478 mark off
3356 Mom will age	3397 my hymn book	3438 home or movie	3479 mark up

259

Directory

3480 merry voice	3521 melon head	3562 Malaysian	3603 matches him
3481 more food	3522 I'm alone now	3563 may I lash him	3604 matches her
3482 morphine	3523 millennium	3564 a mile shore	3605 my chisel
3483 more fame	3524 millionaire	3565 mail Jello	3606 matches shoe
3484 more fury	3525 I'm lonely	3566 a male judge	3607 match sock
3485 marvel	3526 melon wash	3567 mail check	3608 match is off
3486 more fudge	3527 mailing	3568 a male chef	3609 match is up
3487 more fog	3528 melon half	3569 a mail job	3610 matched his
3488 hammer off half	3529 melon pie	3570 milks	3611 I'm shut out
3489 hammer half up	3530 I'm all messy	3571 milk it	3612 I'm shut in
3490 hem rips	3531 malamute	3572 mulligan	3613 may I shoot him
3491 I'm your buddy	3532 mailman	3573 mail gum	3614 my ashtray
3492 my ribbon	3533 mail my ham	3574 mall walker	3615 my huge deal
3493 hammer by him	3534 a mile more	3575 mail call	3616 mash dish
3494 home robber	3535 mail my will	3576 mail cash	3617 my huge deck
3495 marble	3536 mail my shoe	3577 milk cow	3618 much TV
3496 I'm rubbish	3537 mail my wig	3578 mail coffee	3619 match it up
3497 humor book	3538 home will move	3579 mail a cap	3620 machines
3498 more above	3539 home lamp	3580 male voice	3621 my chant
3499 I'm your baby	3540 molars	3581 mail food	3622 may I join in
3500 molasses	3541 mail route	3582 I'm leavin'	3623 match name
3501 I'm lost	3542 mail run	3583 my, I love him	3624 machinery
3502 I'm loose now	3543 mailroom	3584 mull over	3625 emotional
3503 mauls him	3544 mail her hair	3585 I'm lovely	3626 my change
3504 mail is here	3545 mail her heel	3586 a male fish	3627 matching
3505 meal is well	3546 mail her shoe	3587 mail fog	3628 my huge knife
3506 meal is chewy	3547 mail her wig	3588 mail off wife	3629 machine boy
3507 meal is OK	3548 mail her off	3589 mail the VP	3630 mash thumbs
3508 mail is off	3549 mail robe	3590 mail bus	3631 much meat
3509 mail swap	3550 a mile less	3591 mill about	3632 much money
3510 melodies	3551 mail wallet	3592 mall open	3633 mash my thumb
3511 melted	3552 mail a lion	3593 mail bomb	3634 match my hair
3512 mail it in	3553 meal, lamb	3594 male bear	3635 much mail
3513 melt me	3554 a mile lower	3595 mail bill	3636 match my shoe
3514 mild weather	3555 homely lily	3596 Malibu show	3637 match my wig
3515 melt hill	3556 mail eyelash	3597 mailbag	3638 match my half
3516 melt shoe	3557 homely look	3598 Malibu wave	3639 my shampoo
3517 mile to go	3558 my loyal wife	3599 mail pipe	3640 measures
3518 mild wave	3559 a mile loop	3600 my choices	3641 measured
3519 I'm laid up	3560 mail cheese	3601 majesty	3642 my journey
3520 melons	3561 may I lash out	3602 match is on	3643 mushroom

Directory

3644 match your hair	3685 my shovel	3726 I'm gun-shy	3767 make a check
3645 major wheel	3686 match fish	3727 mechanic	3768 mug a chef
3646 my church	3687 much foggy	3728 magnify	3769 make cheap
3647 I'm a jerk	3688 may I shove off	3729 my canopy	3770 make the case
3648 my sheriff	3689 match FBI	3730 make a mess	3771 make a kite
3649 my cherry pie	3690 my jobs	3731 make my day	3772 make again
3650 much loss	3691 my huge boat	3732 make money	3773 make a comb
3651 my child	3692 home Japan	3733 mug Mom	3774 make cry
3652 much alone	3693 mash palm	3734 my camera	3775 make a call
3653 much lamb	3694 mash the bear	3735 my camel	3776 make a catch
3654 much lower	3695 match play	3736 make me age	3777 make cocoa
3655 my shallow well	3696 mash peach	3737 make me go	3778 make coffee
3656 my jail wish	3697 match book	3738 make a move	3779 make a cup
3657 my jail walk	3698 mash beehive	3739 home camp	3780 make a face
3658 much love	3699 my huge baby	3740 I'm crazy	3781 make a video
3659 much lip	3700 makes ice	3741 migrate	3782 megaphone
3660 much cheese	3701 my guest	3742 macaroni	3783 make fame
3661 I may judge it	3702 magazine	3743 macramé	3784 makeover
3662 magician	3703 makes a home	3744 my career	3785 my gavel
3663 much shame	3704 makes war	3745 my girl	3786 make fudge
3664 match chair	3705 my castle	3746 my garage	3787 muggy, foggy
3665 much Jello	3706 makes a show	3747 make her walk	3788 make wife wave
3666 match judge	3707 Mexico	3748 microwave	3789 make wife hope
3667 match check	3708 makes off	3749 I'm crabby	3790 make a pass
3668 match chef	3709 makes up	3750 my clothes	3791 may I keep it
3669 my huge ship	3710 maggots	3751 I'm cold	3792 my cabin
3670 much gas	3711 I'm a cadet	3752 I'm clean	3793 make bomb
3671 my jacket	3712 my kitten	3753 my claim	3794 I'm a keeper
3672 Michigan	3713 make it home	3754 my glory	3795 make a pile
3673 match game	3714 my guitar	3755 my ukulele	3796 make a patch
3674 I'm shakier	3715 make it well	3756 my cliche	3797 make a buck
3675 me juggle	3716 make it chewy	3757 my clock	3798 Ma, keep off
3676 magic show	3717 make it walk	3758 my glove	3799 I'm OK, baby
3677 much cocoa	3718 make it wave	3759 home club	3800 my voices
3678 much coffee	3719 make it up	3760 make a choice	3801 movie set
3679 I'm shook up	3720 my guns	3761 mug shot	3802 movie son
3680 match office	3721 magnet	3762 make a shine	3803 moves home
3681 much food	3722 mug a Nun	3763 make shame	3804 move sir
3682 much fun	3723 magnum	3764 make a chair	3805 moves wall
3683 much fame	3724 mug owner	3765 make Jello	3806 moves watch
3684 much fury	3725 magnolia	3766 mug a judge	3807 movie is OK

Directory

3808 move is off	3849 move her up	3890 move bus	3931 I'm bombed
3809 moves up	3850 muffles	3891 move bat	3932 map man
3810 my videos	3851 home field	3892 amphibian	3933 maybe Mom
3811 I'm faded	3852 my violin	3893 move by him	3934 me hip, merry
3812 move it now	3853 my flame	3894 move by her	3935 mopey male
3813 move it home	3854 Mayflower	3895 move ball	3936 mopey wish
3814 move door	3855 move the lily	3896 move bush	3937 maybe I'm ok
3815 movie deal	3856 my flesh	3897 move back	3938 maybe movie
3816 move dish	3857 my flag	3898 move above	3939 maybe, maybe
3817 move dog	3858 I'm fluffy	3899 move baby	3940 umpires
3818 move the TV	3859 muffle boy	3900 home bases	3941 import
3819 I'm fed up	3860 move shoes	3901 I'm a pest	3942 I'm a Brownie
3820 muffins	3861 move shed	3902 I'm busy now	3943 my broom
3821 move on it	3862 my ovation	3903 mops the home	3944 emperor
3822 move onion	3863 move Jim	3904 I'm busier	3945 umbrella
3823 move in home	3864 move chair	3905 maybe a sale	3946 my brush
3824 move in here	3865 move jail	3906 maybe switch	3947 hamburg
3825 my final	3866 move judge	3907 I'm a busy guy	3948 improve
3826 my funny shoe	3867 muff joke	3908 I'm passive	3949 I'm preppy
3827 moving	3868 move - shove	3909 maybe soup	3950 my pals
3828 muffin half	3869 move ship	3910 empty house	3951 home plate
3829 move on up	3870 move keys	3911 emptied	3952 maple honey
3830 move mouse	3871 move coat	3912 empty wine	3953 emblem
3831 move mitt	3872 move gun	3913 empty home	3954 mop lower
3832 move money	3873 move comb	3914 I'm better	3955 maybe I'll lie
3833 move Mom	3874 move car	3915 embattle	3956 maybe I'll show
3834 move my hair	3875 I'm fickle	3916 empty shoe	3957 maybe I'll go
3835 move the mail	3876 move couch	3917 mop deck	3958 maybe I'll wave
3836 move match	3877 movie kick	3918 I'm paid off	3959 maybe I'll buy
3837 move my wig	3878 my wife gave	3919 I'm paid up	3960 my beach house
3838 move him off	3879 move cup	3920 my bonus	3961 mop the shed
3839 move me up	3880 move vase	3921 homebound	3962 my passion
3840 home fries	3881 move foot	3922 Yum! banana	3963 mop gym
3841 I'm fired	3882 move van	3923 mop in home	3964 mopey jury
3842 my frown	3883 move off me	3924 I'm a pioneer	3965 maybe she will
3843 my farm	3884 move over	3925 map on wall	3966 maybe a Judge
3844 move her here	3885 move file	3926 homey bunch	3967 ambush guy
3845 I'm frail	3886 move the fish	3927 mopping	3968 mopey chef
3846 I'm fresh	3887 move fig	3928 maybe Navy	3969 mop the ship
3847 maverick	3888 move half off	3929 my pin up	3970 my bucks
3848 move her off	3889 move half up	3930 my poems	3971 my bucket

Directory

3972 ham bacon	4013 rest home	4054 wrestler	4095 Rose Bowl
3973 maybe a comb	4014 rooster	4055 wrestle well	4096 rosebush
3974 my big hair	4015 hairstyle	4056 you're a slouch	4097 horseback
3975 my buckle	4016 wristwatch	4057 you're slack	4098 rise above
3976 maybe coach	4017 we're stuck	4058 yourself	4099 hears baby
3977 maybe a cake	4018 raise the TV	4059 you're asleep	4100 red houses
3978 maybe coffee	4019 rest up	4060 horseshoes	4101 artist
3979 may I pack up	4020 raisins	4061 year is shot	4102 redesign
3980 mopey face	4021 Arizona heat	4062 rise / shine	4103 writes home
3981 map of Idaho	4022 resign now	4063 rosy, chummy	4104 rotisserie
3982 maybe Vienna	4023 reassign me	4064 raise chair	4105 yard sale
3983 maybe fame	4024 Arizona air	4065 wears shawl	4106 yard is huge
3984 map fire	4025 arsenal	4066 hires a judge	4107 red sock
3985 map file	4026 you're a snitch	4067 rosy cheek	4108 radio is off
3986 maybe fish	4027 rising	4068 where's chef	4109 ride subway
3987 maybe foggy	4028 raise a knife	4069 raise ship	4110 rodeo days
3988 maybe half off	4029 raisin pie	4070 rescues	4111 red toad
3989 maybe the VP	4030 resumes	4071 risk it	4112 red town
3990 mop the bus	4031 raise my head	4072 raise cane	4113 right time
3991 my baby wed	4032 raise money	4073 rescue me	4114 red door
3992 my baby won	4033 rosy Mom	4074 race car	4115 radio dial
3993 maybe a bomb	4034 raise a hammer	4075 recycle	4116 red dish
3994 my paper	4035 you're smelly	4076 raise cash	4117 heart attack
3995 my Bible	4036 raise my shoe	4077 rescue cow	4118 radio / TV
3996 mop beach	4037 you're smoky	4078 risky wife	4119 road top
3997 humpback	4038 rosy movie	4079 horoscope	4120 red nose
3998 mop above	4039 raise me up	4080 raise voice	4121 right-hand
3999 maybe baby	4040 razors	4081 raise feet	4122 red onion
4000 raises his eye	4041 resort	4082 you're so fun	4123 write name
4001 resist	4042 Rice-A-Roni	4083 receive a ham	4124 award winner
4002 raise a son	4043 rosy room	4084 receiver	4125 thru tunnel
4003 racism	4044 raise her hair	4085 horsefly	4126 rotten shoe
4004 rice, sir	4045 ears hear well	4086 receive wage	4127 writing
4005 hears so well	4046 research	4087 rosy fog	4128 written off
4006 raise switch	4047 rosy rug	4088 receive half	4129 radio knob
4007 you're so sick	4048 raise the roof	4089 raise the VP	4130 your dimes
4008 race is off	4049 our syrup	4090 recipes	4131 red meat
4009 raises up	4050 wrestles	4091 rosebud	4132 rude men
4010 rest easy	4051 result	4092 horse pen	4133 write Mom
4011 rusted	4052 hair salon	4093 air is balmy	4134 here tomorrow
4012 rest in	4053 wrestle him	4094 hair spray	4135 read mail

Directory

4136 right match	4177 red cookie	4218 rendezvous	4259 run, leap
4137 radio mic	4178 throat, cough	4219 roundup	4260 oranges
4138 write him off	4179 rodeo cowboy	4220 runny nose	4261 orange tea
4139 road map	4180 red face	4221 rainy night	4262 rain / shine
4140 writers	4181 red feet	4222 reunion on	4263 run the gym
4141 red heart	4182 red phone	4223 rain on me	4264 rain shower
4142 return	4183 award fame	4224 rain on her	4265 run the jail
4143 redo room	4184 red fire	4225 rain on all	4266 orange shoe
4144 road warrior	4185 rightful	4226 rain on shoe	4267 rain check
4145 rod / reel	4186 red fish	4227 running	4268 ranch wife
4146 road rage	4187 rude, havoc	4228 reunion off	4269 we're on ship
4147 yard work	4188 write half off	4229 run - nap	4270 rings
4148 rude, rough	4189 rose half up	4230 ruin my house	4271 raincoat
4149 ear drop	4190 rodeo pass	4231 run him out	4272 rain again
4150 rattles	4191 heartbeat	4232 Rain Man	4273 ring him
4151 red light	4192 red pen	4233 run Mom	4274 rain gear
4152 ride alone	4193 write poem	4234 rain more	4275 wrinkle
4153 redial him	4194 root beer	4235 run mail	4276 ring wash
4154 retailer	4195 red apple	4236 run the match	4277 ruin cake
4155 red lily	4196 red patch	4237 ruin my walk	4278 ruin coffee
4156 red leash	4197 read book	4238 run him off	4279 run cowboy
4157 right leg	4198 ride above	4239 rain maybe	4280 run the office
4158 hearty laugh	4199 rude baby	4240 runners	4281 ruin food
4159 red lip	4200 rinses	4241 run right	4282 we're in heaven
4160 radio shows	4201 runs out	4242 run run	4283 runny, foamy
4161 radish weed	4202 runs in	4243 our new room	4284 run far away
4162 radiation	4203 ransom	4244 run her here	4285 rainfall
4163 radish, ham	4204 rinse hair	4245 you're unreal	4286 run, fetch
4164 red cherry	4205 rinse well	4246 you're in reach	4287 rainy, foggy
4165 red Jello	4206 runs wash	4247 ruin rug	4288 run off wife
4166 rude judge	4207 ransack	4248 year in review	4289 run the FBI
4167 Radio Shack	4208 rinse off	4249 runner-up	4290 rainbows
4168 rude chef	4209 runs by	4250 run loose	4291 run by it
4169 red chip	4210 warrants	4251 run wild	4292 rain upon
4170 retakes	4211 rented	4252 run alone	4293 run by me
4171 red kite	4212 run-down	4253 our new limo	4294 runaway bear
4172 red wagon	4213 random	4254 run lower	4295 rain pail
4173 red comb	4214 reindeer	4255 here, Honolulu	4296 run the beach
4174 red car	4215 rental	4256 ruin leash	4297 run back
4175 radical	4216 round shoe	4257 run the league	4298 rain above
4176 rude coach	4217 run, eat, walk	4258 ruin love	4299 run puppy

Directory

4300 weary misses	4341 remarried	4382 remove wine	4423 hear your name
4301 you're misty	4342 ram ran	4383 remove him	4424 you're a runner
4302 hire me soon	4343 Army room	4384 warm over	4425 here or in hell
4303 hair museum	4344 hear me roar	4385 removal	4426 their ranch
4304 room is airy	4345 room with rail	4386 remove shoe	4427 roaring
4305 arm is well	4346 arm reach	4387 remove wig	4428 hear runoff
4306 hour massage	4347 room a rug	4388 remove ivy	4429 rear knob
4307 hear music	4348 room with roof	4389 remove hip	4430 war rooms
4308 room safe	4349 hear me rip	4390 ramps	4431 rare meat
4309 arms up	4350 arm loose	4391 armpit	4432 rare money
4310 remedies	4351 Army lad	4392 warm pen	4433 roar Mom
4311 hear my Dad	4352 room alone	4393 room by him	4434 our rumor
4312 her mitten	4353 warm lime	4394 warm beer	4435 rare meal
4313 you're medium	4354 Army lawyer	4395 rumble	4436 rare match
4314 warm water	4355 warm lily	4396 rampage	4437 rare make
4315 armadillo	4356 warm leash	4397 roam back	4438 horror movie
4316 warmed shoe	4357 arm, leg	4398 room above	4439 rare map
4317 arithmetic	4358 you're my love	4399 warm baby	4440 rewire ours
4318 hear my TV	4359 warm lip	4400 her roses	4441 rare art
4319 you're my type	4360 our matches	4401 rear seat	4442 roar rain
4320 romance	4361 room aged	4402 her reason	4443 our war room
4321 remount	4362 row machine	4403 roars home	4444 roar! roar!
4322 hear my union	4363 warm gym	4404 her razor	4445 hear her rule
4323 hear my name	4364 armchair	4405 rehearsal	4446 roar, reach
4324 Roman war	4365 warm chili	4406 rewire switch	4447 rare rug
4325 Roman wall	4366 warm judge	4407 air rescue	4448 hear our review
4326 warm nacho	4367 Army shack	4408 rear is off	4449 roar, rip
4327 harmonica	4368 Army chef	4409 rears up	4450 rare loss
4328 Army - Navy	4369 Army job	4410 your rights	4451 roar lady
4329 roman pie	4370 room keys	4411 rewrite it	4452 roar lion
4330 room messy	4371 Army cot	4412 your radio on	4453 our real home
4331 roommate	4372 Army gun	4413 rare dime	4454 hair roller
4332 Army man	4373 warm gum	4414 rear door	4455 rare lily
4333 hear my Mom	4374 Army car	4415 your rattle	4456 our relish
4334 her memory	4375 you're my gal	4416 our radish	4457 our relic
4335 Army mail	4376 Army coach	4417 rear deck	4458 our relief
4336 Army match	4377 rum cake	4418 hear your TV	4459 we're your help
4337 roomy mug	4378 warm coffee	4419 your radio up	4460 our riches
4338 warm movie	4379 warm cap	4420 reruns	4461 roar jet
4339 Army map	4380 warm face	4421 rear end	4462 our ration
4340 rumors	4381 removed	4422 a rerun on	4463 roar Jimmy

Directory

4464 you're richer	4505 really silly	4546 real rush	4587 roll fog
4465 rare shell	4506 rail switch	4547 real rocky	4588 roll wife off
4466 roar Judge	4507 really sick	4548 real rough	4589 roll halfway up
4467 roar - shake	4508 real safe	4549 roll hair up	4590 ear lobes
4468 hire our chef	4509 rolls up	4550 real loose	4591 rollaway bed
4469 rare ship	4510 relates	4551 real loud	4592 roll pen
4470 hairy rugs	4511 related	4552 real lion	4593 real bomb
4471 wore her coat	4512 roll down	4553 roll lime	4594 real bear
4472 hairy raccoon	4513 real dumb	4554 real lawyer	4595 whirlpool
4473 rework him	4514 realtor	4555 roll lily	4596 real peachy
4474 hear our choir	4515 worldly	4556 real eyelash	4597 rollback
4475 hear your call	4516 real touchy	4557 roll log	4598 real beef
4476 hear ricochet	4517 real dog	4558 real love	4599 real baby
4477 her Oreo cake	4518 worldview	4559 roll lip	4600 reaches house
4478 rare cough	4519 roll the tape	4560 relishes	4601 hairy chest
4479 wore her cape	4520 hairlines	4561 aerial shot	4602 reach the sun
4480 hear reviews	4521 real neat	4562 relation	4603 reaches me
4481 hear her feet	4522 a real nun	4563 real chum	4604 reaches her
4482 hear the raven	4523 real name	4564 roll the chair	4605 reaches all
4483 hear her fume	4524 row the liner	4565 real jail	4606 reach switch
4484 wore her fur	4525 you're lonely	4566 real judge	4607 reaches egg
4485 our raffle	4526 our lunch	4567 real check	4608 your age is off
4486 her raw fish	4527 reeling	4568 real chef	4609 reaches up
4487 rear fig	4528 real naive	4569 real cheap	4610 reach toes
4488 her ear half off	4529 early nap	4570 hairy legs	4611 rich Dad
4489 rewire FBI	4530 real messy	4571 roll a cat	4612 reached in
4490 her ribs	4531 real mad	4572 real gun	4613 reached him
4491 row your boat	4532 real man	4573 you're welcome	4614 reach door
4492 your ribbon	4533 really Mom	4574 roll the car	4615 roach hotel
4493 rewire bomb	4534 a reel mower	4575 roll call	4616 arched shoe
4494 roar bear	4535 early meal	4576 real cash	4617 rich Doc
4495 hear her bell	4536 hourly match	4577 roll cookie	4618 reach the TV
4496 our rubbish	4537 real muggy	4578 real coffee	4619 reached up
4497 rare book	4538 roll movie	4579 roll cup	4620 Russians
4498 rare beehive	4539 real mopey	4580 relieves	4621 rich aunt
4499 rare pipe	4540 rollers	4581 relieved	4622 rich nun
4500 releases	4541 railroad	4582 real funny	4623 arch enemy
4501 really sweet	4542 relearn	4583 real foamy	4624 rich owner
4502 real sunny	4543 real roomy	4584 reliever	4625 rational
4503 roll, swim	4544 real roar	4585 you're lovely	4626 your change
4504 real sore	4545 hourly, yearly	4586 roll fudge	4627 reaching

Directory

4628 arch knife	4669 rich chap	4710 rockets	4751 air quality
4629 rush on up	4670 Hershey Kiss	4711 wear coat / tie	4752 recline
4630 reach my house	4671 wear jacket	4712 rag town	4753 reclaim
4631 rich maid	4672 reach gun	4713 rag time	4754 regular
4632 rich man	4673 recheck him	4714 rocketeer	4755 wreck the lily
4633 rich Mom	4674 you're a joker	4715 rocket oil	4756 archeology
4634 Rushmore	4675 rich gal	4716 rocket watch	4757 rookie league
4635 rush meal	4676 rich coach	4717 rag tag	4758 rake leaf
4636 rush match	4677 rich cookie	4718 rock TV	4759 our club
4637 reach mug	4678 Irish coffee	4719 rocket up	4760 ricochets
4638 rush move	4679 wear huge cap	4720 raccoons	4761 ricocheted
4639 you're jumpy	4680 rich voice	4721 recount	4762 hear action
4640 rich horse	4681 rich food	4722 Reagan won	4763 rock gem
4641 orchard	4682 reach phone	4723 raccoon home	4764 rocky shore
4642 our journey	4683 reach fame	4724 rookie owner	4765 rock jail
4643 your germ	4684 hair shaver	4725 Erie Canal	4766 rookie judge
4644 richer war	4685 our shovel	4726 hurricane watch	4767 our cash cow
4645 richer oil	4686 reach fish	4727 rocking	4768 rookie chef
4646 our church	4687 reach fog	4728 rock the Navy	4769 workshop
4647 you're jerky	4688 reach heavy ivy	4729 year gone by	4770 earthquakes
4648 richer wife	4689 reach half up	4730 hairy combs	4771 earthquake hit
4649 our cherry pie	4690 rich boys	4731 hair - comb it	4772 rock wagon
4650 roach-less	4691 reach boat	4732 rake money	4773 work a game
4651 our child	4692 war with Japan	4733 rookie Mom	4774 wreck car
4652 rush alone	4693 rush by him	4734 wreck my hair	4775 hear gaggle
4653 reach limb	4694 Hershey bar	4735 hairy camel	4776 rookie coach
4654 rich lawyer	4695 reachable	4736 rocky match	4777 wreck cake
4655 reach lily	4696 reach beach	4737 rock hammock	4778 rocky cove
4656 reach leash	4697 reach back	4738 Rocky movie	4779 rookie cop
4657 rich league	4698 reach above	4739 our camp	4780 eerie caves
4658 rush love	4699 reach baby	4740 riggers	4781 wreck food
4659 reach lip	4700 your guesses	4741 required	4782 rock van
4660 hire judges	4701 request	4742 rocky run	4783 rock fame
4661 rush the shot	4702 rakes in	4743 rec room	4784 recover
4662 your huge chin	4703 wrecks home	4744 your career	4785 rock fell
4663 rich chum	4704 wrecks hair	4745 hairy gorilla	4786 rockfish
4664 reach the jury	4705 rakes well	4746 our garage	4787 rocky, foggy
4665 rechew chili	4706 rugs age	4747 rock her wig	4788 throw calf off
4666 rich judge	4707 rookies walk	4748 rocky roof	4789 here, I give up
4667 rich shake	4708 rocks heavy	4749 regroup	4790 rock bus
4668 rich chef	4709 racks up	4750 hourglass	4791 rock boat

Directory

4792 our cabin	4833 rough Mom	4874 refigure	4915 reptile
4793 Iraqi bomb	4834 rough hammer	4875 you're fickle	4916 robbed watch
4794 you're a keeper	4835 rough meal	4876 rough coach	4917 robotic
4795 rock pile	4836 rough match	4877 rough cookie	4918 rubbed off
4796 rocky beach	4837 rough mug	4878 rough cave	4919 wrapped up
4797 rock back	4838 review movie	4879 rough gap	4920 ribbons
4798 rake above	4839 revamp	4880 revives	4921 Robin Hood
4799 rock baby	4840 rivers	4881 revived	4922 wrap onion
4800 rough seas	4841 Harvard	4882 review oven	4923 rob enemy
4801 revisit	4842 refrain	4883 revive him	4924 hire a pioneer
4802 refasten	4843 reform	4884 revive her	4925 harpoon whale
4803 rough sum	4844 rough roar	4885 revival	4926 our bunch
4804 refuse her	4845 you're frail	4886 revive show	4927 wrapping
4805 refusal	4846 you're fresh	4887 rough fog	4928 wrap knife
4806 rough switch	4847 riverwalk	4888 revive wife	4929 ribbon boy
4807 roof is OK	4848 rave review	4889 revive boy	4930 wire bombs
4808 reviews wave	4849 rough rope	4890 review boys	4931 wrap meat
4809 revs up	4850 raffles	4891 rough bite	4932 wrap money
4810 rivets	4851 raffled	4892 review pony	4933 rob Mom
4811 riveted	4852 our violin	4893 review poem	4934 rob hammer
4812 rough town	4853 rough limb	4894 rough bear	4935 wrap meal
4813 rough time	4854 rough lawyer	4895 review play	4936 ruin my shoe
4814 rough water	4855 refill oil	4896 rough peach	4937 rip hammock
4815 rough hotel	4856 rough leash	4897 review book	4938 rip movie
4816 refit shoe	4857 our flag	4898 roof above	4939 air pump
4817 rough dog	4858 you're fluffy	4899 rough puppy	4940 wrappers
4818 rough TV	4859 rough lip	4900 rubs eyes	4941 airport
4819 rooftop	4860 refugees	4901 rhapsody	4942 airborne
4820 ravens	4861 throw fish out	4902 rubs in	4943 wire broom
4821 refund	4862 hear ovation	4903 rips me	4944 wire barrier
4822 rough Nun	4863 rough gym	4904 rubs her	4945 rubber wheel
4823 rough name	4864 rough chair	4905 wraps well	4946 hairbrush
4824 refinery	4865 we're official	4906 rubs watch	4947 air brake
4825 roof nail	4866 rough judge	4907 rubs wig	4948 reprove
4826 orphanage	4867 roof check	4908 rubs off	4949 rhubarb
4827 roofing	4868 rough chef	4909 rips up	4950 rubbles
4828 rough knife	4869 rough shape	4910 rabbits	4951 ear bled
4829 rough nap	4870 rough guys	4911 riptide	4952 airplane
4830 we're famous	4871 rough cat	4912 rebutton	4953 rebloom
4831 rough meat	4872 review again	4913 robbed home	4954 repay lawyer
4832 rough man	4873 our vacuum	4914 wrapped hair	4955 rebel yell

Directory

4956 re-polish	4997 rub back	5038 lays him off	5079 lazy cowboy
4957 wrap leg	4998 rip above	5039 lose map	5080 lose face
4958 our belief	4999 wrap baby	5040 lasers	5081 lose food
4959 rub lip	5000 loses us	5041 lacerate	5082 lose phone
4960 wrap cheese	5001 loses head	5042 less rain	5083 lose fame
4961 rubbish out	5002 lose sun	5043 less room	5084 less fur
4962 rub chin	5003 lose sum	5044 lose rear	5085 lose file
4963 rob huge home	5004 loses hair	5045 lose her will	5086 lose fish
4964 rapture	5005 loose soil	5046 laser show	5087 less fog
4965 wrap Jello	5006 loses shoe	5047 wheels rock	5088 lose half off
4966 robe / judge	5007 loses wig	5048 lose roof	5089 wills of hope
4967 rob shack	5008 yells safe	5049 lose rope	5090 loose pass
4968 rip the chef	5009 loses hope	5050 yellow sails	5091 low speed
4969 weary pushup	5010 lazy days	5051 lose wallet	5092 lose pen
4970 repacks	5011 lazy Dad	5052 lose alone	5093 loose bomb
4971 rebuked	5012 Yellowstone	5053 lose limb	5094 loose bear
4972 rob gun	5013 low sodium	5054 lazy lawyer	5095 oil spill
4973 rub comb	5014 wool sweater	5055 wheel slowly	5096 lazy beach
4974 rob car	5015 last will	5056 lose eyelash	5097 lays back
4975 rebuckle	5016 lost shoe	5057 lose leg	5098 less above
4976 rub cash	5017 elastic	5058 yellow sleeve	5099 lose puppy
4977 wrap cake	5018 lost wife	5059 loose lip	5100 lighthouses
4978 ruby cave	5019 lost hope	5060 less cheese	5101 lights out
4979 wrap cowboy	5020 loosens	5061 lose, cheat	5102 yield sign
4980 rub face	5021 loosen tie	5062 lose shine	5103 leads him
4981 rub feet	5022 listen in	5063 less shame	5104 leads her
4982 ripe vine	5023 loosen me	5064 lazy jury	5105 holiday hassle
4983 rope off home	5024 lazy owner	5065 lose shell	5106 light switch
4984 rub off hair	5025 loose nail	5066 lazy judge	5107 yellow desk
4985 we're hopeful	5026 loosen shoe	5067 lose check	5108 leads off
4986 rub fish	5027 leasing	5068 lazy chef	5109 lights up
4987 repave walkway	5028 loose Navy	5069 lose job	5110 lightweights
4988 rip off wife	5029 loosen up	5070 lose keys	5111 latitude
4989 rip off hobo	5030 loose moose	5071 lose cat	5112 lot to win
4990 our babies	5031 less meat	5072 loose gun	5113 lead it home
4991 rub bat	5032 lose money	5073 lose game	5114 light tower
4992 rip open	5033 lazy mummy	5074 lose car	5115 loud hotel
4993 rob bomb	5034 less / more	5075 Law School	5116 loaded wash
4994 our paper	5035 lose mail	5076 yellow squash	5117 old dog
4995 our Bible	5036 lose match	5077 lose cookie	5118 loud TV
4996 ripe peach	5037 L.A. smog	5078 less coffee	5119 loaded up

Directory

5120 loud noise	5161 loud jet	5202 leans in	5243 align room
5121 late night	5162 Yale tuition	5203 lonesome	5244 lion roar
5122 loud nun	5163 old gym	5204 lancer	5245 lean, roll
5123 old name	5164 loud cheer	5205 hollow nozzle	5246 low energy
5124 loud owner	5165 old jail	5206 lane switch	5247 loan rug
5125 hollow tunnel	5166 loud judge	5207 lion is weak	5248 line roof
5126 old niche	5167 late check	5208 leans off	5249 line her up
5127 oil tank	5168 hail to chief	5209 lines up	5250 lonely house
5128 light knife	5169 old job	5210 walnuts	5251 lonely day
5129 light nap	5170 hail taxi	5211 landed	5252 lonely one
5130 loud mouse	5171 loud cat	5212 London	5253 linoleum
5131 ultimate	5172 load gun	5213 alone at home	5254 lonelier
5132 old man	5173 late game	5214 laundry	5255 lonely eel
5133 loud Mom	5174 Law degree	5215 lion tail	5256 lonely shoe
5134 loud hammer	5175 late call	5216 lion dish	5257 lonely guy
5135 light meal	5176 loud coach	5217 lion attack	5258 lonely wife
5136 light match	5177 loud quake	5218 alone with TV	5259 lonely boy
5137 old mug	5178 light coffee	5219 line it up	5260 lunches
5138 old movie	5179 yellow tea cup	5220 linens	5261 lunch out
5139 old map	5180 loud wives	5221 Halloween night	5262 luncheon
5140 willow trees	5181 lead foot	5222 the lone nun	5263 launch him
5141 loud radio	5182 lot of honey	5223 lone enemy	5264 lunch hour
5142 loud rain	5183 Hollywood fame	5224 lone owner	5265 launch whale
5143 lit room	5184 wildfire	5225 well-known wall	5266 launch a shoe
5144 yellow terrier	5185 lot of yellow	5226 linen wash	5267 loan a check
5145 elderly	5186 light fudge	5227 leaning	5268 lunch off
5146 holiday rush	5187 light fog	5228 lone knife	5269 lone ship
5147 yellow truck	5188 light fife	5229 lion nap	5270 links
5148 low driveway	5189 lot of hope	5230 lion / mouse	5271 linked
5149 ladder up	5190 loud bus	5231 lean meat	5272 Lincoln
5150 ladles	5191 light bat	5232 loan money	5273 lone game
5151 yell outloud	5192 loud piano	5233 lean Mom	5274 lawn care
5152 loud lion	5193 loud boom	5234 lawn mower	5275 yell uncle
5153 little home	5194 wild boar	5235 a lone mile	5276 language
5154 little hair	5195 yellow table	5236 lone match	5277 long ago
5155 little hill	5196 old peach	5237 lion may go	5278 lion cave
5156 little shoe	5197 ladybug	5238 lion movie	5279 link-up
5157 lady luck	5198 loud above	5239 line me up	5280 yellow knives
5158 wildlife	5199 loud baby	5240 liners	5281 lion food
5159 little boy	5200 low noises	5241 lion heart	5282 loan phone
5160 yellow dishes	5201 lines out	5242 lion ran	5283 loan foam

Directory

5284 lion fur	5325 lemon oil	5366 lame judge	5407 yell rescue
5285 low on fuel	5326 lemon wash	5367 lime shake	5408 lowers ivy
5286 alone with fudge	5327 oily mink	5368 lame chef	5409 lower subway
5287 line off walkway	5328 lime knife	5369 lamb chop	5410 lords
5288 line halfway off	5329 lemon pie	5370 yellow mugs	5411 alerted
5289 line halfway up	5330 hail Moms	5371 we'll make out	5412 lower down
5290 lineups	5331 lamb meat	5372 lame gun	5413 alert him
5291 lean body	5332 lame man	5373 lime gum	5414 oily radar
5292 loan pen	5333 helium mummy	5374 lime car	5415 yellow rattle
5293 lone bum	5334 hollow memory	5375 lame call	5416 lower dish
5294 hello neighbor	5335 lame male	5376 lame coach	5417 lower deck
5295 line pool	5336 lame match	5377 lime cake	5418 lower the TV
5296 oil on beach	5337 lime mug	5378 lime coffee	5419 lower top
5297 lineback	5338 lame movie	5379 lime cup	5420 learns
5298 line above	5339 lame map	5380 lime office	5421 learned
5299 alone with baby	5340 all Mothers	5381 lame feet	5422 Law reunion
5300 hello misses	5341 limo ride	5382 lime phone	5423 learn math
5301 lime soda	5342 lime horn	5383 lame fame	5424 learner
5302 limousine	5343 lime room	5384 lime fur	5425 learn well
5303 Law museum	5344 lame roar	5385 limb fell	5426 holy ranch
5304 lime sour	5345 low morale	5386 lime fudge	5427 layering
5305 lambs wool	5346 all march	5387 lime fog	5428 lower knife
5306 oily massage	5347 limerick	5388 I'll move off	5429 lower knob
5307 lime is OK	5348 lime roof	5389 I'll move up	5430 yellow rooms
5308 limb is off	5349 lame rope	5390 lamps	5431 layer meat
5309 limb is up	5350 hilly malls	5391 limped	5432 Holy Roman
5310 limits	5351 limelight	5392 lima bean	5433 lower mummy
5311 limited	5352 yellow melon	5393 helium bomb	5434 lower hammer
5312 yellow mitten	5353 lime, lime	5394 lumber	5435 lower my wall
5313 lime dime	5354 lame lawyer	5395 lamp oil	5436 lower match
5314 lime door	5355 lime lily	5396 lumpy wash	5437 lower hammock
5315 William Tell	5356 lime leash	5397 Olympic	5438 lower my half
5316 lime dish	5357 whole milk	5398 limp off	5439 oily ramp
5317 lame duck	5358 lime leaf	5399 lame puppy	5440 lower / raise
5318 lame TV	5359 lime lip	5400 yellow roses	5441 lower road
5319 all made up	5360 yellow matches	5401 leather seat	5442 lawyer ran
5320 lemons	5361 lame shot	5402 lawyers win	5443 lower arm
5321 lemonade	5362 oily machine	5403 lures me	5444 lower rear
5322 lemon honey	5363 lime chime	5404 lowers hair	5445 lower rail
5323 aluminum	5364 lame jury	5405 lower sail	5446 lower her age
5324 lemon war	5365 lime shell	5406 lowers age	5447 layer rock

Directory

5448 lower roof	5489 lower the FBI	5530 hollow limbs	5571 well liked
5449 lower rope	5490 yellow robes	5531 loyal team	5572 I'll log on
5450 yellow rails	5491 yellow rabbit	5532 yellow lemon	5573 lowly game
5451 whole world	5492 yellow ribbon	5533 lay low Mom	5574 ale, liquor
5452 we'll roll in	5493 lower boom	5534 lay low Mayor	5575 Yale likely
5453 lower limb	5494 all rubber	5535 hail, hail mail	5576 lowly coach
5454 liar, liar	5495 lower pail	5536 we'll all match	5577 lollygag
5455 lower lily	5496 lower bush	5537 loyal mug	5578 lowly cave
5456 lower leash	5497 lower back	5538 we'll all move	5579 I'll lock up
5457 lower league	5498 holier above	5539 oil lamp	5580 yellow leaves
5458 yell relief	5499 lower baby	5540 all lawyers	5581 we all love it
5459 lower lip	5500 all losses	5541 loyal heart	5582 loyal fan
5460 leather shoes	5501 all lost	5542 you'll learn	5583 I'll love him
5461 Lear jet	5502 law lesson	5543 holy, holy rum	5584 I'll love her
5462 low region	5503 we'll lose him	5544 hello, hello roar	5585 yellow level
5463 large home	5504 all loose hair	5545 low heel, really	5586 lowly fish
5464 leather chair	5505 hole, lose wheel	5546 we'll all reach	5587 lowly fog
5465 largely	5506 you'll lose shoe	5547 oily, yellow rug	5588 I'll leave half
5466 large shoe	5507 lily is weak	5548 oily, yellow roof	5589 I'll leave pie
5467 allergic	5508 oil well is heavy	5549 oily, oily rope	5590 oily lips
5468 large wave	5509 oil well is up	5550 lily lace	5591 lily pad
5469 large hippo	5510 yellow wallets	5551 holy, holy lady	5592 lethal weapon
5470 lower case	5511 lay low today	5552 yell, yell lion	5593 I'll lap him
5471 hollow rocket	5512 oil Aladdin	5553 oily, oily, lamb	5594 yell, yell bear
5472 lower gun	5513 oily, oily dime	5554 lowly lawyer	5595 yellow label
5473 I'll work home	5514 yellow ladder	5555 lily lily	5596 we'll all push
5474 lower car	5515 well hello Dolly	5556 holy, holy leash	5597 I'll lay back
5475 we'll work well	5516 loyal teach	5557 oily, yellow log	5598 I'll lie above
5476 lower couch	5517 loyal dog	5558 lowly love	5599 lollypop
5477 layer cake	5518 all let off	5559 holy, holy leap	5600 lashes us
5478 lower cave	5519 we'll let up	5560 lowly choice	5601 lashes out
5479 I'll work up	5520 yellow lines	5561 lay low jet	5602 latches on
5480 lower voice	5521 holy land	5562 oil lotion	5603 lashes him
5481 lower foot	5522 yellow linen	5563 lowly gym	5604 leashes her
5482 lower van	5523 yell, yell name	5564 lowly jury	5605 I'll chisel
5483 lower the FM	5524 loyal owner	5565 lowly jail	5606 lashes wash
5484 lower fire	5525 all lonely	5566 lowly judge	5607 lashes wig
5485 lower file	5526 oily lunch	5567 lowly check	5608 lashes off
5486 lower fudge	5527 all yelling	5568 lowly chef	5609 lashes up
5487 lower fog	5528 loyal Navy	5569 lowly ship	5610 yellow jets
5488 I'll revive you	5529 all line up	5570 lowly case	5611 lashed out

Directory

5612 latched on
5613 latch the dome
5614 latch door
5615 lash tail
5616 lash, touch
5617 leash dog
5618 I'll show it off
5619 all showed up
5620 lotions
5621 legend
5622 leash a Nun
5623 lotion me
5624 lash owner
5625 lotion oil
5626 oil change
5627 whale watching
5628 I'll show knife
5629 latch knob
5630 leash a moose
5631 lush meadow
5632 lash men
5633 leash a mummy
5634 leash my hair
5635 leash mail
5636 lash mash
5637 latch mug
5638 I'll show movie
5639 oily shampoo
5640 yellow jersey
5641 yellow shirt
5642 L.A. journey
5643 yellow germ
5644 I'll shower her
5645 leash rail
5646 Holy Church
5647 latch rug
5648 latch roof
5649 latch rope
5650 yellow shells
5651 oily child
5652 latch line

5653 latch limb
5654 latch layer
5655 latch lily
5656 leash, leash
5657 latch leg
5658 latch love
5659 latch lip
5660 latch cheese
5661 latch jet
5662 latch chain
5663 latch chime
5664 latch chair
5665 latch shell
5666 lash judge
5667 latch check
5668 lash chef
5669 latch job
5670 latch keys
5671 yellow jacket
5672 I'll show gun
5673 I'll check him
5674 yellow shaker
5675 I'll juggle
5676 I'll show cash
5677 yell Chicago!
5678 latch coffee
5679 we'll check by
5680 latch office
5681 latch food
5682 latch van
5683 we'll shave him
5684 hail chauffeur
5685 yellow shovel
5686 latch fish
5687 latch the fog
5688 we'll shove off
5689 lash the FBI
5690 low jobs
5691 we'll ship it
5692 yell Japan!
5693 I'll show bomb

5694 ill shopper
5695 Holy chapel
5696 I'll chew peach
5697 lash back
5698 latch above
5699 leash puppy
5700 Law cases
5701 he likes it
5702 logs on
5703 locksmith
5704 I like his hair
5705 look silly
5706 likes watch
5707 look sick
5708 lock safe
5709 looks up
5710 yellow cats
5711 leg it out
5712 look down
5713 I liked him
5714 alligator
5715 I liked L.A.
5716 lucky dish
5717 locked key
5718 all get off
5719 hello / goodbye
5720 look nice
5721 leaky window
5722 low cannon
5723 leak name
5724 I like owner
5725 hollow canal
5726 look in wash
5727 logging
5728 look naive
5729 yellow canopy
5730 yellow combs
5731 look mad
5732 look mean
5733 look Mom
5734 look merry

5735 hail a camel
5736 I like my age
5737 leaky mug
5738 like movie
5739 lock him up
5740 lacrosse
5741 low grade
5742 Lake Huron
5743 luke warm
5744 Law career
5745 all girl
5746 licorice
5747 legwork
5748 leaky roof
5749 oily crab
5750 legalize
5751 legal aid
5752 all clean
5753 lay claim
5754 like a lawyer
5755 legal will
5756 legal age
5757 wall clock
5758 look alive
5759 lock lip
5760 look cheesy
5761 leaky shed
5762 election
5763 logjam
5764 lecture
5765 lock jail
5766 look, Judge
5767 look shaky
5768 I like the chef
5769 like a chip
5770 lock keys
5771 like a cat
5772 look again
5773 I'll kick him
5774 lock car
5775 lucky gal

273

Directory

5776 I like the coach	5817 love the dog	5858 love life	5899 love baby
5777 lick cake	5818 liftoff	5859 lovely pie	5900 hall passes
5778 I like coffee	5819 leave it be	5860 live shows	5901 leaps ahead
5779 like a cup	5820 love the noise	5861 live shot	5902 I'll buy soon
5780 lock office	5821 elephant	5862 wall of China	5903 I'll buy some
5781 like food	5822 love no one	5863 love the gym	5904 I'll pass her
5782 lock van	5823 love the name	5864 leave the jury	5905 whole puzzle
5783 like fame	5824 Leavenworth	5865 love Jello	5906 lips age
5784 like fur	5825 all vinyl	5866 love the judge	5907 we'll bask
5785 yellow gavel	5826 all finish	5867 leave a check	5908 I'll pass off
5786 lake fish	5827 loving	5868 love the chef	5909 hail busboy
5787 look foggy	5828 leave Navy	5869 leave a chip	5910 yellow beads
5788 we'll give half	5829 I'll have a nap	5870 leave keys	5911 oily potato
5789 I'll give up	5830 love my house	5871 love the kitty	5912 yellow button
5790 look busy	5831 love me too	5872 love again	5913 well bottom
5791 look bad	5832 love a woman	5873 leave game	5914 yellow butter
5792 yellow cabin	5833 love Mom	5874 love the car	5915 we'll battle
5793 like a bum	5834 leave more	5875 live gala	5916 I'll buy dish
5794 look happier	5835 leave mail	5876 leave cash	5917 lap to go
5795 likeable	5836 love match	5877 love cake	5918 leaped off
5796 look boyish	5837 love my wig	5878 love coffee	5919 laptop
5797 lock bike	5838 love the movie	5879 leave cab	5920 whale bones
5798 leak above	5839 leave map	5880 leave office	5921 yellow paint
5799 like a baby	5840 lovers	5881 love food	5922 yellow banana
5800 ill faces	5841 oily, fried	5882 leave phone	5923 help Naomi
5801 love seat	5842 love the rain	5883 hall of fame	5924 the ole pioneer
5802 loves on	5843 law firm	5884 love affair	5925 I'll buy a nail
5803 loves me	5844 love her hair	5885 lava flow	5926 I'll punish you
5804 loves her	5845 ill, frail	5886 live fish	5927 leaping
5805 loves all	5846 all fresh	5887 love fog	5928 I'll buy a knife
5806 leaves a shoe	5847 yell Africa	5888 leave off half	5929 wall pin-up
5807 lovesick	5848 leave her off	5889 life of hope	5930 all poems
5808 loves wife	5849 love her up	5890 leave bus	5931 help me out
5809 loves up	5850 levels	5891 alphabet	5932 help me win
5810 loved the house	5851 leaflet	5892 love piano	5933 help Mom
5811 love Dad	5852 lifeline	5893 live bomb	5934 I'll pay more
5812 leave town	5853 lovely home	5894 love a bear	5935 help me all
5813 we'll feed him	5854 lovely hair	5895 loveable	5936 help my show
5814 elevator	5855 lovely whale	5896 love the beach	5937 help me walk
5815 leave it all	5856 lovely age	5897 love back	5938 help my wife
5816 loved show	5857 yellow flag	5898 leave above	5939 help my boy

Directory

5940 oil price	5981 well behaved	6022 chosen one	6063 choose a gym
5941 leopard	5982 I'll buy phone	6023 chosen hymn	6064 she's cheery
5942 yellow, brown	5983 I'll buy fame	6024 huge snare	6065 she's jolly
5943 yellow broom	5984 I'll be fair	6025 huge snail	6066 shows judge
5944 library	5985 helpful	6026 choose a niche	6067 shows check
5945 liberal	5986 I'll buy fudge	6027 chasing	6068 she's a chef
5946 yellow brush	5987 help the fog	6028 washes knife	6069 she's chubby
5947 yellow brick	5988 leap of faith	6029 huge snap	6070 wash socks
5948 I'll prove you	5989 help the VP	6030 she swims	6071 chase cat
5949 loop rope	5990 hello Pops	6031 chase him out	6072 chose again
5950 labels	5991 help beat	6032 choose a man	6073 chews gum
5951 I'll be late	5992 I'll buy a pony	6033 choosy Mom	6074 chase car
5952 help line	5993 lip balm	6034 huge summer	6075 show a skill
5953 the whole plum	5994 wallpaper	6035 chews meal	6076 huge squash
5954 labeler	5995 Holy Bible	6036 watches match	6077 cheese cake
5955 label wall	5996 he'll be pushy	6037 show smog	6078 juice, coffee
5956 I'll blush	5997 I'll be back	6038 chose movie	6079 juice cup
5957 yellow black	5998 loop above	6039 huge swamp	6080 washes face
5958 label off	5999 help baby	6040 huge sores	6081 washes food
5959 label up	6000 chooses house	6041 chose a route	6082 chase van
5960 yellow pages	6001 chooses it	6042 chase rain	6083 chase fame
5961 we all pushed	6002 chase scene	6043 washes arm	6084 chose fur
5962 I'll buy China	6003 chooses me	6044 washes her hair	6085 she's full
5963 help the gym	6004 chooses her	6045 she's real	6086 she's fishy
5964 help the jury	6005 chooses well	6046 she's rich	6087 she's foggy
5965 whole bushel	6006 shows his age	6047 she's a wreck	6088 she's half off
5966 help the judge	6007 watches us go	6048 shows her off	6089 she's halfway up
5967 I'll buy a shake	6008 chases off	6049 shows her up	6090 chess piece
5968 we'll push off	6009 chooses up	6050 chisels	6091 she's beat
5969 we'll push up	6010 justice	6051 chiseled	6092 chews bone
5970 law books	6011 watch us Dad	6052 chose a loan	6093 chose a poem
5971 lab coat	6012 chase down	6053 chisel ham	6094 she's poor
5972 help - a gun	6013 just me	6054 she's slower	6095 chase ball
5973 I'll back him	6014 jester	6055 chew slowly	6096 she's pushy
5974 help / care	6015 chase tail	6056 she's all wishy	6097 she's back
5975 yellow buckle	6016 washes dish	6057 huge slug	6098 she's above you
5976 loop cash	6017 chase dog	6058 choose life	6099 chase puppy
5977 I'll be quick	6018 watches TV	6059 huge slip	6100 shoots us
5978 I'll back off	6019 juice it up	6060 chews cheese	6101 huge test
5979 we'll back up	6020 show signs	6061 she's shot	6102 jets in
5980 lip / voice	6021 washes window	6062 Jay's chin	6103 jets home

275

Directory

6104 shoots her	6145 huge trial	6186 chewed fish	6227 joining
6105 shot a seal	6146 huge trash	6187 showed fog	6228 join Navy
6106 shoot, swish	6147 sheet rock	6188 showed off wife	6229 shiny knob
6107 jet ski	6148 huge driveway	6189 chewed off pie	6230 Asian mouse
6108 jets off	6149 huge trap	6190 huge tips	6231 wage unmade
6109 shoots up	6150 shuttles	6191 shot put	6232 Asian woman
6110 she dates	6151 she told you	6192 shut / open	6233 Asian mummy
6111 she dieted	6152 shot lion	6193 shut up mouth	6234 shine my hair
6112 shot down	6153 shuttle me	6194 chewed berry	6235 chain mail
6113 cheated me	6154 shuttle her	6195 huge table	6236 join the match
6114 shut door	6155 shot oil well	6196 chewed up shoe	6237 shiny mug
6115 shoddy hotel	6156 chewed leash	6197 shot back	6238 shown movie
6116 chewed dish	6157 jet lag	6198 shout above	6239 Asian map
6117 shot dog	6158 chewed leaf	6199 shout baby	6240 shiners
6118 watched TV	6159 chewed lip	6200 Chinese house	6241 generate
6119 shot it up	6160 wash dishes	6201 Ash Wednesday	6242 ocean rain
6120 show tunes	6161 chit chat	6202 shines on	6243 Gin Rummy
6121 shut window	6162 huge tuition	6203 chains him	6244 shinier hair
6122 chewed onion	6163 she ate jam	6204 Chinese year	6245 General
6123 shout name	6164 huge teacher	6205 Chinese wall	6246 join her show
6124 chewed on hair	6165 judicial	6206 Chinese shoe	6247 generic
6125 huge tunnel	6166 shot judge	6207 Chinese guy	6248 shiny roof
6126 chewed on shoe	6167 should I jog	6208 Chinese wife	6249 shiny robe
6127 shouting	6168 shot chef	6209 shines up	6250 channels
6128 showed a knife	6169 huge touch up	6210 wash hands	6251 shine light
6129 chewed knob	6170 huge dogs	6211 chanted	6252 huge nylon
6130 chewed my ice	6171 shot a goat	6212 Chinatown	6253 chain limb
6131 chewed meat	6172 shotgun	6213 shiny dime	6254 Asian lawyer
6132 shot a man	6173 chewed gum	6214 ocean water	6255 wish - Honolulu
6133 showed Mom	6174 washed car	6215 China doll	6256 shiny leash
6134 huge timer	6175 huge tackle	6216 shiny dish	6257 join league
6135 chewed meal	6176 shot coach	6217 chain dog	6258 shiny leaf
6136 showed match	6177 chewed cookie	6218 shine TV	6259 shiny lip
6137 shot my hog	6178 should I cough	6219 shiny tub	6260 changes
6138 showed movie	6179 chewed cup	6220 shiny nose	6261 changed
6139 huge dump	6180 sheet of ice	6221 shiny window	6262 change wine
6140 shutters	6181 chewed food	6222 shine onion	6263 change him
6141 shattered	6182 shoddy oven	6223 shine name	6264 ginger
6142 shut her in	6183 showed fame	6224 Asian owner	6265 June - July
6143 showed room	6184 shout Fire	6225 genuinely	6266 change shoe
6144 showed rear	6185 jet fuel	6226 show an inch	6267 change wig

Directory

6268 change off	6309 jams up	6350 shameless	6391 jumped
6269 change up	6310 shammed us	6351 huge mold	6392 champion
6270 chunks	6311 jammed toe	6352 huge melon	6393 jump him
6271 junket	6312 huge mitten	6353 jam lamb	6394 chamber
6272 shine gun	6313 jammed thumb	6354 huge mailer	6395 jumble
6273 join game	6314 geometry	6355 jam oil well	6396 jumbo wash
6274 shiny car	6315 she may tell	6356 jam leash	6397 gym bag
6275 wishing well	6316 she may teach	6357 jam leg	6398 jump off
6276 junky show	6317 jammed key	6358 show me love	6399 jumbo pie
6277 shiny cake	6318 show me TV	6359 jam lip	6400 huge raises
6278 showing off	6319 jammed up	6360 huge matches	6401 shower is hot
6279 showing up	6320 jam nose	6361 she may cheat	6402 shower is on
6280 shiny face	6321 chewy mint	6362 age machine	6403 showers home
6281 Asian food	6322 jam onion	6363 shame, shame	6404 shower is here
6282 shiny van	6323 shame on me	6364 show my jury	6405 juries lie
6283 join the fame	6324 shame on her	6365 jam shell	6406 cherries age
6284 Asian fur	6325 jam nail	6366 jam choo-choo	6407 huge rescue
6285 watch the NFL	6326 huge munchy	6367 show magic	6408 shower is off
6286 Asian fish	6327 jamming	6368 show me a chef	6409 shores up
6287 Asian fog	6328 jam knife	6369 show me a job	6410 shirts
6288 shy Navy wife	6329 show man up	6370 jam keys	6411 shirt / tie
6289 she knew a fib	6330 jam mouse	6371 jam coat	6412 shorten
6290 chin-ups	6331 chummy maid	6372 jam gun	6413 short hem
6291 Asian beauty	6332 chummy man	6373 jam gum	6414 short hair
6292 shiny pen	6333 show my Mom	6374 wash my car	6415 short wall
6293 Asian poem	6334 jam hammer	6375 age my gal	6416 shortage
6294 chain bear	6335 jam mail	6376 jam couch	6417 shower dog
6295 shiny ball	6336 jam my shoe	6377 jam cake	6418 shirt off
6296 China beach	6337 show Mom, OK	6378 jam coffee	6419 cherry top
6297 June bug	6338 show my movie	6379 huge make-up	6420 journeys
6298 shine above	6339 show Mom up	6380 show my face	6421 journey ahead
6299 shiny baby	6340 watch Mars	6381 show me food	6422 journey on
6300 huge messes	6341 huge mart	6382 jam phone	6423 geranium
6301 jams it	6342 show me rain	6383 show me fame	6424 wage earner
6302 jams, honey	6343 chew my arm	6384 show me fire	6425 journal
6303 shames me	6344 huge mirror	6385 shameful	6426 huge orange
6304 she may swear	6345 huge mural	6386 show me fish	6427 cheering
6305 huge muzzle	6346 huge march	6387 show me fog	6428 huge run-off
6306 watch massage	6347 shamrock	6388 show movie off	6429 watch her nap
6307 huge mask	6348 jam roof	6389 show him VP	6430 germs
6308 shame is off	6349 jam rope	6390 champs	6431 shower mat

Directory

6432 Germany	6473 chew her gum	6514 shoulder	6555 shallow oil well
6433 sure Mom	6474 sure I care	6515 a child will	6556 chilly leash
6434 charmer	6475 cherry cola	6516 childish	6557 chilly leg
6435 huge airmail	6476 share couch	6517 chili dog	6558 shallow love
6436 jury may age	6477 Cherry Coke	6518 shield off	6559 chilly lip
6437 share hammock	6478 share coffee	6519 shield up	6560 chili cheese
6438 share movie	6479 shower cap	6520 show lines	6561 she'll shoot
6439 cheer me up	6480 share office	6521 chilly night	6562 shallow ocean
6440 huge roars	6481 sheriff wed	6522 huge linen	6563 she'll show him
6441 share the road	6482 share fun	6523 chill on him	6564 chilly shower
6442 show a rerun	6483 sure fame	6524 huge liner	6565 jolly, jolly
6443 share a room	6484 surefire	6525 shy, lonely	6566 jolly judge
6444 shower her hair	6485 cheerful	6526 challenge	6567 shell shock
6445 chair rail	6486 share fudge	6527 shelling	6568 jolly chef
6446 share her wash	6487 sheriff awoke	6528 jelly knife	6569 jolly chap
6447 chair, rug	6488 shower of faith	6529 huge line-up	6570 Shell gas
6448 share her age	6489 shower off boy	6530 chilly moose	6571 huge locket
6449 cheer her up	6490 cherry pies	6531 chili meat	6572 shall we go now
6450 Jerry Lewis	6491 chirped	6532 shallow man	6573 shell game
6451 Charlotte	6492 huge ribbon	6533 chilly mummy	6574 age the liquor
6452 shoreline	6493 cherry bomb	6534 chilly mare	6575 she'll kill you
6453 share a limb	6494 sharper	6535 chilly mall	6576 chilly couch
6454 share a lawyer	6495 share a ball	6536 chilly match	6577 chilly cocoa
6455 jury will yell	6496 share beach	6537 shallow mug	6578 chilly cave
6456 huge relish	6497 sharp wig	6538 shallow movie	6579 shallow cup
6457 chair leg	6498 sharp wife	6539 huge lamp	6580 shelves
6458 huge relief	6499 chirp up	6540 jailers	6581 jail food
6459 cherry lip	6500 shoelaces	6541 huge alert	6582 shallow oven
6460 churches	6501 wish list	6542 chilly rain	6583 shallow fame
6461 charged	6502 chill is on	6543 chilly room	6584 huge liver
6462 huge ration	6503 jails him	6544 chilly rear	6585 shy, lovely
6463 charge him	6504 chills her	6545 chilly rail	6586 jellyfish
6464 charger	6505 chilly seal	6546 she'll reach	6587 chilly, foggy
6465 church wall	6506 chili is chewy	6547 shell, rock	6588 she'll have half
6466 church show	6507 huge - Alaska	6548 chilly roof	6589 jolly VP
6467 church week	6508 chill is off	6549 cello, harp	6590 jail pass
6468 charge fee	6509 chili soup	6550 shallow wells	6591 she'll bite
6469 charge up	6510 shields	6551 shallow wallet	6592 chili bean
6470 jerks	6511 childhood	6552 shallow lawn	6593 she'll bomb
6471 shark tooth	6512 a child won	6553 chilly lamb	6594 chilly bear
6472 sure I can	6513 jail time	6554 jolly lawyer	6595 huge lapel

Directory

6596 shallow beach	6637 judge him, OK	6678 judge coffee	6719 shake it up
6597 she'll bug you	6638 judge movie	6679 huge checkup	6720 chickens
6598 she'll be off	6639 judge my pie	6680 judge office	6721 chew candy
6599 chilly puppy	6640 huge chairs	6681 judge food	6722 huge cannon
6600 judge's house	6641 wash shirt	6682 judge van	6723 check name
6601 judges it	6642 huge journey	6683 judge fame	6724 shock winner
6602 Judge is in	6643 huge germ	6684 huge, huge fire	6725 huge canal
6603 judges me	6644 judge her hair	6685 huge shovel	6726 huge gun show
6604 judges her	6645 judge her well	6686 judge fish	6727 shaking
6605 judges well	6646 huge church	6687 Jewish fig	6728 jackknife
6606 judges show	6647 huge shark	6688 show chef off	6729 jog on by
6607 judge is weak	6648 huge sheriff	6689 judge the FBI	6730 shake mouse
6608 judge is heavy	6649 huge chirp	6690 huge chaps	6731 checkmate
6609 judges boy	6650 huge shells	6691 she shopped	6732 check menu
6610 wash sheets	6651 Jewish lady	6692 show Japan	6733 shook Mom
6611 judged it	6652 judge a loan	6693 judge bomb	6734 jackhammer
6612 huge show tune	6653 judge a lamb	6694 huge chamber	6735 check mail
6613 judged him	6654 judge, lawyer	6695 huge chapel	6736 shake my shoe
6614 judged her	6655 judge a lily	6696 judge beach	6737 shake mug
6615 judged well	6656 show huge leash	6697 huge, huge bug	6738 check movie
6616 judged show	6657 huge, huge log	6698 judge above	6739 shook him up
6617 judge a dog	6658 huge shelf	6699 Jewish Pope	6740 checkers
6618 judged wife	6659 huge, huge lip	6700 shakes us	6741 checkered
6619 she chewed pie	6660 show judges	6701 checks out	6742 huge grin
6620 huge chains	6661 shy judge hid	6702 wage - casino	6743 chew crumb
6621 she joined	6662 judge chain	6703 checks him	6744 huge career
6622 Jewish nun	6663 Jewish gym	6704 checks hair	6745 showgirl
6623 Jewish name	6664 judge, jury	6705 shakes well	6746 huge crash
6624 judge winner	6665 huge, huge shell	6706 checks wash	6747 shag rug
6625 huge shiny wall	6666 Jewish judge	6707 jogs OK	6748 geography
6626 huge change	6667 judge joke	6708 checks off	6749 sugar pie
6627 judging	6668 Jewish chef	6709 checks up	6750 wash clothes
6628 judge Navy	6669 judgeship	6710 checked house	6751 chocolate
6629 huge shiny ape	6670 judge case	6711 checked out	6752 huge clown
6630 huge chimes	6671 judge a cat	6712 checked in	6753 huge clam
6631 judge my hat	6672 show huge gun	6713 checked me	6754 huge gallery
6632 Jewish man	6673 judge game	6714 shocked her	6755 juggle wheel
6633 Jewish Mom	6674 judge car	6715 shake it well	6756 huge clash
6634 judge more	6675 judge call	6716 checked wash	6757 shake a leg
6635 judge mail	6676 judge a coach	6717 shaggy dog	6758 huge glove
6636 judge match	6677 judge cake	6718 shake it off	6759 huge club

Directory

6760 chew cashews	6801 chef's hat	6842 chevron	6883 show off fame
6761 she coached	6802 chef is in	6843 huge farm	6884 show off fur
6762 ejection	6803 chef is home	6844 shave her hair	6885 shove file
6763 gee, cash them	6804 shaves hair	6845 shave her well	6886 show off fish
6764 huge catcher	6805 huge fossil	6846 shy, fresh	6887 shove the fog
6765 check jail	6806 chef's wage	6847 huge frog	6888 shave off half
6766 shock judge	6807 chef's wig	6848 shove her off	6889 shave half up
6767 shaky check	6808 shaves off	6849 shove her up	6890 chief pays
6768 shaky chef	6809 shoves by	6850 shovels	6891 shave body
6769 shaky job	6810 show videos	6851 shovel out	6892 shove piano
6770 huge cookies	6811 shifted	6852 huge violin	6893 shove bomb
6771 Chicago day	6812 chieftain	6853 huge flame	6894 shove bear
6772 chuck wagon	6813 shaved him	6854 huge failure	6895 shove ball
6773 Chicago home	6814 shaved hair	6855 shovel well	6896 shove peach
6774 Chicago hour	6815 chew off tail	6856 huge village	6897 shove back
6775 shake eagle	6816 shove dish	6857 shovel walk	6898 shave above
6776 shake coach	6817 shave dog	6858 shovel off	6899 shave the Pope
6777 shake, kick	6818 shaved off	6859 huge flop	6900 choppy seas
6778 check coffee	6819 shave top	6860 shave cheese	6901 cheap seat
6779 Chicago boy	6820 huge phones	6861 she fished	6902 chips in
6780 shock waves	6821 edge of night	6862 huge ovation	6903 chops ham
6781 shake feet	6822 shave onion	6863 show off gym	6904 chops hair
6782 check phone	6823 shove enemy	6864 shove jury	6905 chips wall
6783 shake fame	6824 shove owner	6865 show off jail	6906 job switch
6784 check fire	6825 watch the final	6866 show off Judge	6907 chops egg
6785 huge gavel	6826 show finish	6867 shave check	6908 chops off
6786 shake fish	6827 shaving	6868 chief, chief	6909 chops up
6787 check fog	6828 shove knife	6869 show off ship	6910 chop toes
6788 shake off half	6829 chew off knob	6870 shove keys	6911 chipped tooth
6789 check half up	6830 she fumes	6871 show off cat	6912 chipped in
6790 chickpeas	6831 shave my head	6872 shove gun	6913 chopped ham
6791 jackpot	6832 shave a man	6873 chew off game	6914 chapter
6792 cheekbone	6833 shave mummy	6874 Chevy car	6915 huge battle
6793 check palm	6834 shave my hair	6875 huge vehicle	6916 chip dish
6794 show keeper	6835 shove mail	6876 show off cash	6917 shop talk
6795 chew cable	6836 shave much	6877 shove cake	6918 chopped off
6796 huge cabbage	6837 shove my key	6878 show off cave	6919 chip tub
6797 check back	6838 shave my half	6879 show off cape	6920 Japanese
6798 check above	6839 shove my pie	6880 shave face	6921 job hunt
6799 check baby	6840 shavers	6881 shove food	6922 chop onion
6800 shaves us	6841 shave her head	6882 shove off now	6923 jab enemy

Directory

6924 show up owner	6965 huge bushel	7006 kisses shoe	7047 kiss her OK
6925 chop only	6966 chubby judge	7007 kisses egg	7048 hockey's rough
6926 huge punch	6967 cheap joke	7008 kisses wife	7049 egg, syrup
6927 shopping	6968 chubby chef	7009 kisses up	7050 castles
6928 chip knife	6969 shipshape	7010 guests	7051 go slide
6929 choppy nap	6970 shoe box	7011 custody	7052 gasoline
6930 huge bombs	6971 huge pocket	7012 keystone	7053 whack, slam
6931 chop meat	6972 shop again	7013 custom	7054 go slower
6932 cheap man	6973 cheap game	7014 kissed her	7055 go slowly
6933 shop Mom	6974 cheap car	7015 coastal	7056 castle show
6934 shop more	6975 huge buckle	7016 go stash	7057 gas log
6935 shop - mall	6976 cheap couch	7017 hockey stick	7058 goes all off
6936 job match	6977 chop cookie	7018 hockey stuff	7059 go asleep
6937 cheap mug	6978 cheap coffee	7019 coast by	7060 key switches
6938 cheap movie	6979 cheap cab	7020 casinos	7061 a guy is shot
6939 cheap map	6980 ship vase	7021 accent	7062 oxygen
6940 shoppers	6981 cheap food	7022 kiss no one	7063 whacks chum
6941 shepherd	6982 cheap fun	7023 kiss enemy	7064 hugs jury
6942 chaperone	6983 cheap fame	7024 eggs on hair	7065 hugs jelly
6943 cheap room	6984 job fair	7025 go snail	7066 hugs the judge
6944 huge barrier	6985 chop, fall	7026 go snitch	7067 walks shaky
6945 cheap reel	6986 chop fish	7027 kissing	7068 kiss the chef
6946 gibberish	6987 chop off wig	7028 Casanova	7069 goes choppy
6947 shipwreck	6988 chop off half	7029 weak snap	7070 kiss, kiss
6948 chop hair off	6989 chop off pie	7030 eggs messy	7071 cascade
6949 ship her up	6990 chop peas	7031 eggs made	7072 ex-con
6950 chapels	6991 cheap bat	7032 kiss a woman	7073 go sock him
6951 show blood	6992 cheap piano	7033 kiss Mom	7074 hockey score
6952 chaplain	6993 cheap bomb	7034 kiss more	7075 thick skull
6953 huge bloom	6994 chew paper	7035 weak smile	7076 egg squash
6954 shapely hair	6995 huge bubble	7036 kiss my shoe	7077 goes coo coo
6955 cheap, lowly	6996 chop up shoe	7037 go smoke	7078 hacks cough
6956 shoe polish	6997 cheap bike	7038 kiss my wife	7079 gas cap
6957 shopaholic	6998 shop above	7039 kiss me bye	7080 kiss face
6958 shapely wife	6999 cheap pipe	7040 kissers	7081 kiss feet
6959 chap lip	7000 excess	7041 kiss the road	7082 hockey is fun
6960 huge beaches	7001 exhaust	7042 kiss her now	7083 hockey's fame
6961 she pushed	7002 cases won	7043 case room	7084 eggs over
6962 show passion	7003 kisses him	7044 kiss her hair	7085 week is full
6963 cheap gym	7004 kisses her	7045 casserole	7086 kiss fish
6964 chubby jury	7005 excel	7046 kiss her shoe	7087 walks foggy

Directory

7088 goes half off	7129 kidnap	7170 walk dogs	7211 ignited
7089 goes half up	7130 cat meows	7171 kitty cat	7212 canteen
7090 gossips	7131 get mad	7172 octagon	7213 canned ham
7091 goes batty	7132 cat woman	7173 good game	7214 country
7092 go spin	7133 a good Mom	7174 good car	7215 candle
7093 goes by me	7134 egg timer	7175 cat call	7216 can't she
7094 Casper	7135 weak oatmeal	7176 good coach	7217 Kentucky
7095 gospel	7136 got a match	7177 good cake	7218 hug new TV
7096 Cosby Show	7137 academic	7178 good coffee	7219 wagon top
7097 goes back	7138 get me half	7179 good cup	7220 cannons
7098 goes above	7139 get a map	7180 cute face	7221 walk on net
7099 goes bye bye	7140 actress	7181 cat fight	7222 walk on onion
7100 cat's house	7141 catered	7182 get the phone	7223 walk on enemy
7101 good city	7142 coat worn	7183 get off me	7224 gain honor
7102 good son	7143 get a room	7184 cat fur	7225 walk on nail
7103 cat's meow	7144 caterer	7185 good / evil	7226 cannon show
7104 gets her	7145 go trolley	7186 got a fish	7227 gaining
7105 waggy tassel	7146 get rich	7187 get off walk	7228 awake on knife
7106 gets wish	7147 coat rack	7188 go dive off	7229 wake no one up
7107 get sick	7148 go drive	7189 get off, boy	7230 weak enemies
7108 go to sofa	7149 ego trip	7190 octopus	7231 gain a maid
7109 gets up	7150 kettles	7191 go to bat	7232 con man
7110 got dizzy	7151 go tell it	7192 good pen	7233 again Mom
7111 cut it out	7152 guideline	7193 get by him	7234 gain more
7112 good town	7153 walk to Lima	7194 go tip her	7235 walk in mall
7113 good time	7154 get a lawyer	7195 code blue	7236 walk in my shoe
7114 good tire	7155 walk to lily	7196 go to beach	7237 can / mug
7115 coattail	7156 good leash	7197 cut back	7238 walk-in movie
7116 cat dish	7157 catalog	7198 cut above	7239 cane my boy
7117 guide dog	7158 get a life	7199 get a puppy	7240 co-winners
7118 good TV	7159 godly boy	7200 Kansas	7241 I can read
7119 good tip	7160 goat cheese	7201 conceit	7242 I can run
7120 kittens	7161 good shot	7202 gain a son	7243 gun room
7121 goodnight	7162 quotation	7203 consume	7244 Cannery Row
7122 good onion	7163 good chum	7204 cancer	7245 walk on rail
7123 good name	7164 good chair	7205 counsel	7246 awake in rush
7124 good wiener	7165 good Jello	7206 wagon switch	7247 go New York
7125 cotton, wool	7166 good judge	7207 cans egg	7248 walk on roof
7126 good inch	7167 good check	7208 conceive	7249 walk on rope
7127 kidding	7168 good chef	7209 can soup	7250 canals
7128 cotton weave	7169 good job	7210 weekends	7251 kenneled

Directory

7252 go online
7253 kennel him
7254 a con, liar
7255 OK, Honolulu
7256 acknowledge
7257 canal walk
7258 gain love
7259 can I help
7260 quenches
7261 quenched
7262 ignition
7263 go in gym
7264 walk on chair
7265 walk on shell
7266 con a judge
7267 gun check
7268 gain a chef
7269 gun shop
7270 kings
7271 conked
7272 going on
7273 king me
7274 kangaroo
7275 going well
7276 wagon coach
7277 going OK
7278 going off
7279 going up
7280 canvass
7281 confetti
7282 confine
7283 walk on foam
7284 gunfire
7285 gainful
7286 awaken fish
7287 walk in fog
7288 again half off
7289 connive boy
7290 walk on bus
7291 walk in boot
7292 walk on piano

7293 canopy home
7294 awaken bear
7295 cannibal
7296 walk on beach
7297 gain back
7298 gun above
7299 awaken baby
7300 calm seas
7301 chemist
7302 hug my son
7303 comes home
7304 combs hair
7305 camisole
7306 OK message
7307 combs wig
7308 comes off
7309 comes up
7310 comedies
7311 committed
7312 comedian
7313 game time
7314 combed hair
7315 comb tail
7316 comedy show
7317 walk my dog
7318 whack my TV
7319 combed up
7320 commons
7321 community
7322 communion
7323 hack my name
7324 cow manure
7325 common law
7326 common show
7327 combing
7328 common wife
7329 common boy
7330 hug the Moms
7331 game mode
7332 hug my money
7333 hug my Mom

7334 comb my hair
7335 come home all
7336 game, match
7337 come home ok
7338 calm movie
7339 come home boy
7340 cameras
7341 comrade
7342 camera on
7343 calm room
7344 calmer weather
7345 calmer whale
7346 camera shy
7347 camera week
7348 camera off
7349 hog my robe
7350 camels
7351 calm lady
7352 hog my line
7353 camel home
7354 camel hair
7355 calm lily
7356 comb eyelash
7357 whack my leg
7358 a game I love
7359 calm lip
7360 game shows
7361 wig matched
7362 commotion
7363 calm gym
7364 calm jury
7365 game show law
7366 calm judge
7367 OK magic
7368 calm chef
7369 go match up
7370 comics
7371 comb cat
7372 come again
7373 calm, calm
7374 comic hour

7375 comical
7376 comic show
7377 gamecock
7378 comic wife
7379 comic boy
7380 game face
7381 OK, move it
7382 OK muffin
7383 go move him
7384 game for you
7385 OK, I'm full
7386 calm fish
7387 calm, foggy
7388 OK, move off
7389 OK, move up
7390 camps
7391 camp out
7392 company
7393 camp home
7394 camper
7395 gumball
7396 comb beach
7397 come back
7398 calm above
7399 calm baby
7400 caresses
7401 crest
7402 greasy hen
7403 greasy ham
7404 grocery
7405 carousel
7406 greasy shoe
7407 crazy week
7408 caress wife
7409 grows up
7410 crates
7411 greeted
7412 accordion
7413 greet him
7414 quarter
7415 Great Wall

Directory

7416 great age	7457 garlic	7498 crabby wife	7539 clump	
7417 critic	7458 cry wolf	7499 cry baby	7540 colors	
7418 gratify	7459 curl up	7500 glasses	7541 Colorado	
7419 great boy	7460 gorgeous	7501 closet	7542 chlorine	
7420 cranes	7461 crashed	7502 calls in	7543 wiggle room	
7421 crowned	7462 creation	7503 coliseum	7544 cooler weather	
7422 corn on the ...	7463 carry shame	7504 calls her	7545 killer whale	
7423 acronym	7464 creature	7505 colossal	7546 cooler wash	
7424 corner	7465 crucial	7506 glass shoe	7547 cooler week	
7425 green wall	7466 crash show	7507 classic	7548 clear off	
7426 greenish	7467 car check	7508 clothes off	7549 call her up	
7427 crying	7468 carry chef	7509 close by	7550 kill lice	
7428 green ivy	7469 crash up	7510 cleats	7551 cool lady	
7429 grown up	7470 crooks	7511 clotted	7552 goal line	
7430 crumbs	7471 cracked	7512 guillotine	7553 kill lamb	
7431 crammed	7472 carry gun	7513 equal time	7554 call lawyer	
7432 crewman	7473 crack him	7514 cold weather	7555 kill a lily	
7433 carry me home	7474 cracker	7515 cold ale	7556 cool leash	
7434 creamer	7475 crackle	7516 gold watch	7557 cool leg	
7435 crummy law	7476 Greek show	7517 cold week	7558 kill / alive	
7436 carry my shoe	7477 crack egg	7518 clay dove	7559 coil lip	
7437 cram week	7478 crack wave	7519 called up	7560 colleges	
7438 carry my half	7479 crack up	7520 clowns	7561 clashed	
7439 Grampa	7480 graves	7521 clarinet	7562 coalition	
7440 careers	7481 gravity	7522 clean hen	7563 clash with me	
7441 car radio	7482 car phone	7523 clean him	7564 glacier	
7442 carry her now	7483 carve ham	7524 cleaner	7565 call jail	
7443 carry the Army	7484 carver	7525 colonial	7566 call judge	
7444 carry her here	7485 careful	7526 clench	7567 kill the joke	
7445 carry the rail	7486 carry fish	7527 clinic	7568 call the chef	
7446 carry her shoe	7487 graphic	7528 clean off	7569 call - show up	
7447 car wreck	7488 carry wife off	7529 cleanup	7570 clocks	
7448 car roof	7489 acrophobia	7530 clams	7571 Calcutta	
7449 carry her up	7490 grapes	7531 climate	7572 clock in	
7450 girls	7491 carpet	7532 coal mine	7573 call game	
7451 grilled	7492 Caribbean	7533 claim him	7574 clicker	
7452 Carolina	7493 car bomb	7534 gloomy weather	7575 go local	
7453 cruel home	7494 grabber	7535 claim all	7576 clock show	
7454 curly hair	7495 grapple	7536 call match	7577 goal kick	
7455 curly wall	7496 garbage	7537 claim key	7578 click off	
7456 girly show	7497 carry bike	7538 claim half	7579 call a cab	

284

Directory

7580 gloves	7621 hockey joint	7662 catch chain	7703 cooks ham
7581 golf tee	7622 lower nun	7663 catch shame	7704 kicks her
7582 kill phone	7623 catchy name	7664 coach jury	7705 cake sale
7583 kill fame	7624 action hero	7665 catch huge eel	7706 cookie is chewy
7584 clover	7625 catch nail	7666 catch choo choo	7707 cooks egg
7585 kill file	7626 wig change	7667 cash check	7708 kicks off
7586 kill fish	7627 catching	7668 catch chef	7709 kick is up
7587 kill fog	7628 catch knife	7669 catch sheep	7710 cactus
7588 glove off	7629 weak chin up	7670 weak jokes	7711 kicked toe
7589 call the VP	7630 catch mouse	7671 hockey jacket	7712 kicked in
7590 claps	7631 gosh, me too	7672 go check in	7713 kicked me
7591 galloped	7632 coachman	7673 catch a game	7714 kick door
7592 clip on	7633 catch Mom	7674 catch car	7715 cocktail
7593 kill bomb	7634 catch more	7675 catch eagle	7716 cake dish
7594 clipper	7635 catch mail	7676 go check wash	7717 kick dog
7595 global	7636 catch match	7677 catch a cookie	7718 kicked off
7596 calabash	7637 catch mug	7678 catch a cough	7719 kick it up
7597 call back	7638 catch movie	7679 catch a cab	7720 cocoons
7598 clip off	7639 go jump	7680 catch vase	7721 coconut
7599 clay pipe	7640 cashiers	7681 catch food	7722 kick no one
7600 catch z's	7641 catch ride	7682 catch phone	7723 kooky name
7601 weak chest	7642 week journey	7683 catch fame	7724 kick owner
7602 cashes in	7643 catch worm	7684 catch fire	7725 kick in wheel
7603 catches him	7644 catch her here	7685 catch flu	7726 Coke on shoe
7604 catchers her	7645 catch, roll	7686 catch fish	7727 cooking
7605 catch seal	7646 ok church	7687 catch thief, OK	7728 cake knife
7606 catches show	7647 go Jerico	7688 go shove off	7729 quick nap
7607 catches egg	7648 weak sheriff	7689 coach the VP	7730 quick mouse
7608 catches wave	7649 weak chirp	7690 catch bus	7731 kick him, too
7609 catches up	7650 eggshells	7691 catch a boat	7732 quick money
7610 coached us	7651 weak child	7692 OK Japan	7733 quick Mom
7611 coached at Iowa	7652 catch a lion	7693 catch a bomb	7734 cook more
7612 cash it in	7653 catch a lamb	7694 cash bar	7735 guacamole
7613 coach team	7654 catch lower	7695 catchable	7736 quick match
7614 coached her	7655 catch lily	7696 catch beach	7737 kick him, OK
7615 catch a tail	7656 catch a leash	7697 cash back	7738 quick movie
7616 catch dish	7657 catch log	7698 whack, chop off	7739 hockey camp
7617 catch dog	7658 catch a leaf	7699 catch baby	7740 Quakers
7618 catch TV	7659 coach help	7700 kicks us	7741 go-cart
7619 go shut up	7660 catch shows	7701 cookie is hot	7742 quick run
7620 kitchens	7661 catch jet	7702 hog casino	7743 quick Army

Directory

7744 OK career	7785 cake file	7826 go finish	7867 coffee shake
7745 cog railway	7786 quick fish	7827 coughing	7868 cough, shave
7746 quicker show	7787 kick off week	7828 cough on wife	7869 coffee shop
7747 weak crack	7788 kick wife off	7829 cough on up	7870 give kiss
7748 quicker wave	7789 kick the VP	7830 weak fumes	7871 go fake it
7749 kick her up	7790 quick pass	7831 go vomit	7872 give gun away
7750 goggles	7791 cockpit	7832 caveman	7873 gave game away
7751 quickly hot	7792 cocoa bean	7833 cough Mom	7874 go figure
7752 quick lion	7793 kick by me	7834 give more	7875 gave a clue
7753 go climb	7794 quick bear	7835 give mail	7876 giveaway cash
7754 quick lawyer	7795 weak cable	7836 give match	7877 coffee cake
7755 quickly yell	7796 quick push	7837 coffee mug	7878 cough, cough
7756 quickly chew	7797 kick back	7838 giveaway movie	7879 coffee cup
7757 quickly go	7798 kick above	7839 give map away	7880 coffee face
7758 quickly wave	7799 kick puppy	7840 givers	7881 gave food
7759 quickly up	7800 wacky faces	7841 go off-road	7882 give van away
7760 kick shoes	7801 OK feast	7842 govern	7883 gave fame away
7761 cookie sheet	7802 caves in	7843 give her ham	7884 give fur away
7762 go / action	7803 gives me	7844 gave her hair	7885 give file away
7763 go catch him	7804 gives her	7845 weak, frail	7886 gave fish away
7764 cookie jar	7805 gives all	7846 gave her age	7887 cough off wig
7765 kick shell	7806 gives age	7847 weak frog	7888 gave wife half
7766 quick judge	7807 gave his OK	7848 gave her half	7889 give off hope
7767 quick joke	7808 hockey faceoff	7849 cover-up	7890 give pass
7768 kick, shove	7809 go fess up	7850 gavels	7891 coffee pot
7769 go catch up	7810 cavities	7851 coffee lady	7892 coffee bean
7770 cakewalks	7811 go feed it	7852 cough alone	7893 gave poem
7771 kick cat	7812 caved in	7853 weak flame	7894 cough up hair
7772 quick gun	7813 go fight him	7854 cavalry	7895 give up Yale
7773 quick game	7814 cafeteria	7855 give a lily	7896 cough up age
7774 quacky car	7815 gave it all	7856 weak flesh	7897 give back
7775 Coca-Cola	7816 give it a wash	7857 UK flag	7898 give up half
7776 quick cash	7817 cough attack	7858 week of love	7899 give up hope
7777 quick kick	7818 give it off	7859 go fly up	7900 capsize
7778 quacky cough	7819 coughed up	7860 gave chase	7901 capacity
7779 kick cab	7820 coffins	7861 go fish day	7902 keeps on
7780 cookie face	7821 go vent	7862 go fishin'	7903 keeps me
7781 quick feet	7822 coffee anyone	7863 go fetch him	7904 keeps her
7782 cook, oven	7823 cough on him	7864 gave chair away	7905 capsule
7783 quick fame	7824 cough on her	7865 give Jello away	7906 keeps a wish
7784 quick fire	7825 weak vinyl	7866 coffee, Judge	7907 keepsake

Directory

7908 keeps off	7949 keep robe	7990 keep busy	8031 office mate
7909 keeps up	7950 cables	7991 cowboy boot	8032 office woman
7910 kept us	7951 gobbled	7992 keep open	8033 face Mom
7911 copped out	7952 goblin	7993 keep bomb	8034 face him here
7912 captain	7953 go bloom	7994 egg, pepper	8035 voice mail
7913 keep time	7954 hockey player	7995 keep the ball	8036 face match
7914 egg, butter	7955 go play well	7996 keep peach	8037 face my week
7915 Capitol	7956 keep leash	7997 keep back	8038 face my wife
7916 keep dish	7957 cable guy	7998 keep beef	8039 office map
7917 keep dog	7958 cable off	7999 wake baby up	8040 officers
7918 captive	7959 go plop	8000 faces us	8041 voice heard
7919 keep it up	7960 cabbages	8001 faces it	8042 officer, no
7920 cabins	7961 keep jet	8002 faces in	8043 face Army
7921 cabinet	7962 caption	8003 faces me	8044 face her here
7922 egg, banana	7963 keep chum	8004 faces her	8045 office rail
7923 keep name	7964 keep jury	8005 voice is well	8046 face her shoe
7924 weak pioneer	7965 keep shell	8006 faces wash	8047 office rug
7925 cabin wall	7966 keep judge	8007 wife is sick	8048 office roof
7926 hockey punch	7967 keep check	8008 faces off	8049 heavy syrup
7927 coping	7968 keep chef	8009 faces up	8050 fossils
7928 keep knife	7969 keep job	8010 wife sits	8051 face lady
7929 cabin boy	7970 hockey pucks	8011 vested	8052 Vaseline
7930 keep mouse	7971 Cape Cod	8012 feast on	8053 half slum
7931 keep my head	7972 go back now	8013 office time	8054 face lawyer
7932 keep money	7973 go back home	8014 visitor	8055 fossil hole
7933 keep Mom	7974 keep car	8015 half stale	8056 fuselage
7934 keep more	7975 wake-up call	8016 fast wash	8057 fossil egg
7935 keep mail	7976 keep the cash	8017 fast guy	8058 fuzzy leaf
7936 keep my wish	7977 cupcake	8018 face TV	8059 fuzzy lip
7937 keep my guy	7978 keep coffee	8019 fist up	8060 office choice
7938 keep my wife	7979 go back up	8020 office noise	8061 ivy was shot
7939 keep map	7980 keep face	8021 face window	8062 physician
7940 capers	7981 cup of tea	8022 face the nun	8063 face huge home
7941 copperhead	7982 keep phone	8023 fasten him	8064 face jury
7942 cabernet	7983 keep fame	8024 fussy owner	8065 face jail
7943 keep warm	7984 Cape Fear	8025 fasten wheel	8066 face Judge
7944 copper wire	7985 keep file	8026 fasten shoe	8067 voice check
7945 copper wheel	7986 keep fish	8027 facing	8068 face chef
7946 copper shoe	7987 keep the fog	8028 fasten off	8069 face - chubby
7947 keep rug	7988 keep off ivy	8029 fasten boy	8070 office keys
7948 keep her off	7989 keep VP	8030 office mouse	8071 fussy cat

Directory

8072 wife is gone	8113 feed team	8154 fiddler	8195 football
8073 wife has gum	8114 foot odor	8155 vital law	8196 fight, push
8074 face car	8115 voodoo doll	8156 foot leash	8197 feedback
8075 physical	8116 food dish	8157 foot, leg	8198 feed beehive
8076 voice coach	8117 feed dog	8158 have to leave	8199 feed baby
8077 office cake	8118 video TV	8159 photo lab	8200 fences
8078 fuzzy coffee	8119 video tape	8160 feta cheese	8201 have nice day
8079 fuzzy cap	8120 video noise	8161 photo shoot	8202 funny son
8080 face offs	8121 footnote	8162 food chain	8203 fun is home
8081 face food	8122 fight no one	8163 feed Jimmy	8204 fancier
8082 fuzzy phone	8123 Viet Nam	8164 heavy teacher	8205 Venezuela
8083 face fame	8124 fight - honor	8165 feed the jail	8206 phone switch
8084 face fire	8125 heavy tunnel	8166 fat Judge	8207 often sick
8085 face full	8126 food - nacho	8167 fat check	8208 phone is off
8086 face fish	8127 fighting	8168 fat chef	8209 fun's up
8087 face havoc	8128 feed Navy	8169 photo shop	8210 vents
8088 ivy is half off	8129 heavy tune-up	8170 fatigues	8211 fainted
8089 face the VP	8130 feed mouse	8171 feed cat	8212 fountain
8090 office boys	8131 feed meat	8172 Vatican	8213 phantom
8091 office bought	8132 vitamin	8173 video game	8214 find your way
8092 office open	8133 feed Mom	8174 heavy tiger	8215 vandal
8093 face bomb	8134 fight more	8175 half tackle	8216 vintage
8094 fuzzy bear	8135 have oatmeal	8176 fat coach	8217 fanatic
8095 vase, ball	8136 fight a match	8177 wife ate cake	8218 funny TV
8096 face beach	8137 food - mug	8178 wife took off	8219 funny toupee
8097 Facebook	8138 video movie	8179 photocopy	8220 often noisy
8098 face above	8139 heavy tempo	8180 feed face	8221 van window
8099 fussy baby	8140 fighters	8181 food fight	8222 funny Nun
8100 fights us	8141 half tried	8182 have TV on	8223 funny name
8101 fatty acid	8142 veteran	8183 fight fame	8224 fun owner
8102 fades in	8143 feed Army	8184 fight fire	8225 funny nail
8103 fights me	8144 heavy terrier	8185 fight a filly	8226 fun in show
8104 feet sore	8145 federal	8186 feed fish	8227 wife winning
8105 fights well	8146 heavy trash	8187 fight fog	8228 funny Navy
8106 food is chewy	8147 off-track	8188 fight off wave	8229 fun nap
8107 food is weak	8148 half drove	8189 feed the VP	8230 venomous
8108 fight's off	8149 heavy trap	8190 feed boys	8231 oven mitt
8109 fights boy	8150 fiddles	8191 fit body	8232 funny man
8110 faded house	8151 fiddled	8192 fight pain	8233 funny Mom
8111 faded hat	8152 fat - lean	8193 fight bomb	8234 have no more
8112 faded in	8153 fat lamb	8194 food buyer	8235 fan mail

Directory

8236 fun match	8277 funny cookie	8318 have my TV	8359 foamy lip
8237 fun mug	8278 fun coffee	8319 have my tub	8360 foamy cheese
8238 funny movie	8279 funny cap	8320 famines	8361 have him shot
8239 fun, maybe	8280 funny face	8321 heavy mint	8362 foamy, shiny
8240 funny horse	8281 funny feet	8322 have my onion	8363 foamy chime
8241 vineyard	8282 fun, fun	8323 have my name	8364 have my chair
8242 fun run	8283 fun fame	8324 fame, honor	8365 have my Jello
8243 fun room	8284 fanfare	8325 foamy nail	8366 foamy Judge
8244 funnier hair	8285 fun fill	8326 have a munch	8367 foamy shake
8245 funeral	8286 funny fish	8327 fuming	8368 VMI chef
8246 funnier show	8287 phone off hook	8328 have my knife	8369 have my job
8247 funnier guy	8288 fun with half off	8329 have my nap	8370 have my keys
8248 funnier wife	8289 funny VP	8330 have my mess	8371 have my coat
8249 funny robe	8290 funny boys	8331 foamy meat	8372 have my gun
8250 funnels	8291 funny body	8332 have my money	8373 have my gum
8251 funneled	8292 funny bone	8333 have my Mom	8374 have my car
8252 phone line	8293 have no bomb	8334 have a memory	8375 have my gal
8253 vinyl home	8294 funny bear	8335 have my meal	8376 have my cash
8254 final hour	8295 have an apple	8336 foamy match	8377 have my cake
8255 vinyl wall	8296 fun beach	8337 have my mug	8378 foamy coffee
8256 final show	8297 phone book	8338 have my move	8379 heavy make-up
8257 final week	8298 fun above	8339 have Mom buy	8380 have my voice
8258 final wave	8299 funny baby	8340 have my rose	8381 foamy feet
8259 funny lip	8300 famous house	8341 FM radio	8382 foamy phone
8260 finishes	8301 have my soda	8342 have him run	8383 have my fame
8261 funny shot	8302 famous wine	8343 have my room	8384 have my fur
8262 finish wine	8303 famous home	8344 have more hair	8385 have my file
8263 have no shame	8304 famous hair	8345 have my roll	8386 foamy fish
8264 venture	8305 famously	8346 heavy march	8387 foamy fog
8265 finish hall	8306 heavy massage	8347 off my rack	8388 foamy fife
8266 finish show	8307 famous guy	8348 off my roof	8389 foamy FBI
8267 funny joke	8308 famous wife	8349 have my robe	8390 have my pass
8268 finish half	8309 foams up	8350 families	8391 have my bat
8269 finish up	8310 vomits	8351 family ate	8392 have my pen
8270 fangs	8311 vomited	8352 half a million	8393 foamy bomb
8271 half-naked	8312 vomit honey	8353 family home	8394 vampire
8272 have no gun	8313 wife, madam	8354 familiar	8395 fumble
8273 fun game	8314 vomit here	8355 family law	8396 foamy peach
8274 finger	8315 heavy metal	8356 family show	8397 off my back
8275 phone call	8316 vomit hash	8357 family guy	8398 foamy beehive
8276 fun coach	8317 have my dog	8358 foamy leaf	8399 heavy mop up

Directory

8400 freezes	8441 forward	8482 free phone	8523 flown him
8401 frost	8442 forewarn	8483 free fame	8524 follow owner
8402 frozen	8443 firearm	8484 forever	8525 flannel
8403 fires me	8444 free her hair	8485 firefly	8526 avalanche
8404 freezer	8445 free roll	8486 free fish	8527 flying
8405 Ferris Wheel	8446 free reach	8487 free heavy guy	8528 Villanova
8406 frees shoe	8447 free rug	8488 free, half off	8529 flown up
8407 fresco	8448 free roof	8489 free half up	8530 flames
8408 frees wife	8449 free ruby	8490 free pass	8531 flamed
8409 Frisbee	8450 frills	8491 everybody	8532 full moon
8410 overdose	8451 frailty	8492 free, open	8533 follow Mom
8411 freed head	8452 fire lane	8493 fire bomb	8534 fly more
8412 free town	8453 farewell, Ma	8494 free beer	8535 flame wall
8413 freedom	8454 frilly hair	8495 free ball	8536 fill my shoe
8414 ivory tower	8455 farewell all	8496 free peach	8537 fill my week
8415 free toll	8456 heavy relish	8497 fire back	8538 fly me off
8416 variety show	8457 fire log	8498 fire above	8539 volume up
8417 fried egg	8458 free love	8499 free puppy	8540 flowers
8418 afraid of	8459 farewell, Pa	8500 heavy loses	8541 Florida
8419 fruit pie	8460 free cheese	8501 velocity	8542 fill her in
8420 ferns	8461 frigid	8502 Phillies win	8543 fill room
8421 friend	8462 Virginia	8503 follows me	8544 flower hair
8422 free union	8463 fresh ham	8504 follows her	8545 floral
8423 fire on him	8464 fresh air	8505 falsely	8546 flower show
8424 fury owner	8465 fragile	8506 false wish	8547 flower week
8425 free nail	8466 fresh show	8507 flu, sick	8548 flower wife
8426 French	8467 fresh guy	8508 philosophy	8549 flower boy
8427 firing	8468 fire chief	8509 false hope	8550 fill lease
8428 heavy run off	8469 fresh up	8510 flood house	8551 full load
8429 free nap	8470 franks	8511 flooded	8552 fully alone
8430 farms	8471 fur coat	8512 fall down	8553 follow lamb
8431 very humid	8472 African	8513 full time	8554 fly lower
8432 fireman	8473 free game	8514 flatter	8555 fill oil well
8433 free Mom	8474 Frogger	8515 flood wall	8556 full eyelash
8434 farmer	8475 freckle	8516 flat shoe	8557 fall league
8435 formula	8476 fire coach	8517 follow dog	8558 fall leaf
8436 very much	8477 free cookie	8518 float off	8559 full lip
8437 frame key	8478 free coffee	8519 float by	8560 fledges
8438 for my wife	8479 free cup	8520 violins	8561 flu shot
8439 off ramp	8480 free office	8521 flint	8562 violation
8440 free rose	8481 free food	8522 flyaway nun	8563 fill huge home

Directory

8564 fill chair	8605 fishes well	8646 heavy charge	8687 fish off walk
8565 full jail	8606 fish switch	8647 heavy shark	8688 fish off wave
8566 full choo choo	8607 fudges week	8648 heavy sheriff	8689 fishy VP
8567 fuel check	8608 fishes off	8649 fish robe	8690 heavy jobs
8568 full shove	8609 fetches boy	8650 officials	8691 fish bait
8569 fill job	8610 heavy jets	8651 official tie	8692 fetch bone
8570 flags	8611 vegetate	8652 official wine	8693 fish bomb
8571 Flag Day	8612 fish town	8653 official home	8694 fish pier
8572 volcano	8613 fudge time	8654 official hour	8695 fishbowl
8573 flag him	8614 fetch water	8655 official law	8696 fish, beach
8574 full car	8615 fish tale	8656 official show	8697 fetch book
8575 half legal	8616 fish dish	8657 official wig	8698 fish above
8576 flag show	8617 fish dock	8658 official wave	8699 fetch puppy
8577 flag week	8618 fugitive	8659 official pie	8700 heavy axes
8578 awful cough	8619 fished by	8660 heavy Judges	8701 off the coast
8579 full cup	8620 fashions	8661 half judged	8702 vaccine
8580 Oval Office	8621 fish net	8662 fish chain	8703 fakes him
8581 velvet	8622 vision honey	8663 fishy gym	8704 fakes her
8582 awful phone	8623 fudge name	8664 fish hatchery	8705 foxhole
8583 fluff him	8624 visionary	8665 fishy jail	8706 fakes age
8584 flavor	8625 fish on wall	8666 fishy judge	8707 fake sick
8585 fulfill	8626 fashion show	8667 fudge check	8708 fogs off
8586 fluffy show	8627 fishing	8668 fishy chef	8709 fogs up
8587 fluffy wig	8628 vision a wife	8669 fish / chip	8710 vacates
8588 fluff off	8629 fish in bay	8670 fishhooks	8711 vacated
8589 fluff up	8630 have shames	8671 heavy jacket	8712 vacate now
8590 flips	8631 fish meat	8672 half jokin'	8713 victim
8591 flipped	8632 fetch money	8673 fish gum	8714 factory
8592 fly open	8633 fetch Mom	8674 fishy car	8715 heavy cattle
8593 flip him	8634 fish more	8675 fish kill	8716 fake dish
8594 flipper	8635 fish meal	8676 fishy coach	8717 fake dog
8595 volleyball	8636 fish much	8677 fish cake	8718 fake TV
8596 flip shoe	8637 fudge mug	8678 fish cave	8719 wave goodbye
8597 fall back	8638 fish movie	8679 heavy shake-up	8720 heavy guns
8598 fly above	8639 huge, jumbo	8680 fish face	8721 vacant
8599 flyaway baby	8640 heavy chores	8681 fish food	8722 heavy cannon
8600 have choices	8641 heavy shirt	8682 fishy phone	8723 fake name
8601 half jest	8642 heavy journey	8683 half shove him	8724 fake honor
8602 have chosen	8643 heavy germ	8684 fish fry	8725 off canal
8603 half chase him	8644 fish thrower	8685 heavy shovel	8726 fake nacho
8604 fishes here	8645 fish roll	8686 fish, fish	8727 Viking

Directory

8728 fake knife	8769 fake job	8810 half off days	8851 wife fled
8729 fake nap	8770 heavy cakes	8811 ivy faded	8852 heavy violin
8730 vacuums	8771 half cooked	8812 heavy futon	8853 heavy flame
8731 vacuumed	8772 fake gun	8813 wife fed me	8854 heavy flower
8732 fake money	8773 fake game	8814 half off tire	8855 half of a lily
8733 fake mummy	8774 fake car	8815 half off hotel	8856 I have flesh
8734 vacuum hair	8775 fake eagle	8816 half off dish	8857 heavy flag
8735 vacuum hallway	8776 fake cash	8817 half off dog	8858 five alive
8736 fake match	8777 fake kick	8818 half off TV	8859 half flip
8737 heavy comic	8778 foggy cave	8819 wife fed boy	8860 half off cheese
8738 vague movie	8779 fake cop	8820 heavy fence	8861 half off jet
8739 fake camp	8780 heavy coughs	8821 have found u	8862 have a vision
8740 figures	8781 fake food	8822 half off onion	8863 half off gym
8741 figured	8782 heavy coffin	8823 half off name	8864 half off chair
8742 foghorn	8783 fake fame	8824 have funny hair	8865 half off Jello
8743 heavy cream	8784 fake fur	8825 heavy vinyl	8866 fife, judge
8744 have a career	8785 heavy gavel	8826 half off nacho	8867 half off shake
8745 heavy gorilla	8786 fake fish	8827 heavy fang	8868 fife, chief
8746 heavy crash	8787 fake, fake	8828 If I have knife	8869 half off a ship
8747 half groggy	8788 wife gave half	8829 half off? Nope	8870 half off gas
8748 fake roof	8789 wife gave up	8830 half famous	8871 half faked
8749 fake ruby	8790 heavy caps	8831 half off meal	8872 half off gun
8750 vehicles	8791 fake bat	8832 half off money	8873 half off gum
8751 fickled	8792 fake pen	8833 half off mummy	8874 half off car
8752 half gallon	8793 fake bomb	8834 half off mug	8875 half off call
8753 heavy claim	8794 heavy copper	8835 half off meal	8876 half off couch
8754 fake lawyer	8795 heavy cable	8836 half off match	8877 half off cake
8755 vehicle law	8796 foggy beach	8837 half off mug	8878 half off coffee
8756 fickle show	8797 vague book	8838 half off movie	8879 half off cup
8757 fake leg	8798 off, keep off	8839 half off, maybe	8880 half off vase
8758 fig leaf	8799 fake pipe	8840 heavy furs	8881 half off food
8759 fickle boy	8800 heavy voices	8841 half off road	8882 half off phone
8760 fake cheese	8801 have a feast	8842 heavy frown	8883 half off foam
8761 fake shot	8802 heavy fasten	8843 heavy frame	8884 half off fur
8762 vacation	8803 half off sum	8844 heavy furor	8885 half of filet
8763 fake jam	8804 heavy officer	8845 half frail	8886 half of fish
8764 heavy catcher	8805 half off sale	8846 half fresh	8887 half off, a fake
8765 foggy jail	8806 half off switch	8847 heavy frog	8888 half off, half off
8766 foggy judge	8807 half off sack	8848 half off roof	8889 half off, half pie
8767 fake check	8808 half off sofa	8849 half off rope	8890 half of bus
8768 fake chef	8809 half off soap	8850 wife flies	8891 half off bat

Directory

8892 half off piano	8933 VIP Mom	8974 FBI car	9015 postal
8893 if, if a bomb	8934 off by more	8975 heavy buckle	9016 upstage
8894 heavy viper	8935 FBI mail	8976 FBI coach	9017 buys a dog
8895 half off bail	8936 FBI match	8977 FBI cookie	9018 best half
8896 half off pouch	8937 FBI mug	8978 FBI cave	9019 passed up
8897 half off bike	8938 FBI movie	8979 heavy backup	9020 business
8898 half off beef	8939 heavy pump	8980 FBI office	9021 poisoned
8899 half off puppy	8940 half price	8981 VIP food	9022 busy Nun
8900 FBI sees you	8941 vibrate	8982 FBI phone	9023 poison him
8901 heavy post	8942 VP ran	8983 VIP fame	9024 peace on earth
8902 heavy poison	8943 heavy broom	8984 FBI fire	9025 basin wall
8903 VP is home	8944 February	8985 FBI file	9026 buys new watch
8904 VP is here	8945 halfway by rail	8986 half by fish	9027 passing
8905 heavy puzzle	8946 heavy brush	8987 half by fog	9028 poison ivy
8906 heavy passage	8947 fabric	8988 FBI wave off	9029 buy a snap
8907 wife buys wig	8948 FBI rough	8989 FBI, FBI	9030 boy is messy
8908 VP's wife	8949 FBI rope	8990 heavy pipes	9031 boy is mad
8909 VP is up	8950 fabulous	8991 FBI pad	9032 busy man
8910 heavy bats	8951 heavy plate	8992 FBI pen	9033 busy Mom
8911 FBI Dad	8952 heavy plane	8993 FBI bomb	9034 pays more
8912 heavy baton	8953 heavy plum	8994 heavy paper	9035 happy smile
8913 off by a dime	8954 heavy player	8995 heavy Bible	9036 pays much
8914 FBI door	8955 FBI will yell	8996 VIP beach	9037 buys a mug
8915 heavy battle	8956 heavy blush	8997 FBI bag	9038 boy's movie
8916 FBI dish	8957 FBI log	8998 FBI above you	9039 buys map
8917 FBI dog	8958 VP will wave	8999 VIP baby	9040 pass her house
8918 half paid off	8959 FBI alibi	9000 passes us	9041 bus ride
8919 half paid up	8960 ivy bushes	9001 passes it	9042 boys ran
8920 heavy pianos	8961 VIP jet	9002 passes on	9043 boy's room
8921 viewpoint	8962 heavy passion	9003 passes him	9044 boys roar
8922 heavy banana	8963 FBI shame	9004 bosses her	9045 boys are well
8923 VIP name	8964 FBI jury	9005 passes law	9046 boys are huge
8924 heavy pioneer	8965 FBI jail	9006 buys his watch	9047 busier guy
8925 off by a nil	8966 fib the judge	9007 passes egg	9048 pass her off
8926 heavy punch	8967 FBI joke	9008 passes off	9049 passerby
8927 fibbing	8968 VIP chef	9009 passes up	9050 puzzles
8928 FBI, Navy	8969 VIP ship	9010 pests	9051 puzzled
8929 wife - a pin-up	8970 heavy books	9011 posted	9052 baseline
8930 heavy bombs	8971 heavy bucket	9012 Boston	9053 buys lime
8931 VP met you	8972 heavy bacon	9013 passed him	9054 pays lawyer
8932 FBI man	8973 FBI game	9014 poster	9055 buys lily

Directory

9056 buys leash	9097 pass the buck	9138 bad movie	9179 pet guppy
9057 boy's league	9098 pass above	9139 beat him up	9180 about face
9058 busy life	9099 pass baby	9140 powders	9181 bad food
9059 boys leap	9100 body size	9141 patriot	9182 Beethoven
9060 passages	9101 Pizza Hut	9142 patron	9183 beat VMI
9061 busy jet	9102 bad sun	9143 bedroom	9184 paid for
9062 position	9103 potassium	9144 better hair	9185 beautiful
9063 busy gym	9104 Budweiser	9145 patrol	9186 pet fish
9064 busy jury	9105 beats well	9146 better show	9187 paid off guy
9065 busy jail	9106 bad switch	9147 buy truck	9188 paid off wife
9066 busy judge	9107 buy desk	9148 paid her off	9189 paid the FBI
9067 pass check	9108 paid his wife	9149 batter up	9190 bad boys
9068 busy chef	9109 bad soup	9150 beetles	9191 bad bite
9069 busy job	9110 bad days	9151 paddled	9192 bought pen
9070 basks	9111 potato head	9152 battalion	9193 paid up Ma
9071 basket	9112 bite down	9153 battle hymn	9194 bad breathe
9072 pass the gun	9113 bedtime	9154 butler	9195 beatable
9073 boy's comb	9114 bad odor	9155 paddle wheel	9196 body patch
9074 buys a car	9115 paid toll	9156 bite leash	9197 bad back
9075 bicycle	9116 bad dish	9157 bad leg	9198 bad beef
9076 hopscotch	9117 bad dog	9158 bad love	9199 bad puppy
9077 boys kick	9118 bad TV	9159 bite lip	9200 hypnosis
9078 buys coffee	9119 potato pie	9160 bad cheese	9201 poinsettia
9079 pass the cup	9120 buttons	9161 bad shot	9202 happy in sun
9080 boy's face	9121 buttoned	9162 beautician	9203 pains me
9081 pussy foot	9122 bad onion	9163 bought a gym	9204 bouncer
9082 buys van	9123 bad name	9164 badger	9205 pencil
9083 boy's fame	9124 boutonniere	9165 bad jail	9206 opens show
9084 pacifier	9125 bought a nail	9166 bad judge	9207 been sick
9085 pass file	9126 bad nacho	9167 bad check	9208 open safe
9086 boys fish	9127 biting	9168 bad chef	9209 bounce up
9087 Pacific	9128 beat Navy	9169 pet shop	9210 pants
9088 passive wife	9129 button up	9170 pay tax	9211 bandit
9089 busy VP	9130 bottoms	9171 beat egg white	9212 happy Indian
9090 bus pass	9131 bottom out	9172 beauty queen	9213 bantam
9091 busy body	9132 Batman	9173 bad game	9214 painter
9092 buys pony	9133 beat Miami	9174 pit crew	9215 ponytail
9093 pass by him	9134 bought more	9175 bad call	9216 bandage
9094 pass by her	9135 bad meal	9176 paid cash	9217 paint egg
9095 baseball	9136 bad match	9177 patty cake	9218 paint wife
9096 pass the peach	9137 epidemic	9178 bat cave	9219 open top

Directory

9220 bananas
9221 open window
9222 banana, honey
9223 banana, ham
9224 banana hair
9225 banana oil
9226 penny in shoe
9227 opening
9228 been naive
9229 banana pie
9230 been messy
9231 been mad
9232 piano man
9233 been a Mom
9234 open more
9235 open mail
9236 open match
9237 open hammock
9238 open movie
9239 open map
9240 pioneers
9241 pony ride
9242 pony ran
9243 piano room
9244 bony rear
9245 buy new rail
9246 been rich
9247 bye New York
9248 buy new roof
9249 buy new robe
9250 panels
9251 penalty
9252 been alone
9253 been lame
9254 been lower
9255 bye Honolulu
9256 be on leash
9257 bony leg
9258 be in love
9259 bony lip
9260 banjos

9261 punched
9262 pension
9263 punch him
9264 puncher
9265 punch wall
9266 bunch wash
9267 punch a guy
9268 bunch ivy
9269 bunch up
9270 banks
9271 banged
9272 penguin
9273 bunk them
9274 bunker
9275 bungalow
9276 bang shoe
9277 pancake
9278 bank fee
9279 bang up
9280 open face
9281 benefit
9282 been funny
9283 been foamy
9284 bonfire
9285 painful
9286 bon voyage
9287 pain of a week
9288 pain of a wave
9289 ban the FBI
9290 open bus
9291 open pit
9292 open, open
9293 open up home
9294 piano bar
9295 pineapple
9296 open pouch
9297 beanbag
9298 open above
9299 bony baby
9300 bombs house
9301 bombs it

9302 up Amazon
9303 bombs them
9304 bombs her
9305 bombs wall
9306 buy a massage
9307 buy music
9308 bomb is off
9309 bombs up
9310 bombed house
9311 bombed out
9312 buy mitten
9313 happy medium
9314 palm tree
9315 bombed all
9316 bombed show
9317 buy me a dog
9318 buy me a TV
9319 bombed up
9320 boy, a menace
9321 payment
9322 bomb no one
9323 bomb name
9324 bomb owner
9325 bimonthly
9326 buy me nacho
9327 bombing
9328 bomb Navy
9329 bomb NBA
9330 bomb mouse
9331 pay my maid
9332 pay Mom now
9333 pay my Mom
9334 pay me more
9335 buy me a meal
9336 bum match
9337 bomb hammock
9338 bum movie
9339 beam me up
9340 bombers
9341 palm read
9342 a bomb ran

9343 bomb room
9344 buy mirror
9345 buy me a roll
9346 happy march
9347 bomb Iraq
9348 bomb roof
9349 buy me a ruby
9350 boy, I'm lazy
9351 boy, I'm late
9352 buy a melon
9353 buy me a lime
9354 pay my lawyer
9355 buy me a lily
9356 buy my leash
9357 bum leg
9358 buy me love
9359 palm, lip
9360 buy matches
9361 buy me a jet
9362 pie machine
9363 bomb chime
9364 pay my share
9365 bombshell
9366 bum judge
9367 buy my shake
9368 be my chef
9369 buy me a ship
9370 buy my gas
9371 buy me a coat
9372 buy me a gun
9373 bum game
9374 buy me a car
9375 bum call
9376 pay me cash
9377 buy my Coke
9378 buy me coffee
9379 buy me a cup
9380 happy movies
9381 buy me food
9382 bomb van
9383 bomb VMI

295

Directory

9384 buy me fur	9425 perennial	9466 prejudge	9507 please go
9385 bomb valley	9426 branch	9467 brush wig	9508 plays off
9386 bomb fish	9427 pruning	9468 brush off	9509 bless boy
9387 pay me half, OK	9428 prune ivy	9469 brush up	9510 plates
9388 pay my wife off	9429 brown ape	9470 breaks	9511 pleated
9389 palm of boy	9430 brooms	9471 barricade	9512 platoon
9390 bumps	9431 Bermuda	9472 broken	9513 palladium
9391 pumped	9432 poor man	9473 pro game	9514 apple tree
9392 bump in	9433 premium	9474 breaker	9515 bloody wall
9393 pom-pom	9434 primer	9475 broccoli	9516 blue dish
9394 bumper	9435 poor meal	9476 pro coach	9517 pillow talk
9395 pimple	9436 pro match	9477 break egg	9518 played off
9396 Palm Beach	9437 borrow mug	9478 break off	9519 blood bath
9397 Bah humbug	9438 borrow movie	9479 breakup	9520 balloons
9398 bump off	9439 primp	9480 privacy	9521 plant
9399 pump up	9440 barriers	9481 approved	9522 plain honey
9400 bruises	9441 priority	9482 proven	9523 plain ham
9401 priest	9442 poor Iran	9483 perfume	9524 planner
9402 person	9443 bar room	9484 braver	9525 plainly
9403 bruise him	9444 bury her here	9485 profile	9526 buy lunch
9404 appraiser	9445 poor rule	9486 preview show	9527 playing
9405 Brazil	9446 bury her shoe	9487 preview week	9528 plain wife
9406 power switch	9447 poor rug	9488 brave wife	9529 plain boy
9407 brisk	9448 poor roof	9489 brave boy	9530 blooms
9408 abrasive	9449 barrier up	9490 props	9531 playmate
9409 bar is up	9450 burials	9491 burped	9532 blue moon
9410 pirates	9451 bear will hide	9492 bourbon	9533 blame me
9411 braided	9452 bury lion	9493 prep me	9534 bloomer
9412 baritone	9453 apple, lime	9494 barber	9535 blue mail
9413 boredom	9454 poor lawyer	9495 propel	9536 play match
9414 braid hair	9455 parallel	9496 prep wash	9537 blame guy
9415 bridle	9456 bear will age	9497 barbecue	9538 blame wife
9416 Broadway show	9457 prologue	9498 prop wife	9539 blue map
9417 boardwalk	9458 barely off	9499 prep up	9540 players
9418 borrow a TV	9459 poor leap	9500 pleases	9541 blue, red
9419 pretty boy	9460 brushes	9501 pool side	9542 ballerina
9420 brown eyes	9461 parachute	9502 bless wine	9543 play room
9421 burnt	9462 operation	9503 bless him	9544 bluer hair
9422 pronoun	9463 brush him	9504 blazer	9545 blue rail
9423 brown ham	9464 brush hair	9505 blow whistle	9546 blue arch
9424 brown hair	9465 brush well	9506 please wash	9547 blue rock

Directory

9548 blue roof
9549 blue robe
9550 blue whales
9551 play late
9552 play alone
9553 apple, lime
9554 pale lawyer
9555 blue lily
9556 blue leash
9557 pull leg
9558 belly laugh
9559 blue lip
9560 apple juice
9561 blushed
9562 pollution
9563 Belgium
9564 bleacher
9565 palatial
9566 play judge
9567 play joke
9568 play chef
9569 blue chip
9570 black eyes
9571 blackout
9572 pelican
9573 ball game
9574 apple core
9575 black hole
9576 black shoe
9577 apple cake
9578 block wave
9579 bulk up
9580 bluffs
9581 pillow fight
9582 blue van
9583 blue foam
9584 play fair
9585 playful
9586 bluefish
9587 pelvic
9588 bluff wife

9589 believe boy
9590 apple pies
9591 pulpit
9592 play piano
9593 bleep him
9594 blueberry
9595 play ball
9596 blue patch
9597 play back
9598 plop off
9599 blue baby
9600 beach houses
9601 hope chest
9602 pushes on
9603 pushes me
9604 pushes her
9605 patches hole
9606 bashes show
9607 pushes guy
9608 pushes off
9609 pushes up
9610 beach days
9611 pushed ahead
9612 beach town
9613 pushed him
9614 PGA Tour
9615 beach towel
9616 push, touch
9617 poached egg
9618 pushed off
9619 pushed up
9620 passions
9621 patient
9622 push onion
9623 push name
9624 push owner
9625 push nail
9626 happy change
9627 pushing
9628 bash with knife
9629 bash the NBA

9630 bash mouse
9631 bash meat
9632 pushy woman
9633 peachy Mom
9634 push more
9635 push the mail
9636 push match
9637 push mug
9638 bash movie
9639 happy champ
9640 pagers
9641 patch road
9642 patch worn
9643 patch room
9644 patch rear
9645 push her well
9646 happy church
9647 patch rug
9648 patch roof
9649 peach robe
9650 bushels
9651 happy child
9652 push alone
9653 peach, lime
9654 bachelor
9655 push lily
9656 bash eyelash
9657 bush league
9658 patch love
9659 push, help
9660 happy judges
9661 boy judged
9662 push chain
9663 bash gym
9664 push chair
9665 bash jail
9666 push judge
9667 push check
9668 push, shove
9669 bash job
9670 up she goes

9671 bushwhacked
9672 beach wagon
9673 beach game
9674 buy sugar
9675 beach gala
9676 push couch
9677 bye Chicago
9678 patch cave
9679 push cup
9680 beach office
9681 beach food
9682 push van
9683 beach foam
9684 push far
9685 push, follow
9686 push fudge
9687 beach fog
9688 push wife off
9689 a pushy VP
9690 push ups
9691 bash bat
9692 push open
9693 bash palm
9694 push bear
9695 beach ball
9696 push, push
9697 push back
9698 push above
9699 push baby
9700 boxes
9701 back seat
9702 backs in
9703 buxom
9704 boxer
9705 bake sale
9706 packs shoe
9707 back is weak
9708 backs off
9709 picks up
9710 pockets
9711 polka dot

297

Directory

9712 backed in	9753 pick lime	9794 pick berry	9835 happy female
9713 pocket them	9754 pick lawyer	9795 pick apple	9836 above match
9714 back door	9755 pick lily	9796 book page	9837 above hammock
9715 big deal	9756 backlash	9797 backpack	9838 above my wife
9716 pocket watch	9757 happy go lucky	9798 pick up wife	9839 above the map
9717 back deck	9758 pick leaf	9799 bagpipe	9840 beavers
9718 picked off	9759 buckle up	9800 happy faces	9841 pave road
9719 packed up	9760 packages	9801 happy feast	9842 above the rain
9720 pick nose	9761 buck shot	9802 above sun	9843 buff arm
9721 back window	9762 pack china	9803 above his home	9844 above rear
9722 buy cannon	9763 back gym	9804 buy VCR	9845 buff rail
9723 beckon him	9764 picture	9805 paves well	9846 beverage
9724 bikini wear	9765 pack shell	9806 buffs watch	9847 above rock
9725 up the canal	9766 back judge	9807 buffs wig	9848 above roof
9726 bygone age	9767 back check	9808 pay off, save	9849 above rope
9727 picnic	9768 pick a chef	9809 buffs up	9850 bevels
9728 pack knife	9769 pick job	9810 happy vets	9851 beveled
9729 pack'n up	9770 peacocks	9811 paved it	9852 pavilion
9730 big mouse	9771 back gate	9812 above town	9853 above limb
9731 pack meat	9772 pack gun	9813 above dome	9854 buff lower
9732 Pacman	9773 pack comb	9814 above door	9855 above lily
9733 big Mama	9774 pack car	9815 above hotel	9856 buff eyelash
9734 pack more	9775 back the call	9816 wipe off dish	9857 above leg
9735 pack mule	9776 pack cash	9817 paved walkway	9858 above leaf
9736 back my show	9777 bake cake	9818 above TV	9859 above lip
9737 boy comic	9778 pack coffee	9819 above tub	9860 buff shoes
9738 back my wife	9779 pack a cape	9820 above nose	9861 buff jet
9739 back me up	9780 pack office	9821 above window	9862 wipe off chin
9740 bikers	9781 back foot	9822 above no one	9863 buff, gym
9741 backyard	9782 poke fun	9823 above name	9864 above chair
9742 buy grain	9783 buck fame	9824 beefy wiener	9865 above the jail
9743 back room	9784 book fair	9825 buff nail	9866 above Judge
9744 happy career	9785 pack file	9826 happy finch	9867 beefy cheek
9745 boy / girl	9786 pack fish	9827 paving	9868 above chief
9746 pack her wash	9787 buck the fog	9828 buff knife	9869 above ship
9747 bike rack	9788 pick off ivy	9829 above knob	9870 buy fakes
9748 biography	9789 pie, coffee, pie	9830 above mouse	9871 above the coat
9749 pick her up	9790 peek a boos	9831 pay off maid	9872 above wagon
9750 pickles	9791 pack boat	9832 buff money	9873 above comb
9751 piglet	9792 back pain	9833 above Mom	9874 happy figure
9752 back line	9793 pack bomb	9834 pave more	9875 above the call

Directory

9876 above coach	9917 baby Doc	9958 puppy love	9999 pop pop
9877 above the cake	9918 popped off	9959 bubble bath	
9878 above cave	9919 baby top	9960 peep shows	
9879 above cap	9920 baboons	9961 baby jet	
9880 above office	9921 baby net	9962 baby Jane	
9881 above foot	9922 buy banana	9963 baby gym	
9882 above phone	9923 baby name	9964 baby shower	
9883 above fame	9924 baby winner	9965 buy a bushel	
9884 above fire	9925 pop nail	9966 baby Judge	
9885 above file	9926 buy a bunch	9967 baby jog	
9886 above fish	9927 popping	9968 baby chef	
9887 above fog	9928 baby knife	9969 baby job	
9888 pave half off	9929 baby nap	9970 P.O. Box	
9889 above the FBI	9930 baby mouse	9971 baby, cute	
9890 above the boss	9931 baby mad	9972 pop gun	
9891 beef patty	9932 baby money	9973 baby game	
9892 pave open	9933 baby, Mommy	9974 baby care	
9893 above palm	9934 baby hammer	9975 baby eagle	
9894 above the bear	9935 baby meal	9976 baby couch	
9895 above the ball	9936 baby match	9977 baby cake	
9896 above beach	9937 baby mug	9978 buy back half	
9897 pave back	9938 baby movie	9979 baby cup	
9898 pave above	9939 pop him up	9980 baby face	
9899 behave baby	9940 papers	9981 baby food	
9900 baby sis	9941 paperweight	9982 baby phone	
9901 babysit	9942 pepperoni	9983 baby fame	
9902 pops in	9943 baby room	9984 pop over	
9903 baby's home	9944 baby rear	9985 pop fly	
9904 baby's hair	9945 pep rally	9986 baby fish	
9905 baby's well	9946 buy a brush	9987 pop off, OK	
9906 baby's age	9947 paprika	9988 pop half off	
9907 baby is awake	9948 baby - rough	9989 baby the VP	
9908 pops off	9949 baby robe	9990 baby wipes	
9909 Papa's boy	9950 bubbles	9991 baby bat	
9910 puppets	9951 buy a plate	9992 pop open	
9911 popped head	9952 Babylon	9993 pipe bomb	
9912 pipe down	9953 pop limb	9994 Papa Bear	
9913 wipe bottom	9954 popular	9995 buy Bible	
9914 puppeteer	9955 baby lily	9996 pop, push	
9915 baby hotel	9956 publish	9997 baby back	
9916 puppet show	9957 public	9998 pop above	

Conclusion

Each year, near the battlefields of Gettysburg, a group of ordinary people with extraordinary minds compete in the USA Memory Championship.

A ticket to compete is less demanding than qualifying for the Boston Marathon. If you've celebrated your 12th birthday and have paid a modest fee, you're in.

Throughout the day, contestants memorize names and faces, long-digit numbers, over one hundred words, a long poem, and within five minutes attempt to memorize the order of a shuffled deck of playing cards.

Those in attendance, as well as the score of national media covering the event, are amazed at the incredible feat the human mind can produce. If they only knew. Contestants have less in their minds than those holding the program because they never try to remember more than two things at the same time. They have trained their mind to associate new information to what they already know. They're skilled with strong anchors, strong imaginations, and strong links.

Learning the techniques in this book can put you in front of the cameras, too. More importantly, it will increase your productivity no matter your life's goals.

A trained memory increases the productivity for an attorney, waitress, bellhop, salesperson, student, clerk, physician, police officer, mechanic, librarian, engineer, and anyone else who gets out of bed to go to work.

These systems work, and they'll work for you. Spend time learning each system. Realize that every example, every exercise in this book linked only two things at the same time.

MEMORY is too big to ignore.

INDEX

A

Abdul, Paula, 51
Absent-mindedness, 92
Academy Awards, 8, 55, 142
Acosta, Alex, 78
Acronyms, 52-3, 75-6
Acrostic, 76
Alarm Clock, 108
Alderson, Naomi, 185
Aldrin, Buzz, 77
Alita, Samuel, 75-6
Allowance, 119
Alphabet Anchor Method, 41
Alzheimer's, 9, 162
American Idol, 51
Anchor, 19
Appointment
 picking up child, 175
Armstrong, Neil, 77, 210
Arthur, Chester A., 208
Associations, 10
Autumn, 185

B

Barkley, Charles, 223-4
Bean, Alan, 77
Beatles, The, 67
Bell, Alexander, 218
Belt, 164, 177
Bible, 128
Bill of Rights, 31-33
Bills, 154
Body Anchor Method, 24

Bon Air Library, 4
Books
 authors, 185
 library, 25
 pages, 21
 recalling what you read, 114
Bouvier, Jacqueline, 219
Brady, Tom, 223-4
Breyer, Stephen, 75-6
Burns, Ken, 76
Business Cards, 56, 109, 124

C

Calendars, 215
Capitals, 148
Car
 gas cap, 184
 oil change, 125
 turn signal, 183
Carey, Mariah, 223-4
Carlin, George, 45
Cernan, Eugene, 77
Chaffee, Sydney, 77
Chao, Elaine, 78
Clothing
 recalling what's worn, 186
 sizes, 124
Coffee
 filters, 187
 turning off, 172
Color-Coding, 161
Conrad, Pete, 77
Cooking
 stove top off, 143

thawing, 136
Coupons, 149
Crestar Bank, 209

D

Dallas Cowboys, 207
Dance Steps, 122
Danes, Claire, 223-4
Definitions, 116
DeGeneres, Ellen, 45
Descriptions
  eye witness, 134
DeVos, Betsy, 78
DiMaggio, Joe, 203
Diet
  fiber, 102
Directions, 101
Disney World, 63, 137, 203
Dolby Theatre, 55
Door
  mall, 93
Duke, Charles, 77

E

Eden Park School, 4
Empire State Building, 47-50
ET, 9
Evans, Janet, 76
Evert, Chris, 203
Exaggeration, 12
Exit West, 185

F

Fabric Softener, 127
Fallon, Jimmy, 45
Felix, Allyson, 76
Ferrell, Will, 223

Food
  orders, 158
  purchase, 107

G

Gas Cap, 184
Gettysburg Address, 50, 140
Ginsberg, Ruth Bader, 75-6
Glasses
  locating, 132
Glenn, John, 208
Golf Strokes, 123
Gorsuch, Neil, 75-6
Grant, Ulysses, 59
Gym Pass, 126

H

Haley, Nikki, 78
Hamid, Mohsin, 185
Hayes, Jahana, 77
Heaton, Patricia, 223
Houdon, Jean, 60

I

Ideas Remembered, 147
Identical Twins, 94
Introduction, 165
Iron, 118
Irwin, James, 77

K

Kagan, Elena, 75-6
Kennedy, Anthony, 75-6
Kennedy, Jacqueline, 67
Kennedy, John F., 13, 45, 218

Index

Keys
 locating, 120
 locking doors, 188
King, Martin Luther, 45

L

Language, 121
Laps
 pool, 106
 track, 133
Laundry
 dry cleaners, 160
 fabric softener, 129
 remembering, 176
Lawn
 watering, 182
Lawrence of Arabia, 67
Lee, Bruce, 223
Lennon, John, 67
Lights, 96
Lincoln, Abraham, 50, 140
Lindbergh, Charles, 210
Linking, 48
Loci Method, 20
Lopez, Jennifer, 68
Lorayne, Harry, 4
Louganis, Greg, 76
Lucas, Jerry, 4

M

Madison Square Garden, 47
Mailings
 bills, 154
 postcards, 168
Markle, Meghan, 222-3
Manning, Mandy, 77
Mathematical Formulas, 131
Mattis, James, 78
Mattress, 180
McCartney, Paul, 67

McComb, Sean, 77
McKinley, William, 209
Medication, 170
Meetings
 keeping awake, 159
Memory
 keeping active
Middleton, Kate, 223
Mileage Recording, 157
Milk
 put away, 169
Mitchell, Edgar, 77
Money
 allowance, 119
 checkbook, 111-181
 entries recorded, 111
 paid back, 96
Mothers Against Drunk Driving
 (MADD), 75
Mount McKinley, 209
Movie Times, 191

N

Names
 accepting award, 142
 acronyms, 142
 boyfriend's name, 117
 concentration, 57-8
 couples, 68-9
 eye contact, 58-60
 first names, 81-90
 focusing, 57-8
 groups, 75-77
 interested in others, 55-7
 introduction, 58-60, 165
 last names, 69-74
 neighbor's name, 146
 noticing, 63-4
 occupation, 70-1
 pronunciation, 150
 relating to, 67-8

Index

story, 76
visualization, 63-7
Names & Association, 81-90
Navratilova, Martina, 203
New York Knicks, 47-9
New York Stock Exchange, 210
Nicklaus, Jack, 229
North Atlantic Treaty Organization (NATO), 75
Number Directory, 236-305
Number / Rhyme Method, 34-6
Number Shape Method, 30

O

O'Brien, Conan, 45
Oil Change, 124
Oven
  taking food out, 100

P

Pachinko, 185
Packing
  for trip, 173
  leaving from trip, 105
Parking
  airport, 139
  mall, 94
  work, 193
Peeples, Shanna, 77
Perdue, Sonny, 78
Perry, Katy, 223
Phonetic Alphabet, 196-10
  anchors, 201
  rules, 199
Pi, 235
Plants
  bringing them in, 192
Playing Cards, 226-34

Pompeo, Mike, 78
Presley, Elvis, 52, 223
Prince William, 223

R

Receipts, 111
Recipes, 144
Refrigeration, 190
Repeating Oneself, 110
Richmond Toastmasters Club, 4
Roberts, John, 75-6
Rockefeller Center, 47

S

Secretariat, 218
Schmitt, Harrison, 77
Scott, David, 77
Scully, Vin, 76
Seat
  Stadium, 98
  Theatre, 112
Seymour, Jane, 223-4
Shepard, Alan, 77
Shields, Brooke, 223-4
Shopping Lists, 167
Sing, Unburied Sing, 185
Sinise, Gary, 76
Smith, Ali, 185
Society for the Prevention of
  Cruelty to Animals (SPCA), 72
Sotomayor, Sonia, 75-6
Space Needle, 210
Speeches
  acronyms, 52-3
  plays, 140
  key points, 156
Statue of Liberty, 194
Super Bowl XII, 207
Swift, Taylor, 223-4

Index

T

Taylor, Elizabeth, 218
Taylor, Zachary, 207
Telephone
 concentrating, 166
 re-charging, 101
Television
 listing, 98
Tennis, 137
Tent, 152
The Memory Book, 4
The Power, 185
Thomas, Clarence, 75-6
Timberlake, Justin, 223
Toastmasters International, iii, 4
Train of Thought, 151
Trump, Donald, 67, 78
Turn Signal, 183

U

Umbrella, 104
USA Memory Championship, 305

V

Virginia State Capitol, 60
Visualization, 16-8
Vocabulary, 116

W

Ward, Jesmyn, 60
Washington, George, 60
Watson, Thomas, 218
Webster, Noah, 7-8
Welch, Raquel, 223-4
What's My Line? 78
Wheel of Fortune, 202

White, Brooke, 51
Williams, Serena, 223-4

Y

Young, John, 77
YouTube, 45

Z

Z, Jay, 223
Zamperini, Louis, 76
Zuckerberg, Mark, 223-4
Zipper, 164

Made in the USA
Columbia, SC
12 July 2018